# ALL THINGS
# BEING EQUAL

## LENNY MOORE

WITH
### JEFFREY JAY ELLISH

www.SportsPublishingLLC.com

ISBN: 1-58261-781-3

Publishers: Peter L. Bannon and Joseph J. Bannon Sr.
Senior managing editor: Susan M. Moyer
Contributing editor: Dona Avery
Acquisitions editor: Joseph Bannon Jr.
Developmental editor: Doug Hoepker
Art director: K. Jeffrey Higgerson
Dust jacket and insert design: Joseph Brumleve
Project manager: Kathryn R. Holleman
Imaging: Dustin Hubbart
Photo editor: Erin Linden-Levy
Vice president of sales and marketing: Kevin King
Media and promotions managers: Mike Hagan (regional),
 Randy Fouts (national), Maurey Williamson (print)

Printed in the United States of America

Sports Publishing L.L.C.
804 North Neil Street
Champaign, IL 61820

Phone: 1-877-424-2665
Fax: 217-363-2073
Web site: www.SportsPublishingLLC.com

This book is dedicated to my son, Leslie Moore
(September 11, 1957 – January 15, 2001)
His bout with drugs ended when he took responsibility to care for his niece,
Nikki. Les was a brilliant student who searched for truth and higher educa-
tional levels. Many times I went to him to seek answers and wisdom. Now, as
then, I'd like to say, "Thanks, My Man."

To my wife Edith,
the woman I always wanted. She is my best friend. She changed my life. I
thank God for our union. At a time when I was crumbling, God moved her
into my life. I learned how to grow and be the man I
needed to be. I love you Dear!!!

To my children, whom I love with all my heart. Carol, my oldest daughter,
Toni my middle daughter, Terri my youngest daughter.

To my stepchildren, Brenda, Ronnie, Ray, and Butch.

My oldest son, Lenny Jenkins,
through some empty early years we have built a relationship.

To my granddaughters Rachel, Nikki, and Lindsey.

To my sisters, with love, Virginia (Honeygirl), Margaret (Mickey), and
Constance (Connie).

# CONTENTS

# FOREWORD

Often I am asked who is the best football player I ever coached. I am reluctant to answer that question for two reasons. First, I have been fortunate to have coached many great players who were also wonderful people. Second, I have always felt that Lenny Moore's coach at Penn State, Rip Engle, and his high school coach, Andy Stopper, deserve the credit for Lenny's development as one of the five or ten greatest football players of all time.

That is who he is: a great amongst greats, and the greatest player with whom I have ever worked. Lenny could do it all on offense and could have been a wonderful defensive player.

But Lenny's impact on Penn State and the people he has touched goes beyond what he could do on the football field. He has always cared deeply about people. Throughout his life, he has reached out to help those in need. His style, his loyalty to his school, college, and to the Baltimore Colts, and his willingness to share the glory with his teammates are truly unique qualities that endear him to us.

I first met Lenny on the sideline of a football game between Villanova and Penn State in 1951. He was a senior in high school and Sever Toretti, our line coach, was recruiting him. I remember looking at him—a lanky kid in a zoot suit and key chain—and asked Coach Toretti, "Who is the 'Dude?'" Sever answered, "That's Lenny Moore and he is going to make us good coaches!" He was right on the mark.

From the first time that Lenny stepped onto the practice field in State College, he was electric. If I coach for another 50 years, I will never forget the battle he and Jim Brown had in 1955 when Penn State beat Syracuse, 21-20. You talk about the "battle of the Titans." I saw it.

Lenny and I share another experience. Weeb Eubank, who brought Lenny to the Colts, had been my backfield coach at Brown University during my freshman year. Later, when Weeb and I got together, most of our conversations led to telling stories about Lenny's exploits.

If Andy Stopper, Rip Engle, and Weeb Eubank were alive, they would join me in telling the world how lucky we were to have coached Lenny

Moore and how much we love him because of his humanity. He's as good as God makes them.

Enjoy his book. It is the story of a superb athlete and human being.

–JOE PATERNO

Penn State football coach
March, 2005

# PREFACE

What does it take to become a legend and member of the Pro Football Hall of Fame? Lenny Moore knows! Gifted with extraordinary talent, he has electrified football fans with his exploits throughout the high school, college, and professional ranks. It is my great honor to know him as a friend for over 50 years. We were high school rivals in football and track. Later we became roommates and teammates while playing football at Penn State University. We became close friends from that time on.

Born in Reading, Pennsylvania, in 1933, during an era of the Great Depression, his proud and hardworking parents had little money to support their large family. Like most American children of that devastating period, Lenny did not understand what was happening during those stressful years. Many years later, he remembered traveling with his mother, sisters and brothers to the Relief Office for food. The handouts consisted of flour, potatoes, powdered milk, eggs, fruit juice and day-old bread.

His athletic career began at an early age, playing sports in the streets, sandlots and vacant lots in Reading. We saw him blossom as an athlete in high school as he struggled against poverty and racism. By his senior year in high school, 1951, he had become a star on the football team and an outstanding sprinter and long jumper on the track team. At that point in time, he was perhaps Pennsylvania's greatest school boy long jumper. He could have easily won the State championship in the long jump, but he decided to go to his senior prom instead. That same year, Lenny was selected as a member of the All-State Football Team. Sports writers of the day nicknamed him "The Reading Rocket." In college, he became one of the greatest running backs in Penn State's history.

Lenny's trademark was making tacklers miss with ghostlike moves, embarrassing opponents on his way to a touchdown. He continued to tape his shoes throughout his career, even during his 12 professional campaigns with the Baltimore Colts, right into the Pro Football Hall of Fame. He also set a National Football League record by scoring at least one touchdown in 18 straight games, as his legend began to grow.

*All Things Being Equal* is not just a memoir of an African American football player, it is a social and cultural history as well. It is impossible to understand his life story apart from his time. In the pages of this book, the readers will meet and come to know both the major and the minor personalities in Lenny Moore's life. With each groundbreaking performance as an athlete, he added to his laurels, despite racial prejudice, personal dilemmas and professional rivalries. The dynamics of his story hinge on an uncommon look into the little known story of pioneering African American professional football players such as Fritz Pollard and Paul Robeson, who were often taunted with racism during the early years of the profession. The racial burden was tremendous, but the few pioneering African American collegiate and professional players shouldered the burden of bigotry with remarkable skills and courage. Gradually, as the country changed during the Civil Rights Movement, so did football. Today, almost 70 percent of the players in the National Football League are African American, with the number of African American coaches increasing slowly each year.

Mystery is truly the backdrop of life, and with deep thought and pain Lenny explains for the first time to the public the disturbing and treacherous behavior of his former friend and fellow professional football star, Claude "Buddy" Young. Always forthright, he also shares some new insights on the facts pertaining to the mysterious death of his friend Eugene "Big Daddy" Lipscomb. But football was merely one aspect of Lenny Moore's life. We see him today as a dedicated husband to his family, his role as program specialist for the schools in Baltimore and his commitment to the elderly and poor as every year during Thanksgiving and Christmas, Lenny and his wife Edith deliver turkeys to the poor.

In the end, the measure of Lenny Moore is not on the football field, but in the character and courage of his family and in the hearts and minds of the at-risk youth he tries to touch every day. So join me in celebrating the life and times of a remarkable person who has taken his celebrity and tried to make a difference—no matter small or large—in the hope that he can brighten someone's day. The world would be a better place with more people like Lenny Moore.

—CHARLES L. BLOCKSON

# PROLOGUE

The death of my best friend, former New York Giant football star Rosey Brown, who was inducted along with me and two others in 1975, was shattering since we had planned on being at the Hall of Fame in Canton for our 30-year induction anniversary in August of 2005. That despair, though, was tempered by the joy I felt in hearing that Fritz Pollard, a great pioneer for African Americans in football, will be inducted into the Pro Football Hall of Fame this year.

It was a long time coming, but it is a reality now. He has a special place in my heart. Once I learned of his accomplishments, and that it was on his shoulders those of us who came later would stand, he became a shining beacon of hope to me throughout my career. Not only was he the first black head coach in the NFL, which was overlooked in the history books, he was the second black to play professionally after Charley Follis. What attracted me most to him wasn't the groundbreaking football career, but the fact that he was an astute businessman and well educated during a very difficult time for any black to advance in society. His induction is another achievement for black citizens of this country to be proud of as we continue to fight for equal opportunity: socially, economically, and spiritually. If we have to rewrite every history book in order to note the achievement of Blacks throughout time in the name of full and fair disclosure, then it will be a battle worth fighting.

I had the great privilege to interview Fritz Pollard at his home in New Rochelle, New York, in 1973, before his dementia had set in. It was during these conversations I would learn about the multitalented Paul Robeson, a close friend of Fritz. He would regale me with stories of other peers such as Duke Slater, Ozzie Simmons, Herb Mc Donald, Joe Trigg, Ray Kemp, Brad Holland, Ink Williams, and Joe Lillard, who was the last black to play professionally in 1933. It wouldn't be until 1946 that another black set foot on an integrated football field. Not coincidentally, Major League Baseball would go through this same metamorphosis during this time period.

I've tried to pay homage to many of these legends in telling my life's story. I am of the opinion that their stories cannot be retold enough. One contemporary of mine who doesn't receive the respect he deserves is Johnny

Bright. As you'll read later, he paid the price for being a standout black athlete. The morbid hit he received in a college game almost killed him. Because of the racism he encountered, he continued his career not in the NFL, but in Canada, where he fled to find some peace. It was this same path that I, and many others, were tempted to follow.

Sadly, the struggle for equality not only predates the NFL, but it also predates this country. Ever since the Renaissance Period, European artists such as Da Vinci, Raphael, and Michealangelo, painted Christ in their own image—although new and current evidence proves otherwise. Unfortunately, this time-honored manipulation of the truth has assisted in the psychological bondage that so many blacks live with even today. If my story can inspire just one black youngster to break through the chains, then this book will have served its purpose.

Thank you, Fritz. Thank you, Charley. Thank you to all of the courageous black athletes of the 1920s and 1930s. Thank you, Jackie Robinson and Larry Doby. Thank you to those who have fought to make things equal: Martin Luther King, Jr., WEB Dubois, James Baldwin, etc.

All things being equal, where would sports, better yet society, be? I hope we all live long enough to find out the answer to that question.

# INTRODUCTION

I've studied the lives of several great sports stars of the past and present, and so often they are identified at an early age as someone with special athletic skills. Whether it is speed, hand-eye coordination, or unusual height, such an athlete is singled out very quickly by a coach or a physical education teacher as a prodigy with "star" potential. Along with the special attention now lavished on our youth, there is intense pressure for him or her to consistently perform at a superhuman level. It is a precious few who are able to handle that grind. Every year, as new generations take the field, the star pressure becomes more overwhelming at each level of competition. At some point, salary often becomes more of a motivator than the enjoyment of the game. Nowadays, many million-dollar salaries are made—and then lost—thanks to all the sneaker pushers and the so-called "street agents," who swarm around athletes like bees to honey. We have all seen how fame at an early age, and the inordinate pressure that comes along with it from friends and family, can lead to drug addiction. Only the strongest souls can avoid being permanently damaged, both physically and psychologically. Before you know it, these young athletes, who were once on the fast track to fame, end up scorned for their lack of success and are ill-equipped to handle the rigors of being a normal person and not a superhuman athlete. They eventually realize that their talents and/or body just can't meet the unrealistic demands placed upon them either by themselves or others, and tragedy often sets in. In the milder instances, you'll find a case like Todd Marinovich, who has been in and out of drug rehabilitation centers. The harshest examples may lead to murder, as in the sad case of Rae Caruth.

Luckily for me, I was no obvious superstar in my youth. My childhood wasn't filled with the constant pressure to achieve on the football field, because in my day there were very few black players who achieved any degree of stardom and acceptance in America. Another fortunate factor in my being saved from early superstar burnout is the fact that, growing up in the 1940s and '50s, there were no such things as Nike-sponsored summer camps or traveling AAU teams. Sure, we had summer leagues, but they were designed to keep kids busy and out of trouble during the months we were out of school, not to parade young athletes around like show ponies. I was able to remain relatively innocent and insulated, my skin color making me immune to the superstar phenomenon that has overtaken high school athletics today. I was the shy, lanky kid standing in the back of the crowd, admiring the Anglo achievers, like everyone else. I was a pretty good athlete, but no one ever looked at me and immediately imagined a collegiate, much less a professional, football player—and that was fine with me, because neither did I.

My generation of African Americans was filled with the self-loathing that was inherited from a history of slavery, compounded by the void of information about contemporary blacks who were, in actuality, achieving fantastic things despite an outrageous racism that permeated society. In countless ways, we were prevented from imagining what possibilities actually existed for us as African American youths.

The first person outside of my family who helped boost my self-esteem and who helped give my life direction was my high school track and football coach, Andy Stopper. Later, after a remarkable turn of events, I attended Penn State and played for another great man, coach Rip Engle. From this solid foundation, I went on to meet some of the greatest figures American culture has ever seen: Jim Brown, Johnny Unitas, Miles Davis, Jimmy Smith, Jackie Robinson, Rosey Grier, Charlie Blockson, Big Daddy Lipscomb, Buddy Young, and Charlie Parker, to name a few. The list of my acquaintances goes on to include governors, owners, commissioners, coaches, professors, and even some U.S. presidents.

For a variety of reasons, my life turned out very differently than one might have expected, given my race, my country, and the times. Hopefully, my life story can add something to the history of sports in America, especially regarding the impact of black athletes who helped to establish a new standard of performance in all sports—football, in particular. As an African American, playing collegiate and then professional football, during the 1950s and '60s, I experienced some of the most turbulent times in this country's history. The Korean War; the Civil Rights Movement, the Vietnam conflict, and the shocking deaths of JFK, Robert Kennedy, Martin Luther King, Jr., and Emmett Till—all of these events undoubtedly influenced many of the choices I made in my journey through life. The volatile issues swirling around our nation during this era would not soon be resolved; I have found that racist ideologies and practices colored my life even in the 1970s and '80s, and well into the new millennium.

I feel that now that I have been on this earth for more than seven decades, I need to tell this story. Do not expect this book to be comprised solely of sports-related anecdotes and Hall of Fame hype. There are many issues that concern me deeply because I confronted them repeatedly at different times in my life. This book will shed some light on where the athletic culture has been, where it is now, and where it needs to go. Without a doubt, the world of sports is a microcosm of society, and I feel that my first-hand knowledge of this incredibly insulated universe has some value in the ever-present cultural conversation in this country.

The book you are reading now is just a snapshot of my journey thus far, starting as one of nine offspring of a dirt-poor, but learned, handyman and his hard-working wife, both of whom were only two generations removed from slave ancestors. I'll talk a bit about being the first in my family to go to college, about playing football, and learning about life with the likes of Rosey Grier, Jesse Arnelle, Sam Green, and Charlie Blockson, at Penn State. Then there's my time spent with the Baltimore Colts, and the future Hall of Fame inductees I played with and against. I'll also give you a taste of my post-football life: meeting my current wife, Edie, representing the state of Maryland in working with troubled youth, and being elected to the NFL Hall of Fame. But you'll also learn about some losses in my life, the deaths of some very special people, such as my first and second wives, my second oldest son, my brothers and oldest sister, and some of my best friends: Rosie Brown, Sherman Plunkett, and Eugene "Big Daddy" Lipscomb. I'll talk about my being hired (and abandoned) by CBS, and about being a community relations director for the Baltimore Colts—before they left town in 1984 (taking my job, and many others', with them).

One goal for this book is to pass on to the reader the real story of what went on in my life and in the League, from the '50s to the present, a story that, all things being equal, wouldn't be quite as compelling without the emotions, actions, and language of the day. You, the reader, will be placed in some conversations and situations that took place more than 50 years ago. The people involved in these stories may remember the events differently; but I relay my point of view, not in an attempt to prove someone right or wrong, but to reconstruct what I know in my heart to be true. I recognize that it was a much different time than that in which we now live. People change, I'm aware of that. I myself am a different and (I hope) better person than I was 40 or 50 years ago. Sadly, though, much of the

Eurocentric and color-oriented ideologies of half a century ago have not changed all that much.

Before we start, I'd just like to thank you for taking the time to pick up this book and to care enough to journey through life in my cleats. I hope you enjoy hearing about my life as much as I have grown, living it.

# ONE

# AN INNOCENT CHILDHOOD IN READING

Although I've called Baltimore my home for most of my adult life, I was actually born in Reading, Pennsylvania. My hometown is a unique melting pot, in more ways than one. By the turn of the 20th Century, Reading was your typical blue-collar town, focused on the manufacturing of steel—work that turned people hard, both physically and emotionally. By the 1920s, and into the 1930s, there was a larger variety of goods being produced there, which created an economic boom that would be unmatched in the town's history. It was a banner period of time for the city, and its vibrant economy attracted all colors, races, and creeds. Although Reading's original population was mainly German, many other immigrants—the Dutch, Irish, Polish, Italians, Greeks, and Ukrainians—soon made Reading their home. Due to the explosion of jobs, many blacks (mostly from the south) migrated to Reading as well. During a time when racially mixed communities were rare, Reading was the exception. It was not unusual for different races to live side by side. The Italians dominated the northern part of town, and the Pennsylvania Dutch were sprinkled throughout. Because most blacks didn't have their own transportation, most of them settled on the south side of town, because it was closer to the railways, where the manufacturing was taking place. For the most part, though, nobody worried about who lived where and next to whom. It was very simple.

Don't get me wrong; segregation was a very real way of life; but everyone lived in relative peace. Nonetheless, the tone of the neighborhood was not defined by the separation of blacks and whites.

Pennsylvania, in general, has always been a friendly place for blacks. It is true that when the state was just a colony, like the other Eastern regions of America, in the seventeenth and eighteenth centuries, there were African slaves in Pennsylvania. But whether it was the result of the Quaker faith, small farms instead of huge plantations, or an acute awareness of right and wrong, the state was very conscious when it came to race. As if it were preordained, Pennsylvania eventually became the first northern state to enact emancipation laws, in 1780. In time, Pennsylvania would hold the North's largest free black population.

Furthermore, Pennsylvania was, in fact, a key hub in the Underground Railroad, which helped countless black slaves escape their masters in the South to achieve their freedom. As the Civil War tore the country apart in the late 1800s, members of Reading's own Bethel African Methodist Episcopalian (AME) Church would open its doors to the runaway slaves. The AME congregation was a safe harbor for those hundreds of blacks each year who made their exodus from the South, fearing for their very lives.

In the twentieth century, the church that my family and I attended was Union Baptist, which was right up the street from Bethel AME, between Third and Fourth Streets on Washington Avenue. Remarkably, I did not learn about Bethel's honored place in black history while I was growing up. Bethel Church was designated a historical landmark and celebrated for its role in the Underground Railroad long after I became an adult and had left Reading for Baltimore. Regrettably, it would take almost a century for Bethel to assume its rightful place among the pantheon of landmarks now recognized for its importance to the cause of civil liberties.

It was the Civil Rights movement of the 1960s that propelled Bethel AME into the spotlight. Unfortunately, the same sixties era of Civil Rights marked a dramatic shift in the racial tone within Reading's city limits. Where there was once understanding and interaction between the races, there was now suspicion and paranoia. While I would be the last person to condone segregation, I do remember that life in Reading was more comfortable in the fifties. Everyone knew the accepted boundaries, and we had very distinct and understood rules to live by. It was easier then, because we knew where to go and, more importantly, where not to go. Most of the time, the message was clearly displayed in the store windows: there were signs that read, "Colored not welcome," or "For Whites Only." It is foolish to think that the feelings of those proprietors who practiced segregation for the majority of their lives would change their behavior with the stroke of a pen in Washington D.C., with Civil Rights legislation. After desegregation, blacks were uncertain about where they could go and how they would be treated. There also emerged an unhealthy competition within the race: When I was a youth in Reading, blacks knew they had to stick together; but with "equality" as the new buzzword, it became one black against another, each trying for that "equal" position in society. The result was a weakening of the fabric of the black population. A subsection of tension soon developed, and is still evident today, between fair-skinned blacks and darker blacks. With the proliferation of social programs, those blacks who attempted to make something of themselves were scorned and those who preferred to be left behind in the "neighborhood" were seen as some type of anti-hero. No longer were we pulling in one direction, but now scattered in our thoughts as we, as a people, are today. Sometimes change brings both good and bad consequences, but that is a story for another book.

Just as Bethel's Underground Railroad had helped black slaves to a better life, my own family benefited from the more visible, literal railways that helped put Reading on the map and provided its lifeblood. My parents, George ("Jack") and Virginia Moore, actually met in York, Pennsylvania, just as the country was settling into the Great Depression. "Jack" had ridden the rail from rural South Carolina, to start a life in the less oppressive North. While working at a variety of odd jobs, including playing the piano in a local band and being the head chef at one of the local hotels, Jack met Virginia one steamy summer night at the music hall that Virginia's parents operated on the outskirts of York. At that time, Virginia was recently widowed from her first husband, Richard Wilson, who died at age 29 of dropsy, which is a debilitating condition that results in the deadly build-up of fluids in the tissue of a human's body that ultimately results in death. Sadly, this affliction overtook him shortly after he and my mother had started a family together. Virginia, still a young woman, had a world-weary look that came from the burden of being responsible for five children. Luckily, she received much help and support from her parents, Anderson and Bessie Tally. Jack felt that Virginia was nonetheless still a vision of beauty. They fell in love at first sight, and married after a short courtship. The couple moved east to Reading. Unfortunately, Jack and Virginia didn't have enough money to support all five of the children at that time so it was decided that the two daughters—Virginia ("Honey Girl") and Bessie—and a son named Charles ("Sonny"), would move to Reading with them, while Richard and Joe would stay with their grandparents in York.

It wasn't long before my father was able to bring in an income as a tradesman, plying his wares around Reading. Initially he worked odd jobs as a handyman; but he soon hooked on with one of the local railroads and worked there throughout the 1930s. With a steady income, the family soon moved into a home at 17 Poplar Street. Virginia, finding great satisfaction in raising her children, was a proud housewife. It was a priority for both Jack and Virginia to raise a healthy and happy family, and it was this focus on "family first" that was quickly instilled in me and all of my siblings at a young age. Even in my earliest recollections, ours was a family unit that was tight and protective.

Jack and Virginia had four children together, to add to the five from Virginia's first marriage: Georgie was the first child of this union, and one was lost due to pneumonia. Then I came into the world. I was the third child, joining the family as Leonard Edward "Lenny" Moore, on November 25, 1933. (My oldest sister, Bessie, to whom I would eventually grow the closest, chose my name. To this day, no one knows for sure where she came up with "Lenny." What we do know is that she liked it so much that she later named one of her own children "Leonard" as well.) My sister Margaret ("Mickey") was next, and the last Moore child would be Connie.

We nine children spanned quite a time horizon. When I was born, my oldest brother Richard was already 13. But we were a very close-knit family. An example of this togetherness is that although for the majority of my childhood, Richard and Joe were still living with my grandparents and were technically stepbrothers, we always referred to them as "brothers," and we saw them constantly. The same holds true with my "stepsisters." My brothers and sisters were my best friends and, being the baby boy, I was doted on by all of my siblings. With 11 people in the family, we were poor, but I lived a very pleasant childhood.

I didn't spend all of my formative years in Reading. My father chased work wherever he could find it and, for a short two-year term when I was four years old, we lived in Brooklyn, New York. My father found some steady work there at a large industrial laundry and brought the family with him. The Brooklyn job paid very well, enabling my mother to continue to stay home with us children. But my mother had a strong distaste for city living. She was very adamant about not raising her children in the city. When she became pregnant with my sister Connie, she said that she refused to bring a child into this world in Brooklyn, New York. The declaration became a moot point, though, as my father was injured in an accident at the laundry when he took a spill and severely hurt his shoulder. He was laid up for an extended period of time and had to apply for welfare in order to feed his family. This meant that the whole family had to pack up and move back to Reading in order to collect a welfare check.

Finding a way to feed seven children without any money or expectations of income was a very stressful time for my parents. The solution, at first, was to have my dad, my brothers, and I sleep at the Hope Rescue Mission, while my sisters and my mother slept at the Salvation Army. We were together for every meal, though, gathering at Scottie's Restaurant on South Ninth Street. With the vouchers my parents collected from the welfare office, we were able to have a fine breakfast, lunch, and dinner every day at Scottie's. I can still taste the cream of wheat that our waitress served in the mornings, and I recall the greasy odor of the restaurant even to this day.

Fortunately, this arrangement lasted only about a month. Soon my father found some steady employment through FDR's "New Deal" program, and he worked with the Works Progress Administration (WPA), doing public works projects of all sorts throughout the area. With this steady employment, our family was happy to move into an apartment at 526 Laurel Street. Later on, we moved into an old wooden home on 43 Pear Street, where we lived during my time in elementary school, then my parents finally found a home in northeast Reading, at 540 Poplar Lane. This sturdy red brick house, one of eight in a row, was where my family lived for the rest of my childhood.

On Poplar Lane, there were four black families and four white families. Growing up amidst white neighbors left a lasting, positive effect on me. Ours was an idyllic neighborhood, for we all watched out for one another. If it was time for dinner and I was out playing baseball in the big field by the railroad tracks, it wouldn't take long for word to spread that my mother wanted me to come home.

Without even knowing it, at an early age I was a pioneer of sorts. I attended a school that was just recently integrated. Northeast Junior High was an all-white school until my siblings and I arrived; but I don't remember the transition as being anything but "normal." As a kid in Reading, I probably had more white friends than black, even though it really wasn't anything I thought about. I had plenty of friends of both races: Paul and

Bennie Boswell, Granville and Percy Price, Will McRae, the Geigers, Dorothy Robinson, and Alan Merkle. These souls would be friends of mine for life, although, sadly, Alan is no longer with us. But Dorothy still lives in Reading, and she has a remarkable collection of newspaper clippings that track my football career from start to finish. We were as close as brothers and sisters, and we did everything together—played stickball, football, or went to the movies. "Civil Rights" and "desegregation" were concepts that would not reach Reading for another decade or so, but our little mixed-race group was happy and innocent.

In fact, the first time I felt my color, the first time I really felt different from my schoolmates, was during an assembly at Northeast Junior High. The school's Glee Club was performing for the students and, at one point, asked the student body to participate in a sing along. We were singing some standard, easy-listening songs of that era. I remember the lyrics of one song, though, that exaggerated the common stereotypes of Southern black people. The song was "Swanee River," the classic that was made popular in the 1939 movie of the same name that featured Al Jolson, who was all too famous for his "black face" impersonations of my race. Although I was familiar with the song from my frequent trips to the movie theater, it was as if I were hearing the words for the first time. In a daze, I looked around this assembly of predominately white kids (there were only about 15 of us black kids in the school at that point) and all eyes seemed to be looking at me. I realized for the first time that I was black and that my friends recognized the difference in me. This really made an impact on me. I can remember it as if it happened yesterday. I vividly remember the waves of emotion that shot through me as the eyes of the auditorium all seemed to focus on me when the lights went up. I wasn't the only black kid at the assembly, and although I never shared my feelings on that day, I imagine that the others felt the same inferiority that I did from that point forward.

When a simple song can make you aware of racial difference, you realize how entrenched racism is in America. You begin to understand why changing people's perceptions about skin color can take so long—it's because of the subtle indoctrination that has permeated society for centuries. Stereotypes and myths are reinforced and perpetuated through our popular culture, even if new laws assert that we are "equal." The old beliefs and feelings are evident everywhere, even in a silly song, performed at a school assembly.

Whether or not I was conscious of the cause, at the time, I now remember that it was in those years before high school when I felt the innocence of childhood fading away. Up to that point, as a young child, I didn't think of color barriers; I mean, my friends—both black and white—and I habitually licked off the same ice cream cone and shared everything, as though we were kin. It's important to realize that not all racism is loud and in your face; it could be an off-hand remark or the lack of perspective by another person that triggers painful emotions or sadness, without warning. Somewhere along the line, though, as if a light bulb had switched on abruptly, I began to resent the slurs and insults that I had ignored before. I started to get into fights in and out of school, and I felt conspicuous, more of a target of derision, than at any point in my life. I had learned that I was "colored." I was suddenly a minority in my own school, with few people like me who I could connect with.

Very few of my friends were aware of how my view of life had changed, even the people closest to me. A few years ago, before my dear friend Alan Merkle passed away, I met him and his wife in Reading in preparation for a leisurely drive to Happy Valley, and we reminisced about those years as youngsters. Throughout the conversation, I explained to him some of the things I had gone through as a young adult—sometimes referencing times and places that Alan had in fact been with me—that have left scars even today. As our dialogue drifted into an uneasy silence, Alan, with tears in his eyes, turned to me and said he genuinely didn't realize how much I had been affected, how much I had hurt. He never really had any idea. How could he have known? It is not like we sat around and talked about these situations as we were growing up. Alan felt badly that he was ignorant of my feelings and that he wasn't there for me. His concern touched me. I wished we could have talked about these things while they were happening, but it is hard to deal with these issues as adults, much less as teenagers. Over the years, I've learned to handle racist remarks and actions; but even to this day, I cannot prevent the emotions they evoke.

In my high school years, my response was to become more introverted. I kept more to myself to avoid the confrontations and the subsequent brooding. My only diversion—in fact, my salvation—was to be found in sports. On the playing field, there was no "color," other than the practice jersey you wore. On the football field, I had no race. Players were separated only as far as their abilities, and I found that I could always hold my own.

If I had a football hero back then, it was Glenn Davis, the great running back from Army who won the Heisman Trophy in 1946. He was part of the famous duo, with Felix "Doc" Blanchard, that was aptly nicknamed "Mr. Inside and Mr. Outside." Davis was fast, elusive, handsome, successful, and famous. I loved how graceful he was! We had no instant replay back then; heck, we didn't even have television. But movie theaters often showed black-and-white newsreels—featuring sports and current events—after every motion picture feature. I lived for the newsreels that showed Glenn Davis dodging all the would-be tacklers, from Navy to Notre Dame. I could have watched Davis on the gigantic screen in front of me on a continuous loop if I could. I was so obsessed that many times, once the movie that I had paid to see was over, I would hide in the darkness of the Ritz Theater and wait for the second movie to start, just so I could see the newsreel all over again.

On the Saturdays when I wasn't hiding out in movie theaters, waiting for a shot of Davis on the big screen, I imitated his moves out in the fields of Reading, playing football with my gang of friends or horsing around with my brothers. Many times, I would go down to the field all by myself and throw the ball up in the air and catch it, then dash to an imaginary end zone. Looking back, it was those days out in the field, all alone, where unbeknownst to me, I was training my body to move the way I would eventually move on the field at Baltimore's Memorial Stadium. That time in solitude was when I truly found my passion and excitement for the game of football.

Years later, at one of my first Pro Bowls, I had a chance to meet Glenn and tell him how he really sparked my interest in football. It was a great thrill to meet him and is something I'll always remember. It's ironic, though, that back in those high school years when I was awestruck by Davis, I never took football seriously as a career for myself. Glenn Davis was white, and I was not. There was little chance that I'd ever play in college, much less in the pros. In fact, when I was a kid, I didn't think blacks played any professional sports in the United States, because I never really saw or heard about them. The notion that there were people of color, just like me, achieving some tremendous things in the sports world, was beyond my imagination.

I do remember Jackie Robinson (who is someone else I had the pleasure to get to know later on in my life) breaking the color barrier in Major League Baseball with the Brooklyn Dodgers in 1947. But there was not another black person, man or woman, featured in those sports newsreels, until then. There were not many black people even in the movies, except those characterized as butlers or criminals, maids or prostitutes. And the blacks I knew in real life worked as blue-collar laborers in factories, or they scrubbed floors, or they were unemployed and did nothing at all. The only blacks I admired were my older brothers, who had all joined the military. Without any other frame of reference, I expected to join the army myself; I had no other plans for my life after high school.

Looking back, that absence of blacks in sports, movies, or respectable careers had a profound effect on me. I had no idea what life had in store for me, but I wasn't very optimistic. I can't begin to fathom how much I could have accomplished if black role models had been visible in my youth; and I know there were many more kids just like me who thirsted for inspiration. All of my brothers, for instance, were excellent athletes who might have had futures in the public spotlight. My brother Rich played baseball and my brother Sonny played football; but my brother George was the most athletic of the bunch. At Reading High School, he was definitely the star of the team. I enjoyed being in his shadow. In eighth grade, when I made the team, I was George's back up at running back. He was a fantastic, all-around athlete, but colleges didn't recruit the way they do today; and even if George had dreamed of playing college athletics, or of going to college at all, the recruiters wouldn't look at him. Once he'd completed 11th grade, he thought that Uncle Sam offered him a better opportunity than a high school diploma, and he joined the army. In those days, there were only two goals that my brothers had—to get out of Reading and to send money home to the family to help out. The army was the only way to reach both goals.

What if George had been aware of other possibilities? What a different life he might have had. The potential was just bubbling out of him, but the surface was only scratched during his years in the army. If he had known that, since the 1800s, blacks had been achieving success all over the Eastern Seaboard, would he have wanted something better for himself? Would he have pursued an athletic career? For that matter, would I have dreamed of a football career, had I known other blacks had done it? It frustrates me that I was an adult researching for myself what it meant to be an African-American, before I learned about the great black sports figures who litter American history as forgotten pioneers.

Black jockeys, for instance, had been winning riders in the Kentucky Derby since 1875. The first jockey to win three Derbys was Isaac Murphy, an African American who was celebrated in the Winner's Circle in 1884, '90, and '91. Another black man, William H. Lewis, played football at the University of Amherst, then at Harvard; and he was eventually named in

1892, as the first black All-American player, by the legendary coach Walter Camp. Lewis later became a lawyer and then the Assistant U.S. District attorney in Boston. Many other outstanding players were to follow in both the collegiate and professional ranks. Among them were Joe Lillard, "Dolly" King, Robert Marshall, Duke Slater, and Brice Taylor. Then, in the early 20th century, there was "Fritz" Pollard and Paul Robeson—more uncelebrated black football players. Fritz Pollard broke barriers at Brown University and went on to become the first black running back to be named All-American, as well as the first to play in the Rose Bowl. He went from Brown University to the Akron Pros, and promptly led the latter team to the League championship in 1920. Pollard also became the first black professional head coach in 1921, as he assumed the helm for the Akron franchise. But there wouldn't be another black head coach in professional football until the LA Raiders hired Art Shell in 1989.

Paul Robeson, a contemporary of Pollard's and a teammate on the Akron Pros, received a scholarship from Rutgers in 1917, and enrolled as only the third black student in the school's history. He went on to win 15 varsity letters in four sports (football, basketball, track, and baseball), then joined Walter Camp's All-American Team. After playing professionally for a brief time with Akron (in order to pay for law school), he became a world-renown actor, vocalist, orator, and activist.

And in any history of black athletes, who could forget Joe Louis, heavy-weight champ of boxing? Or Jesse Owens, whose astonishing broad jump won the gold medal at the 1938 Olympics? How could such black brilliance have escaped my notice as a child?

For one thing, the press of those days did not get out the word; whites comprised most newspaper subscribers, owned the major media outlets, and purchased most of the radios. As a result, there were few black journalists to speak of. Since there were no black advertisers paying for newspaper space or radio commercials in the mainstream media, there was no incentive to cover the positive activities of people of the black race. Thus, the accomplishments of countless blacks were obscured and minimized, and any news about blacks was more likely connected with issues of crime and poverty.

Another reason we never heard about successful blacks in sports was because there were so few. The history of segregation in professional football is especially muddied because of the racism of team owners like George Halas of the Chicago Bears, and George Preston Marshall of the Washington Redskins. These men are often referred to in reverential terms because of their roles in building the League, but they were also responsible for not allowing blacks to compete in the NFL for a very long time. It wasn't until Jackie Robinson broke the color barrier that desegregation in professional sports became an issue. In 1947, Robinson opened the floodgates for black athletes to play in professional sports.

In 1947, I was 14 years old and had just began to learn that I was "colored." Once I had that knowledge, thanks to the "Swanee River" song I heard at a junior high school assembly, any ambition I might have had seemed to dissolve. My grades began to slip; I had no goals and no reason to push myself. The one thing I enjoyed about school was football; but even there, I never really excelled. It wasn't a priority for me as it is now for many teenagers. I was just happy to be part of the team. I was marking my time, floating aimlessly through school. In order to play football, I needed a passing grade of 60 percent; and, somehow, I maintained a 65 percent or 67 percent—just enough to skate by. If I had an upcoming test, I would study the night before. I wasn't interested in good grades because I didn't see the point; I had no clue that some colleges gave football scholarships. How did I know what was possible, when I knew of no one like me out there doing well? All I knew was that I loved playing sports, especially football; and if maintaining decent grades guaranteed my access into that world, I would stay in school. Once my junior year was up I'd follow my brother George into the army.

The one thing that made me happy was to go to football practice every day and hang out with the guys. Unlike the rest of my life, the camaraderie I enjoyed on the field was always better than off, so I never wanted it to end. Apart from football, my life was a day-by-day existence. Without much of a plan for my life in place, outside of preparing for the next game day, I was headed nowhere. All things being equal, I was on the verge of becoming just another number. Luckily for me, things changed in a hurry.

# TWO

# THE READING COMET

My life changed when an angel with a clipboard and a whistle appeared to me, halfway through my junior year at Reading High. For some reason, a football coach—the unstoppable Andy Stopper—saw some potential in me. I didn't know what he was looking at, but I truly appreciated the time he spent with me. Everyone needs someone special in his life, to believe in him and nudge him farther than he thinks he can go. For me, that person was Coach Stopper. He was one of the most unique men I have ever come across in my life. In many ways, he saved an aimless kid from Reading from drowning in mediocrity.

Coach Stopper was a special person in the community. Beneath his quiet exterior was a romantic at heart, someone with a sense of fair play and equality. He genuinely cared about all the kids he came in contact with, no matter what part of town they came from. Helping foster a community that wasn't divided by race, as most of the country was in 1950, was very important to Andy Stopper. He was totally "color blind." He wanted us all to succeed. I really think he saw sports (he coached football and track) as a way to come into contact with kids who were destined to a life of being judged by their skin tone. Then draw those kids into an environment that was based not on race, but on running, jumping, catching, and blocking. On Coach Stopper's field, we were rewarded by our speed and agility, not by our ancestry. He built our confidence; and he strove to develop us adolescents not only into athletes but, more importantly, into responsible men.

To prove he wasn't all talk, one summer he took a job as a lifeguard at a swimming pool down on 7th and Laurel. It was a swimming pool that at that time was all black. He felt it was important to know how the black kids on his team were living, how they communicated with each other, how they acted outside of a school environment. Everyone thought he was crazy, but this action impressed me. Up to that point in my life, I hadn't witnessed many white adults anxious to learn our language and see what it was like to walk a mile in our shoes.

What I didn't know about Andy at the time was his devotion to our city of Reading and to the kids he coached. After a standout career at Villanova as a halfback, he turned down an opportunity to play with the New York Giants so that he could coach high school football in Reading. Married to his high school sweetheart, Sophie, he came to Reading with the intent of putting down roots. In fact, later in 1951, when his alma mater came calling to ask him to lead their varsity squad, he turned them down out of loyalty to his kids at Reading High. A more ethical man I never met.

As a youngster on his team, I didn't have to listen to Andy, but the interest he took in me made me hold him in such high regard that he became a measuring stick for me. Forever after, whenever I would confront a harsh situation growing up, or when there were times I didn't know how to handle myself, I would think about how Andy would have dealt with the issue. As a benchwarmer going into my junior year, I didn't have as much contact with him as the starters did, but I watched how he treated everyone with the same amount of respect—it didn't matter if you were the star of the team or the last man on the roster. And he demanded the same respect among the players: no one was to be either privileged or disrespected. I thought he was amazing, even before I really was able to get to know him well.

While I dreamed of moving into the starting lineup, however, much to my dismay, it seemed I was pretty firmly planted on the bench. I developed a strong distaste, even at a young age, for sitting on the bench. It was not that I had dreams of going to college on an athletic scholarship; I just wanted to be out there on the field competing and having fun. The one consolation about my time spent on the bench was that I was backing up my brother George. As I've mentioned before, I respected him so much for his athletic talent. It was just a privilege to be on the same team with him. I learned so much being around him; it was like having a full-time football tutor. He would do anything to help me succeed, and I would listen to anything he said. It was a match made in heaven.

In backing up George before he enlisted, I played junior varsity football in tenth grade under Charles Dunkelberger and Bill Reese. Once George left, I ended up playing behind our twin star backs in my eleventh grade class, Phil Mathias and Ben Kemp, who were the two most celebrated and prolific athletes in Reading at the time. Ben starred in all sports, from football to baseball, basketball and track. And Phil was not far behind him. Even with this star power, though, the team was going nowhere by the time we met our rivals from Steelton High in the middle of the year. Little did I know that game would be one of the first defining moments of my young life—a moment that helped shape the person I am today.

The Steelton Steamrollers were beating us pretty badly. At one point during the game, Ben and Coach Stopper became embroiled in a very heated disagreement on the sideline. Coach Stopper typically remained calm during the games: it wasn't his style to display much emotion, much less argue with a player in front of a packed house. I knew Ben must have said something outrageous for the coach to lose his composure. In short order, and with ill-disguised fury, he ordered Ben to the bench. Then he glanced in my direction and told me to get in the game. I was shocked by the whole turn of events. It was strange enough to see Andy Stopper lose his temper; but for him to call me in to replace Ben, without my having played much up to this point in the season, bowled me over. I was stunned and still gape-jawed merely from the sight of Coach Stopper losing his cool. Nonetheless, I gathered up my helmet and started toward the field.

In hindsight, Coach didn't do me any favors by sending me into the game at that moment. I was still a scrawny little guy who didn't strike fear into the opposition by any means. Lord knows, Steelton always gave us a whipping. When Andy called my name, I thought to myself, "Oh, Lord, here we go." I bravely went in and let Steelton beat up on me for the rest of the game. Regardless of my inexperience and fear, it was a great learning experience. I never backed down; I just kept running as hard as I could whenever they gave me the ball. I didn't want to let Andy down. It was the first time that anyone outside of my family had shown so much faith in me, and I was determined not to disappoint my coach.

Steelton ended up beating us 34-0. True to form, though, Andy had let the team know, in no uncertain terms, that there would be no prima donnas on his team. Andy was the coach and leader and didn't allow anyone to challenge him! Reading was, and still is, a very small town that takes its high school football very seriously. It took a lot of guts for Coach to stand up to

Ben. In the rest of my time, I would never see another player challenge Coach Stopper again.

When we got back to Reading after the game, Coach stopped me as I was getting off the bus, saying, "I knew you wouldn't let me down. We'll show 'em! Now we've got some work to do." At practice the following Monday, I took Ben's spot and lined up alongside Phil. As if I needed to see it in print to believe it, I rustled through the newspaper the next day to find a very brief description of the screaming match between Ben and the coach. I was amazed, as I read further, to see that Coach Stopper had disclosed to the papers that I would be awarded the starting position for the rest of the year. Furious with the decision, Ben quit the team immediately.

I didn't make it easy on Coach in my debut performances as the new starting running back. In my first four games as a starter, I didn't score any points. Most other coaches would have wavered and benched me in hopes that someone would replace Ben competently, but Coach Stopper, as I'm sure you know by now, wasn't your average coach. I may not have been a quick study in the classroom, but I was on the field. I made it my mission not to let Coach Stopper down. I would soon reward him for the faith he exhibited in me, and it would be better than either one of us thought it could ever be.

My first varsity touchdown came against Bethlehem High in mid-October, on a 27-yard scamper. After that game, something clicked for me, and two games later I scored two more touchdowns—one on a Statue of Liberty play, and another on a pass-reception. Nonetheless, it was still trial by fire. I wasn't as polished as Ben had been, and Andy had to spend a lot of time coaching me throughout the season. Relying mainly on my raw ability, I would usually revert back to my bad habits by game time; but finally, by the end of the season, I returned a punt 85 yards for a touchdown by starting down the sidelines (as Andy had taught me) and breaking back toward the middle of the field when I saw a hole. Afterwards, I couldn't wait to get back to the sideline and tell Andy how I finally knew what he had been talking about. I would finish my junior year with seven touchdowns and a dramatic increase in my confidence as a player and as a person.

Going into my senior year, Andy had high expectations for the team, and so did the rest of Berks County, Pennsylvania. Throughout the season, we regularly played in front of crowds as large as 7,500 people. In our first game that year, I contributed three touchdowns against Norristown High. Later I was able to exact some revenge on Steelton High by scoring a touchdown on the opening kick-off, en route to a 33-6 victory. Our only blemish that entire season was a 21-16 loss to Williamsport High. We finished our season 9-1, with a 19-7 victory over Pottsville, in front of 10,000 people at Veteran's Memorial. All three touchdowns in that victory were mine. Remarkably, we wouldn't be invited to the Central Penn Championships because of our one loss, but Andy and his Reading High team had the time of our lives.

That year, there were many standouts on the team, such as John Jenkins (who went to Arizona State) and Ed Albright (who went to Syracuse); yet, I was thrust into the spotlight as the star of the team. I earned the nickname "the Reading Comet," and I was awarded the Astor Theater Trophy as the best athlete in Reading in 1951. All the attention made me feel a little uncomfortable. This may sound immodest now, but I really didn't know what all the fuss was about. I always thought playing college ball was for someone else. I never envisioned myself in a position to take my success any further. With a solid one and a half seasons under my belt, my numbers were good. I broke the single-season touchdown record with 22; and I stood out on offense as a flanker/running back, on defense as a defensive back, and on special teams as a kick and punt returner. Had any colleges taken notice? I didn't know or really care; I didn't even know how the recruiting process worked.

As though there were an invisible hand guiding my fate, though, a number of colleges began showing their interest. The postmarks came from all over: Tuscaloosa, Ann Arbor, Columbus, and Grambling, just to name a few. Recruiting wasn't quite the year-round job it is now for college coaches. Back in the 1950s, if there were kids putting up big numbers around the country, the major schools would send out feeler letters as a matter of routine. That is why I received a letter from Notre Dame—who wasn't even allowing blacks on their team at that time—which assumed, with a relatively generic name, that I was white. My family and I got a laugh out of that!

I really didn't pay any attention to the letters from various universities until one day, halfway through my senior season; Coach Stopper called me into his office and said, "Lenny, you need to think about going to college." That was really the first time I gave the idea much thought. Andy told me that I had a lot of talent and that I needed to use that talent to make an opportunity for myself. He asked if it would be okay with me if he made some calls. I reluctantly agreed.

All the attention from the community, such as the write-ups in the newspapers, awards from local civic groups, and the growing number of recruiting letters still didn't impress me very much. Even into the spring semester of my senior year (although Coach Stopper didn't find out until much, much later), I was sure that I would be well on my way to the military, soon after high school graduation. I knew that if I were to pursue college and not go right into the army, the tuition and living costs would be a burden on my parents. I had pretty much determined that I would follow in the footsteps of my brothers and help support my family through military wages.

Luckily for me, Coach Stopper knew my personality and never pushed. He didn't push me to go to Penn State, or to Villanova, his alma mater. He never pressured me to go to any college. He just had a way of subtly nudging me in the right direction until I made the decision on my own. Andy knew that he could do no better than to give me the sense that I was master of my own destiny.

One of the assistant coaches at Reading High was Bob Perugini, a mountain of a man and a former lineman for Penn State. He still had contact with his alma mater, and he and Coach Stopper would routinely send that university some of their better players. Bob contacted Sever Torretti, an assistant coach at Penn State; and it wasn't long before Coach Torretti became extremely interested in me. Late in the 1951 season, when Penn State's game against Villanova was moved to Allentown, Pennsylvania, Coach Torretti urged me to meet Penn State's coach, Rip Engle, before the game.

Although I still wasn't sold on the idea of going to some university that was far away in the Pennsylvania mountains, I nonetheless didn't want to show up at our meeting wearing torn blue jeans and an outsized sweatshirt; so my older brother Sonny let me choose an outfit from his wardrobe. He was quite a dresser and always sported the newest fashions. I borrowed his best suit and topped it off with a brand new furry beaver hat from my brother Rich. I thought I looked dashing! I had no idea where this was going to lead me, but I certainly wanted to impress this coach. If nothing else, I wanted to do my family proud.

Unfortunately, I was late to the lunch meeting at the team hotel and missed meeting Coach Engle before the game. Coach Torretti was still interested in me—and very persistent. He was convinced that I was worth the trouble and insisted that I go to the game and let me stand on the sidelines until the game was over. I didn't mind. Hey, I was just along for the ride! In short order, though, I was awed by the speed with which these massive college players played. I was mesmerized and enjoyed the game thoroughly; so much so that I forgot all about Coach Engle. According to Ridge Riley, in his great book, *Road to Number One*, Coach Engle kept looking down the sideline at me, finally asking Coach Torretti, "Who's he?" Coach Torretti is said to have replied, "Don't worry about 'who's he.' 'Who's he' is going to win a lot of games for you know who."

If it had been anyone but Coach Torretti, that type of smart response wouldn't have gone over very well, but it certainly got Rip's attention. Over the next few weeks, Coach Engle came to several of my games to watch me play without my even knowing. He was interested. When we finally met, I was very impressed with him. He reminded me a lot of Coach Stopper. Not as a coach, but as a man. That meeting stuck in my mind and would play a major part in my decision regarding a forthcoming offer to play for Penn State.

Because my grades never were fantastic, Coach Stopper told me that a scholarship to Penn State depended on my passing an entrance exam for the university. He asked if I could do it, and I said, "No problem." Late in the spring of my senior year, I went to Happy Valley to see the campus and take the exam; I passed it on my first try. It wasn't that I couldn't get good grades. I was very capable. I was just disinterested.

Although I was still apprehensive about leaving home and being a burden on my parents, I accepted the scholarship to Penn State to start my collegiate career and venture into uncharted territories. No one in the Moore family had ever been to college. Even more daunting: outside of that two-year stint in Brooklyn, when I was a preschooler, I had never voluntarily lived outside Reading city limits. I had no desire to be far away from my family; I was very much accustomed to the quaintness of the small burg I called "home," and I had worries about adjusting to life in a big city. I had few expectations from life; I certainly had no dreams of fame or prosperity. But suddenly I was on the verge of playing major college football and pursuing a college education. I wondered how my life would change now that I had taken an active role in choosing an untried course for my family.

My whole life up to then had been lived on a day-to-day basis: When I graduated from grade school, I thought to myself, "Now what?" I moved on, to Northeast Junior High School, like everybody else. When I graduated from Northeast, I thought to myself, again, "Now what?" The next step was to enter Reading High. Now I was at a crossroads, with an either-or choice: go to Penn State or enlist in the army. The only difference between my brothers and me was that I had a second choice. At that point, I didn't know if continuing my education was the better path or if it was just the one that I chose. In retrospect, the motivating factor was the chance to play football. With the game as my guiding light, it was not a difficult decision after all.

With my focus now on playing for Penn State, did I have visions of becoming another Jackie Robinson? Not a chance. Ask any black person alive in the fifties, and you will learn that the entire black population in this country was aware of how Jackie had changed the sports world. His achievements were a source of pride for us and were truly historic moments, without question. Because of Jackie, the Brooklyn Dodgers were the toast of the town every summer in most black homes throughout the country. But watching Jackie in the latest newsreel was very different from imagining success for any other black individual at that point in time. For a dose of reality, most blacks still had to watch those flickering images of Jackie from the balcony of most movie houses, because in most cities we weren't allowed in the main seating area. So, yes, he was a role model and a hero for us on the screen; but it was life as usual once we left the darkened theater and hit the streets. To us, Jackie's achievement was almost mythical. It was as unreal as those Westerns that ran in the theaters every Saturday. He blended into those other flickering images on the newsreels before and after the main attraction.

The exploits of a cowboy on a white horse, riding into Dodge to fight the bandits, were on a par with Jackie's home runs for the Dodgers. The two "stories" held equal weight on Main Street, USA, in terms of reality. To me, and many others in my position, Jackie was an anomaly. A poor black kid from Reading had little hope of repeating his success. My going to Penn State was a privilege, but not a sure path to fame. It was just another option, another station to visit, on my journey through life.

~ ~ ~

Once I had accepted my scholarship to Penn State, however, fate had another surprise in store for me, and I almost never made it to campus after all.

In high school, my sweetheart was a girl named Lorraine. She was the apple of my eye. As an adolescent, I was just learning how to love and be loved, but Lorraine was the only girl I had ever been serious about in all my teenage years. I cared about her, and us, very deeply. I was very naïve about sex and literally had no idea what I was doing. Like most teenagers, my friends and I would talk about our sexual exploits; but whether or not my friends were just spinning yarns, I didn't know. I didn't really elaborate on my own experiences, because I hadn't had any. To deflect any attention, I just played along with them. Then, one summer night, between my senior year at Reading High and my freshman year at Penn State, I made love to Lorraine for the first time. That magical night felt like a comedy of errors to me. Due to my lack of experience, I was very nervous. I really wasn't even sure what was supposed to go where. The whole experience was very awkward and very quick; but it was important to us that we shared the experience, because I believed that we loved each other very deeply.

A few months after that passionate evening, and after I had made my commitment to attend Penn State, I started to realize that this might be a difficult transition for Lorraine and me. We talked about it often and agreed that distance would not drive us apart. She accepted that I would be leaving, and I promised to come home to Reading whenever I could. A few weeks before I was set to leave for Happy Valley, Lorraine came to my house, looking despondent and scared. She demanded that I sit down. Bewildered, I followed her orders; I knew something was very wrong. She started crying as she told me that she was pregnant.

I was shocked and terrified after hearing the news. My life was turned upside down in one short sentence. I didn't know what to do. We went immediately to our parents out of sheer desperation, ready to face any consequences that might await us. At that time in America, having children out of wedlock was just not acceptable. In those days, no matter how old two people were, when a young lady was pregnant, there were no other options; the couple was expected to marry, and the young man was expected to support the family. That was it—case closed. With my pending college career a nice option, but not a lifelong goal, I was prepared to marry Lorraine and get a job as soon as possible to support the young family that was instantly thrust upon us.

The days after Lorraine came to me with the news that I was going to be a father were difficult and heart-wrenching for both of us, to say the least. It did not take long for me to give up the idea of attending college. I told myself that I needed to focus on getting used to the idea of being married. I grew to be very excited about what the future would hold. My focus had shifted: my goal now was to find work to support a family.

Thus, I was shocked when one day out of the blue my parents said to me in private, "We want you to go to Penn State." They felt so strongly that this was an opportunity that I couldn't pass up, that they would take responsibility for the child Lorraine and I were about to have. "We will do our best to support our grandchild in any way possible," said Dad.

I was stunned. I didn't know what to say or how to react. "That isn't fair to you," I finally said. "It's my responsibility, and I'll deal with it."

But my parents would not change their thinking. In their minds, I was going to Penn State and that was that. In a day or two, I found myself sitting with my mother, Lorraine, and her mother, having a very direct conversation.

Lorraine's mother asked, "So what are you going to do?"

My mother responded politely, but matter-of-factly, "My son is going to college. He is the first one in our family to have the opportunity and we are not going to deny him the chance. We don't have a lot of money, but Jack and I will do what we have to do, with whatever money we have available."

I held my breath in anticipation of a response from either Lorraine or her mother. They both sat silent for what seemed to be an eternity before Lorraine's mother spoke. In the end, Lorraine's mother seemed satisfied. It was almost surreal how cordially these two women took control of the situation and made the decision for Lorraine and me. But as I have said, my family has always been a remarkably tight group. Growing up, I learned that sacrifice, for a family member in need, was a given. Whether it meant my mother scrubbing floors, my father working multiple jobs, or my brothers enlisting in the military so they could send their allotment check home to help support the family, we always put family first. The gift my parents gave me in this situation, though, was inordinately invaluable. The Penn State scholarship was a special opportunity presented to me, and it wasn't lost on any of the family. Each would give anything to see me succeed.

I had no idea that a college education meant that much to my parents. We had never talked about my going to college before because we all knew it was financially impossible. Looking back, though, I recall that my father was well into middle age before he learned how to read—and it was my mother who taught him. He demanded literacy from himself and an education for his children.

My father was born into poverty in South Carolina and was on his own from an early age. His parents were sharecroppers, the first generation of blacks to be on their own after the Emancipation Proclamation determined their freedom. But as black people all over the country were set free, they realized they didn't have any place to go. They weren't educated. They didn't own anything. The only solution, for many, was to rent land from a plantation owner and set about raising small crops. The landowners exacted a heavy price, though, and the sharecroppers were dirt poor. It was a very dark period in my father's life, and he never wanted to burden his family by talking about it. All we knew is that he pushed us children farther than he had been able to go. He said, "All of you are going to school so that you can read and write."

When he learned to read and write, around the age of 30, it was like unlocking a Pandora's Box of activity. I have never seen anyone with such a thirst for learning and self-improvement. There were stacks of *Popular Mechanics* books around the house for as long as I can remember. He taught himself to be an excellent electrician, plumber, and mason. He not only improved our home by wiring it for electricity, installing indoor plumbing, and adding extra rooms to our house, but he did the same for other people in town as well. He taught himself all about auto mechanics, too. When he bought our first car, he didn't know how to drive, but he took that old junker up and down our street, reading the owner's manual as he went, trying to understand how the vehicle worked, until he'd mastered it. He learned on his own how car engines worked, and he soon purchased another used car and practically rebuilt it. Then, once televisions became affordable, in the 1950s, he used his electrical knowledge to keep our television in good repair, along with fixing those owned by our neighbors.

In short, there was nothing my father couldn't do once he learned to read.

What would he have accomplished if everything had been equal? If he had been allowed to go to school and learn like white children? A lawyer? An engineer? A business owner? Because of the scars he carried from his childhood as a sharecropper's son (both physically and mentally), a life not far removed from legalized slavery, he didn't want to dwell on his own lack of education. Instead, he always maintained a positive and forward-looking attitude. And when one of his sons got the opportunity to go to college, he was not about to let that gift be rejected.

This is why, over the four years that I was at Penn State, my parents cared for my first son, Leonard Jenkins, as if he were their own child. Not once did they complain, hold it over my head, or make me feel guilty. It is only because of their unwavering support that I have had the experiences that occasion the writing of these memoirs. The selfless love that my parents always showed me was especially crucial at the time of my life when I was about to become a father, a university student, and a college football player. All things being equal, I was about to become a man.

# THREE

# PENN STATE BOUND

To this day, many emotions well up inside of me whenever I visit the Penn State campus in Happy Valley, Pennsylvania. Like so many others before me, I am overwhelmed with the beauty of the campus. It is, without a doubt, a picture postcard in all seasons. As a collegiate setting, it is second to none, and I felt very fortunate to be there. In my mind's eye, I can still feel the crisp, fall breeze as it rattled through the ancient trees that beautify the campus. The pastoral mountain ranges surrounding the area serve to frame the community, and they also seem to help insulate this place from the march of time. Those mighty hills protect the community from the dregs of unmitigated sprawl and blatant commercialization that would otherwise spoil this idyllic setting.

At the same time, those grand old mountains may have protected the residents from cultural progress and enlightenment. It is as though racial equality, for one thing, possibly ran out of steam while trying to climb Mount Nittany: black students and athletes of today endure much the same treatment as my buddies and I experienced back in the fifties. Like Sysiphus, pushing his rock uphill for eternity, the issue of race struggles against a slippery slope of Eurocentric ideologies in this central Pennsylvania town. As a result, in my opinion, true race equality has never really quite reached Happy Valley. Racism was an issue before I arrived on campus, and there has been only stilted improvement in the town's attitudes since I left.

Perhaps my hometown of Reading spoiled me; it was as close to Nirvana for a black child as one could expect in the 1950s. The prejudice I confronted in my primarily white high school was tempered by the fact that there was a strong base of families just like mine, facing the same discrimination. The occasional rude remark or stare certainly hurt; but I never felt isolated, because all of us in the large black community supported each other and erased the psychic wounds.

My whole perspective on what it meant to be a young adult of color in the 1950s would change, though, once I arrived at Penn State.

It should be no surprise that homesickness dominated my first year at college. As I'm sure you've deduced, I am an admitted momma's boy, and proud of it. I missed everyone back home: my parents, my brothers and sisters, my friends, and Lorraine. Although my family tried to attend as many of my games as possible, it was still a tough adjustment. I didn't have a vehicle my freshman year, which was probably a good thing: If I had had a car, I'd have gone home every weekend and, most likely there would have come a time that I'd have decided never to return to campus. As it was, I traveled back to Reading by bus whenever I had the money; but for the most part I was on my own, far away from my support system of family and friends.

As a freshman I practiced with the football team, attended meetings with the coach, and even played two games against other freshmen squads at Bucknell and at the Naval Academy. The structure of practice and the anticipation of playing in the next game were all that kept me interested in school. I made sure my grades were where they needed to be—not a bit higher—in order to remain eligible for football. It was still not evident to me how a college degree would benefit me in life, so I only put in the effort that was required of me, and not much more.

I took a different path of education than my teammates at Penn State, as I matriculated through the liberal arts program. Most members of the team majored in physical education, because they figured they'd be gym teachers if their football careers didn't take them any farther than Beaver Stadium. I had no interest in running a gym class for the rest of my life, nor was I ready to pursue a curriculum that, at the time, was practically a pre-med program. I was glad I went the liberal arts route, because most of the guys in physical education were disappointed to learn that what they thought would be courses about athletics were, in fact, lectures about chemistry and biology. The program eventually scared many of my teammates away after two years. Most would eventually join me in liberal arts.

I liked liberal arts because I was allowed to take a wide variety of classes. I particularly enjoyed psychology and English literature. In psychology, we students were forced to look at ourselves and those around us to find out why we acted the way we did. Learning about human nature was fascinating to me. Reading stories that always had a human element in English literature held my attention for the same reason: I wanted to learn what makes human beings tick. Mostly, I wanted to learn about myself—but it didn't take long for me to realize that there was scarce emphasis on African-Americans in any of the course options. Back then there were no "Black History" months or "African American Studies" courses. Even if these programs did exist, I don't recall there being any black professors on campus to teach them.

Looking back, a big reason why I never finished my course of study was because I was sick of learning about the history of my white classmates. Based on the lesson plan set out for me every semester, you would think that blacks just appeared out of nowhere to be slaves to their white masters. I knew all about Christopher Columbus and George Washington. I knew that my people had to have a history, but it was totally ignored at that time. I felt a tremendous void in my education for this reason, and that led to much of my disinterest.

I wanted to know where I had come from—why I was who I was. Everywhere I looked, I could see that my peers knew who they were, because they saw themselves in history. Moreover, most white people I knew had a family history full of accomplished ancestors. The knowledge of my own family history barely stretched back two generations. My father was loath to talk about his poor sharecropper parents. My grandmother, who actually lived with us for a while, also refused to talk about that early part of her life. As a result, I knew very little about my uncles, aunts, and cousins. I felt almost orphaned compared to the other students, who knew, for the most part, who they were and where they came from. It made me feel lonely and empty.

It was at this point that I started a journey of self-discovery in earnest that would never end. I took what I could get out of the classes I attended, but I knew the information I was thirsting for would have to come from nontraditional places. In my search for self, I created a support system that I still have today.

The cornerstone of my Penn State support system was someone I had known well even before I set foot on campus. Charlie Blockson, against

whom I competed when playing Norristown High School, was my roommate that first year. Although we didn't end up at Penn State together on
purpose, it was one of those happy accidents in life that has led to decades
of friendship that I cherish greatly.

What I learned about Charlie immediately upon moving into our dorm
room together was that he would pray every night before he went to bed.
That to me showed what type of person he was. I knew that I would be
sharing my room with a person of strong moral convictions. Looking back,
it is clear that Charlie also helped ease the transition for me and helped me
stay grounded. For one thing, he was always acutely aware of his surround-
ings—meaning that he was aware of the quietly consistent racism that permeated this town we lived in, our temporary hometown, but he chose to
transcend it by avoiding confrontations.

Charlie was also a fantastic athlete and shared my passion for sports. But
at that point in our lives, he was much more advanced academically than I
was. He didn't rest on his athletic laurels; he applied himself to his studies
with a passion for learning that I never possessed. Throughout our time at
Penn State, there were many instances when I would be looking for Charlie
to see if he wanted to grab a bite to eat at the Student Union or go to a
movie—but I couldn't find him. He was usually in the library reading. Or
sitting under a tree reading. Or walking across campus—with his nose in a
book. He was a very good influence on me at a time when I didn't seem to
have a plan or a purpose outside of waiting for the next football game or
practice.

In time, Charlie became a confidant who knew me as well as anyone;
he was a pal to whom I could tell my innermost feelings. One of the major
adjustments Charlie and I faced on campus was getting used to the lack of
other people who were like us, with whom we could socialize. There were
very few places for black students to congregate in those years. The room
that Charlie and I shared at McKee Hall became a hub for many of the
black students on campus—even those who were not on the football team.
Other than our dorm room, there were a few black fraternities: Alpha Phi
Alpha, Omega Psi Phi, and Kappa Alpha Psi. There were two black sororities on campus, as well: Delta Sigma Theta and Alpha Kappa Alpha. The
white fraternities and sororities on campus did not allow blacks as members;
and the only time we were allowed to mix with the white "Greeks" was at
open house during Rush Week. We were able to walk through a fraternity
house, but it was a quick tour, believe me. It didn't bother me because I did-

n't have any interest in participating in Greek life of any kind. I would attend many of the functions I was invited to; but when I saw what the pledges had to go through during "rush," it struck me as a total waste of time.

So it was in our dorm room, the Student Union, the Rathskeller (a local restaurant), and at the Kappa house, that a small number of us blacks on campus would meet between classes, homework, and football practice. We watched out for each other. Jesse Arnelle and Rosey Grier, who were sophomores, tutored Charlie and me on how to navigate campus; where we could go to have ice cream or watch a movie or get a haircut. For any black person, finding a place to get your hair cut was not easy; but a few years before I arrived, Penn State had drawn national attention when all the local barbers refused to cut hair for any black people. They claimed that it would ruin business and that they didn't know how to cut "Negro" hair. Most of the blacks on campus, along with a few liberal whites, gathered in protest one day, and finally some of the barbers gave in. By the time I got to Happy Valley, though, there was only one place in town that would give me a haircut. As a result, some of us learned to cut hair and we could give each other a shave. With a few amateur barbers among us, it was better than worrying where we would be shut out next. If it wasn't such a bonding experience for us, we could have dwelled on the sad commentary this presented of our isolation on campus, but we didn't look at it that way. We were survivors, and this experience, albeit a small and inconsequential one, helped each of us build our character.

By the time I arrived on campus, it had been only five years since Penn State had allowed black players on the team. The first was Wally Triplett. He and Denny Hoggard played for Penn State in the late 1940s, breaking through significant color lines, not only on campus but also nationally. Wally and Denny were the first blacks to play in the Cotton Bowl in Dallas in 1948. When I came on board, there were more blacks on the team, including Rosey, Jesse, Bob Pollard, and Sam Green. Although we represented only a small percentage of players on that team, we were actually one of the largest contingent of black players on a traditionally white football squad, at any college in the nation.

By the second semester of my freshman year, I had my bearings on campus, and I knew where I could and couldn't go in downtown Happy Valley. For the most part I loved being a part of Penn State Football, and being exposed to the coaches and the veterans on the football team increased my football knowledge daily. With every passing moment I grew more anxious to play football for the varsity. Each small taste of the action made me want it even more. For the sake of football, I was staying focused on keeping my grades up and staying out of trouble. I could not wait for my chance on the varsity team.

Then one blustery March day I received a letter in the mail from a close friend back in Reading. That letter broke my heart.

Lorraine and I had made it a point to keep in touch while I was at school. I came home as often as I could, and our relationship seemed to be all right. Our son, Leonard Jenkins, had been born in January of 1953, and I was so proud to be a father. But that spring I received a letter that alerted me to the fact that Lorraine had been unfaithful to me. I was devastated. Instead of handling this in a long distance phone call, I bought a ticket on the next bus to Reading to confront her in person. I asked her point blank if she had been unfaithful, and she admitted that she had.

I told her that we were through. I didn't want her to call me, send me letters, or try to contact me in any way. It was the hardest thing I'd ever done, but I couldn't maintain a relationship with someone I couldn't trust. It tore my heart apart. I boarded the bus back to Penn State and cried my eyes out, but I never looked back—only ahead to the end of my freshman year.

That summer, I went back to Reading and found a job stocking shelves at the local grocery store. It was a pattern that would continue, as every summer I traveled back home to find menial employment. It was the most depressing time of every year, for I would see my mother and father struggling to put food on the table and working endless hours to make ends meet. I would see other black people in Reading working at minimum-wage jobs. It all made me wonder, "What is the point of my going to college, studying white people's history or white people's literature, listening to lectures by white professors, surrounded by white students if I will only end up doing mindless labor like other blacks?" Other than maintaining a consistent grade point average so that I could play football, I didn't see that I was doing anything useful at Penn State.

When I returned to school in the fall of my sophomore year, the coaches sensed that I was less than enthusiastic about continuing this academic charade. They paired me up with Jesse Arnelle as my roommate at McKee Hall, for the next two years. Jesse was All-Everything. He was a year older than I was; but from a maturity and focus standpoint, he was light years ahead of me. He not only played football, he also was the best player on the basketball team, leading the university to its only Final Four appearance to date. He also excelled at track. He would burn the midnight oil and maintain excellent grades. He was approachable, well-spoken, and handsome. He had all the tools for success, and he would continually sharpen them. More importantly, he opened many doors that had never been tested by black students at this college. It was his goal to challenge the traditionally white organizations on campus to accept him. He achieved this when he was invited to join the Lion's Paw, which was an ultra-exclusive academic club on campus. And he eventually ascended the ladder at Penn State to become the first black student body president of a major university with a predominately white student body. I think he got his determination from his father, a black police officer who, having to be better than average in order to succeed, managed to instill in Jesse a work ethic that was second to none.

The coaches apparently hoped that by having Jesse and me room together, his work ethic and study habits would rub off on me. It didn't happen. Although I truly admired and respected Jesse, I did not adopt his approach toward studying, even after two years as his roommate. Outside of not wanting to get kicked off the team and disappointing my family and my high school mentor, Coach Stopper, I really had no use for my studies.

What did stoke my passion was the start of the 1953 season. I couldn't wait. After spending my freshman year playing only two games and doing nothing but scrimmaging against the varsity, I couldn't wait to test myself against live action.

The previous summer, the NCAA had re-instituted the two-platoon system in college football, which meant that players had to be able to fill dual roles on the field. This change was due to the dearth of athletic talent, which was a result of so many college-aged men being drafted for the Korean War. Although this new system meant a tremendous shift in the way college football would be played and coached over the next few years, I can't say it really bothered me. Playing both sides of the ball was nothing new to me. In high school, once Coach Stopper gave me a chance to play my junior year, I not only took over the halfback position at Reading, but I also started playing defensive back, and I returned kick-offs and punts. I did whatever the coaches told me to do; all I wanted to do was get out on the field and help the team win. There were many games that I played nearly the whole 60 minutes, and I loved every second of it.

I was as eager to play multiple roles at Penn State. I didn't have a lot of expectations; I didn't spend a lot of time thinking about winning a national championship or going to a Bowl game (those were primarily shut out to teams with black athletes anyway, since most were held in the South). All I wanted was to be a better player than I was the year before. The battle I was looking to win was within my own mind, and all I hoped for was the chance to show the coaches that I belonged. When Coach "Rip" Engle listed me as the starting tailback in my first varsity game, I entered camp not knowing if I was good enough. I felt I had to prove that I could compete at this level.

The sport was different back then. Penn State University wasn't PENN STATE. The school was independent, and we played most of our games against Eastern seaboard colleges. Coach Engle wanted to change that perception and wanted to expand the schedule so we could start playing the powerhouses in the Midwest and in the South. It was a good season to stretch those boundaries, because the 1953 team had a ton of potential. At that point, we had 16 returning lettermen, with the likes of Jesse Arnelle, Tony Rados, Don Malinak, Don Bailey, Rosey Grier, Sam Green, and Dan De Falco, in addition to my class, which had Charlie Blockson, Bobby Hoffman, Frank Reich, and Otto Kneidlinger. It would be a season worthy of the work that the senior class had done in helping Coach Engle build a respectable Penn State football program, after inheriting a team that was in disarray when he was hired in 1950.

We opened the 1953 season against a formidable Wisconsin team starring my future teammate and Heisman Trophy winner, Alan Ameche. Alan was a nationally recognized superstar already; and in this game he showed why he was a premier tailback in college athletics. Little did we know that, in a few short years, he would be my running mate on the Baltimore Colts team, and then a College Football Hall of Fame inductee.

A large crowd filled Camp Randall on a typically humid, Midwestern fall afternoon. It was the kind of day that made you sweat just by taping up your ankles. By the time we walked out of the tunnel and into a sea of red, I was already drenched in perspiration. I had played in some big games at Reading in my junior and senior years, but this was different. Wisconsin was the defending co-champ of the Big Ten, and they had just come off an appearance at the Rose Bowl. I remember catching a glimpse of Alan warming up on the other end of the field and thinking he was larger than life. It was commonplace to see running backs at a playing weight of 215 pounds, which is where Alan was back then. But by comparison, I only weighed 182 pounds. When playing on defense against him, you took your life into your own hands because he was such a punishing runner that if you made a mistake you were going to get hurt.

I know I wasn't the only player wondering if we had a chance against this team. The butterflies had created a maelstrom in my stomach, but I couldn't wait to get my hands on the ball and get hit. That's what it would take to purge my system of the nervousness.

My first offensive action came early in the second quarter of a scoreless contest. Our quarterback, Tony Rados, pitched me the ball, and I broke a few tackles and eventually scampered down the sideline for a touchdown. It was thrilling to be ahead but, more importantly, the activity helped me break the tension I was feeling about starting the game. Unfortunately, because of an illegal-motion penalty, the touchdown was called back and nullified. But it didn't matter to me, as my confidence had been energized. Even though we ended up losing 20-0, and I only had 10 yards on 10 carries (my collegiate low, in my first game), the team felt like it belonged. We had given Wisconsin a battle for the whole game. If that first touchdown hadn't been called back, I'm convinced it would have been a different story and we could have won.

That was the first of three games on the road that year. We next traveled to Philadelphia to face the Quakers. Being a young man from Reading, this was a special contest for me. The Quakers were very popular when I was growing up; every boy in Pennsylvania knew the likes of Chuck Bednarik and all the great players who came before him. Moreover, we were playing at Franklin Field: To play at this historic site made you realize that you were stepping into history. It gave me chills.

As a team, we felt that this was a game we should win; given the talent we had that year. Physically, we were clearly the dominant contender; but the Quakers had a little bit of a mental edge as their coach, George Munger, was retiring at the end of the season and he had not yet been able to beat Penn State.

We jumped ahead by a touchdown early in the game; but the offense was still not in sync, so we stalled after that. With the game tied in the second quarter, I fumbled the ball on our own 39, and the Quakers struck quickly a few plays later, for a 26-yard touchdown. They won the game, 13-7. Although my mistake cost the team the game, my experience on varsity was beginning to be a scaffold for self-confidence. Leo Riordan, of the *Philadelphia Inquirer*, wrote of the performance, "In Leonard Moore, it

[Penn State] has a menace. Moore is overdue and future opponents will get it."

Personally, I thought that to start the season 0-2 was quite a disappointment. I grew frustrated with the way I was playing. I knew I had so much more to give, but things just weren't clicking. Our next game was to be against Boston University, and I hoped I could turn things around by then. We all felt that the Terriers didn't have the talent to compete with us. With the help of a total team effort, I scored the first two touchdowns of my collegiate career.

The rest of the season flew by, and playing in front of the home crowd was always exciting. Though it was easier to play on the road because there were fewer distractions, playing for the home fans added another level of tension, which boosted my adrenaline. The crowd at Beaver Stadium was electric when we faced Syracuse, the first home game of the season. Syracuse dominated the first quarter by eating up most of the clock with a 78-yard drive down the field to take a 7-0 lead. The Syracuse offense scored another touchdown late in the third quarter. But then Charlie capped our first touchdown drive with a 45-yard gallop off tackle. Jesse scooped up a fumble on Syracuse's next possession at their 45-yard line, and Charlie and I pushed them back to the 3-yard line. Tony Rados called a timeout to discuss the play with Coaches Paterno and Engle; and on the next play Rados pitched the ball to me. I managed to tie the score with ten minutes left in the game.

We traded possessions over the next few minutes of play; then, with Syracuse pinned deep in their territory, my former teammate from Reading High, Ed Albright, came out to punt. The punt was blocked and our team recovered. In a brutal series of downs, we fought to regain the lead, 20-14. But Syracuse was a formidable opponent and wasn't done with us yet. They capitalized on a penalty and combined a long pass to be within striking distance of the end zone. The Syracuse quarterback then faded back and heaved up a pass, which I intercepted. I had stopped the drive and sealed the victory until I was pushed out of bounds and someone on the sideline jumped me with a cheap shot. Suddenly, both benches cleared and fans were on the field. Fists were flying. Finally though, when order was restored, we walked away victorious.

Meeting one of my former teammates from Reading High on the college circuit wasn't an uncommon event, as many of us went on to play college ball. Some players, like John Jenkins who went to Arizona State and starred with John Henry Johnson, moved away from Pennsylvania. Some went to all-black colleges in the South. But most stayed in the area and played at Villanova or Drexel—or at Syracuse, like Ed. Like most of the white players on the Reading team, Ed was a teammate but we didn't have much of a relationship. Just because you are on a team together and have common experiences, it does not make you friends. This would be a theme I would see throughout my playing days. Once the game is over or practice is done, everyone goes their separate ways. I didn't dislike Ed, but I can't say that he was a friend in a literal sense. The same goes for a lot of the other white players I've shared the field with. By contrast, my black teammates at Penn State were, and remain, some of my best friends. Charlie, Rosey, Sam, Jesse, Bob Pogues, and I were close throughout the school year, on the field and off.

During that 1953 season, we went on to play Texas Christian University in our homecoming game where, with the help of my teammates, I rushed for over 100 yards, totaling 127 yards on 16 carries.

Probably our toughest opponent yet came in the form of fifth-ranked West Virginia, who had their best team in quite a while. The Mountaineers were an offensive juggernaut at the time. They were leading the NCAAs in total offense and were a solid favorite to start the game. As usual, the odds-makers underestimated us, and with a solid game plan from Rip, we played them toe to toe. As late as the third quarter, we were leading them 12-6 when Lady Luck started to frown on us.

With West Virginia at the goal line, the defense dug in and appeared to stop a sneak by Fred Wyatt, their outstanding quarterback. Although game film would show his knee was down well before he crossed the goal line, the play would nonetheless stand. To make matters worse, on a later possession, the Mountaineer 11 held us on three downs and forced us to punt. Prior to the snap, their middle guard clearly jumped offside. No whistle was blown, and with that quick start he busted through our line in time to block our punt. West Virginia recovered the loose ball in the end zone for what would be an insurmountable lead. Although we outnumbered them in every major category, we lost in the most important comparison, the final score, losing 20-19. West Virginia was a bitter rival; we played every year and it was always a dog fight, but this was especially heartbreaking.

One bizarre experience that did help bond all the players on our team occurred over junior prom weekend that year. Coach Engle wanted to help the team regain its concentration after a very lethargic week of practice, so he loaded us onto a couple buses and took us out to a hunting camp located about 30 miles away. The *Daily Collegian* had reported mild weather, both "clear and cold"; but unfortunately, the forecast was far from accurate. By 8 a.m. the next day—game day, when we were to host Michigan State—we were snowed in. The team awoke to over 20 inches of snow. We were stranded at that hunting camp for hours before the caretaker in charge of the grounds found us. Eventually, Coach Engle organized us and led us on foot out of the camp and onto the buses. It took us a half hour, marching in columns, like grunts going to war.

Back at Beaver Stadium, where the snow drifts reached as high as 13 inches, a number of student volunteers had helped clear the field for the game. We finally arrived—at game time. Both teams agreed upon a short 45-minute warmup, and then we took the field. I managed to rush 108 yards on 11 carries, and I scored our first touchdown, in the second quarter. We won the contest, 28-21, none the worse for wear, after being so close to frostbite, not to mention forfeit, had the forecast not been so incorrect.

My teammates at Penn State will also remember the game at Rutgers that season. Late in the first half, Rutgers actually held a 14-6 lead, and Coach Engle just exploded. He ripped into the team as a whole, and we responded by scoring three touchdowns before the half. We rolled to a 54-26 victory. And then there was our finale, against Pittsburgh, which was a cakewalk. The final score, 17-0, involved three interceptions deep in Pitt territory, by Tony Rados. It was an exciting game for me, as well: I opened the first scoring drive with a 21-yard punt return. Two plays later, from scrimmage, I took the hand-off on a draw play up the middle and eluded a defender for a 79-yard touchdown—the longest run in 15 years for the team. I ended up with 120 yards, my third 100-yard game of the year. I also broke the school record for the number of 100-yard games in a season. My average was 5.6 yards a carry, and I finished with 601 yards for the year. It was a defining year for me, and I have my teammates to thank for their support.

It was during my time with Penn State that I earned the nickname "Spats." During practice one day, I saw Bob Pollard wrap tape around the outside of his shoes. I asked him why he did that, and he explained that he'd suffered a high-ankle sprain earlier in the season. He said he never wanted to have that type of injury again, so he provided extra support by wrapping his ankle, inside and outside of his shoe. Coach Engle had decided everyone should dress the same, so we all had to wear black, high-cut Riddells, which gave the illusion of providing maximum support. I adopted Bob's trick of wrapping my feet to prevent injury. Some reporter noticed the black-and-white effect on my cleats, and mentioned that it looked like I was wearing spats, a popular style of shoe in the Roaring Twenties. The name stuck. I actually liked the look; and it was, by then, a ritual: taping my feet helped me put on my "game face" before each contest.

All things being equal—my gains on the field, the camaraderie of my teammates, the attention by the press—my sophomore year had provided me an unbelievable amount of confidence. Reality hit again, though, as I returned to Reading and got a job working in a quarry, splitting rocks for a pitiful wage. It was a tedious summer, because all I could think about was my faraway year as a junior. With every rock I split, I counted down the days until I would board the bus and head back to school. The tough physical labor strengthened my still-developing body. It would be months before I would realize how this hard physical labor would benefit my play and help Penn State be recognized as a developing national power.

# FOUR

# COMING INTO MY OWN

Although the personnel on the team was in transition from the 1953 to 1954 seasons, I was even more excited to get through the summer of 1954 to start the season. After a pretty solid first year starting for the varsity, I really felt like I had proven to the team and myself that I belonged as a starter among them. I felt confident enough in my abilities that even with all the changes taking place on the team due to graduation that I could perform at a high enough level to help keep the team competitive.

The most glaring transition was going to be at the quarterback position. The team's steady star quarterback, Tony Rados, was gone; and the coaches were in a bind, trying to decide between Milt Plum, Don Bailey, or Bobby Hoffman, to replace Tony. Coach Paterno, the offensive coordinator, wanted Milt, because he had worked hard to recruit him from New Jersey. Don had a lot of heart but wasn't as talented. I thought Bobby had the most talent of the bunch. He was quick on his feet and very athletic, to the point that Rip envisioned him as a third running back in the backfield even as a quarterback (Coach had added a quarterback option into the playbook, in fact, in order to open more running lanes for Charlie Blockson and me), but he was young and very raw. Rip knew there would be a tremendous learning curve and was fearful the team wouldn't be able to rebound from a slow start to the season if Bobby faltered.

But even after a full training camp, nothing was settled, and the quarterback controversy was still raging. We opened the season against the Big Ten champion: the University of Illinois. They were the preseason pick to repeat as Big Ten champs once again, and they had some tremendous athletes on their team, including J.C. Caroline. Caroline was a dynamic runner who had led the nation in rushing in 1953, and he had set many school records at Illinois.

Rip went against his better judgment and started Bobby at quarterback that first game. Almost as if scripted, in our first possession he was soon intercepted. Illinois took the ball, and after a few plays scored on a 28-yard screen pass. Coach Engle decided to cut his losses and pulled Hoffman and sent in Don Bailey; but he, too, was intercepted. Playing defensive back, I stymied the ensuing Illinois drive by forcing a fumble by Mickey Bates. My new roommate, Jesse Arnelle, recovered the fumble at the Illinois 28 and the tide had shifted. After a rocky start, Don settled in and led the team to our first score on a 24-yard pass to Jesse to put us on the board. From there Rosey and Earl Shumaker took over and dominated the line of scrimmage and the tempo of play. On one series, Caroline did break away into the secondary and was on his way to a touchdown when I chased him down to make a shoestring tackle. At that point, our defense started clicking on all cylinders.

The offense wasn't as smooth, but for what we lacked in cohesion, we made up for in toughness and determination. After my touchdown-saving tackle on J.C., we took back possession on an Illinois punt. With only a few minutes left in the half, Rip was aggressive and tried to put some more points up. Rip called for an end around by Bailey. He faked a lateral to me, and I followed him down the field. What he thought was open field dissipated quickly as the Illini defenders swarmed our plodding signal caller. He was hit hard at the eight but had the sense to turn and lateral the ball back to me. I broke several tackles and bullied my way into the end zone, to give us a lead going into the half. That was the turning point in the game. We were firmly in control of the momentum from then on. Illinois would manage one more touchdown but missed the extra point. Penn State won the game, 14-12. Not only did we beat the defending Rose Bowl champs, which raised the recognition of the university a few notches, but I started the season off right with 137 yards on 18 carries. It was one of the most hard fought victories I had experienced in my short collegiate career to that point. This game was very special for me because of my opponents, a trio of outstanding black running backs: J.C. Caroline, Mickey Bates, and Abe Woodson. I met them for the first time before that game and we each felt a connection as kindred spirits who were going through the same awkwardness. It was special for me to play against people whom I admired and would eventually grow very close to.

Coming off the Illinois game, our team felt like world-beaters. In our annual battle against Syracuse, this time at Archbold Stadium, Rosey and the boys were up to the task and put together a great defensive effort. Limiting Syracuse to 75 yards on the ground and 22 yards through the air, the Orangemen were no match for us this day. The team was energized and controlled the game by accumulating over 200 yards rushing. At one point, we drove the field 76 yards, all on the ground, to be capped off by my 22-yard touchdown run. I missed having another 100-yard game by just seven yards, but the team's second consecutive road victory was all that mattered to me.

For our home opener, we hosted the Cavaliers of Virginia, who came in undefeated but would not leave that way. We thrashed them 34-7, as I notched 120 yards and two touchdowns, due to the great blocking of the offensive line. For the first time since I had been at State, we were able to break into the AP Top Ten; we would tie Navy for the ninth spot. Although we took pride in the ranking, it really wasn't as big a deal back then as it is now. As cliché as it might sound, no one really gave a damn about the stats on our team. In today's game, many players know their game stats before the final whistle is blown, but it just wasn't an emphasis for us. We may have been different than other teams, but we just looked forward to the next game.

We did feel good for Rip, though. That top ten national ranking was a culmination of hard work on his and the other coaches' part. Prior to Rip's hiring, the school had a tendency to play mostly teams in our region, which didn't lead to much national attention. Rip felt that we were being overlooked and tried very hard to gain some notoriety by playing a difficult schedule with a variety of teams. It took him five years, but it was finally paying off. Nonetheless, the university's lack of notoriety made it difficult for the team to be awarded any All-American honors. Full recognition of the team's talent wouldn't come until I moved on to the NFL.

West Virginia was on the schedule next, and we couldn't wait. After outplaying the Mountaineers so thoroughly the year before and not coming out with a victory, revenge was on our minds. West Virginia came in highly touted and undefeated. They were led by a gangly linebacker recruited from the coal mines—Sam Huff. Even the casual fan would recognize that name, as we would meet again in the NFL, most specifically, the 1958 and 1959 NFL Championship Games.

This was our homecoming game, and the stadium was jam packed. The skies were clear and a fresh Indian summer breeze filled the air, even though Hurricane Hazel had just passed through town. The Nittany Lions were favored by six points, but the Mountaineers must not have read the spread, for they jumped ahead 6-0. Doing my best to change the momentum, I took a punt 19 yards to serve as the catalyst for a 24-yard pass from Bailey to Younker. Soon after that, our defense stopped West Virginia, and we started on a 76-yard drive, including a breakaway on my part for 41 yards on one play, and then catching an option pass from Bailey for an eight-yard touchdown. Without any drama from the refs, the first half score of 14-6 left us confident that we'd finally beat the Mountaineers and avenge last season. Unfortunately, it wasn't meant to be. The West Virginia defense bottled us up and held us scoreless. Two touchdowns later, the Mountaineers left Happy Valley with a 19-14 victory.

Next, the team traveled to Fort Worth for a contest with Texas Christian. This was the first time an integrated football team had ever played in Fort Worth. A few years earlier, in 1947, Penn State had visited Dallas, to play in the Cotton Bowl—another first for an integrated team— as Wally Triplett and Denny Hoggard met up with Southern Methodist University. In Fort Worth, though, we played a wretched game, as we lost the ball four times on fumbles and interceptions. I scored a touchdown and finished with 109 yards on 19 carries, and the team managed to outgain TCU in total yardage; but the Horned Frogs came away with the victory, 20-7. This was clearly one of the most frustrating games we had that year.

To make matters worse, the only hotel that would accommodate blacks was far out of town. Because Coach Engle was striving for team cohesion and wouldn't let the team be separated, we all stayed beyond the city limits. There was some press about the way Fort Worth treated us. Throughout the game, our sideline was riddled with insults and racial slurs. The whole team tried to ignore it, but it was difficult to tune it out. Listening to the vitriol being spewed from the "host" fans really made me feel awful and left a very bad taste in my mouth for the state of Texas (which would be evident to me again as a member of the Colts years later), but as usual, I got through it the best I could. A few weeks later I received a nice note, which I still have, from a lovely lady who said that not all Texans are bigots. It was a small gesture that meant a lot to me.

Happy to be back north of the Mason-Dixon Line, we played at Franklin Field in Philadelphia next. This game was nationally televised, an inaugural experience for Penn State. It was in many ways my national coming-out party, and with a great deal of blocking I ran all over the Quaker defense, scoring three touchdowns and finishing with 143 yards on the ground. The first touchdown came at the end of the first half with the score tied 7-7. On a trap play, I took the ball and broke a number of tackles, forcing my way into the end zone. The second touchdown came on our first possession in the second half. On a pitchout from Bailey, I took the ball around the end and down the sideline for a 60-yard score. The last touchdown was the result of an interception I made off the Quakers' quarterback to seal the victory. I took the ball 53 yards the other way to make the final score 35-13. After the game, Herb Good of *The Philadelphia Enquirer* wrote, "Spindle-legged Lenny Moore, a hot rod in football togs, ran wild on Franklin Field yesterday . . . Moore, extremely fast and very elusive, proved . . . why he is rated one of State's all-time greats."

In our next game I elbowed myself into the Penn State record books by breaking the single-season rushing record in a rout against Holy Cross, a 39-7 victory. I scored two touchdowns and finished with 127 yards on nine carries. That total gave me 843 yards for the year. Ridge Riley, of *The Football Letter*, wrote:

"This game belonged to the lithe . . . Lenny Moore, the most exciting performer in Penn State football for more than a quarter of a century. Someone overheard a few of our players discussing what makes Lenny run: 'I guess,' Jesse Arnelle said, 'It's Lenny just doesn't like to be tackled.'"

When we met Rutgers on our home turf the following Saturday, I continued my season-long roll by besting State's single-game rushing record, with 171 yards on 12 carries. This would be my tenth 100-yard game over the last two seasons. What made it all the sweeter was that we were trailing 7-6 late in the second quarter before mounting a long, 80-yard drive. In that drive I ran for 36 yards, took a seven-yard reception, and made a three-yard run for the touchdown. In the fourth quarter, I set a few more State records by capping the game's score with a 54-yard run for the touchdown. I thus tied the school record for touchdowns in a single season, with 13. That run also pushed me over 1,000 yards for the season, the first Nittany Lion to do so.

In our final game against Pitt, I was confident I could overtake the nation's rushing lead, starting the game only 11 yards behind the leader, Art Lupino, of Arizona. I also intended to break Penn State's touchdown record. But Pitt had designed a defense to key in on me. Coach Engle caught on to this fact very early in the contest and decided to use me as a decoy for most of the game. By the time Coach gave me the go ahead, the field was pretty slippery from a steady rain, and I couldn't quite get any footing or momentum. I ended without any touchdowns and notched only 68 yards rushing. Yet what I lacked on the offense, I made up for on the defensive side of the ball. I had what might have been my best game from the defensive side all year. I recovered a fumble and intercepted two passes to stall three Pitt drives as we won 13-0. At the end of the game, Coach Engle came to me and apologized for misusing me during the game. He said, "Maybe your yardage wasn't as high, but you never played a better game." The press, too, were aware of what had happened: Chet Smith wrote in *The Pittsburgh Press*:

"Used for part of the game as a decoy, State's great halfback Lenny Moore still played a vital role in the victory and was rewarded . . . [with] a new University record for offense over one season, . . . [totaling] 1,082 yards in nine games to break the mark of 1,031 set by Shorty Miller in 1912 . . . Moore was also worth his weight in gold defensively, turning in a pair of pass interceptions that helped in taking the heat off his team."

Statistically, this was my best season ever, but it did not come without a heavy price: my grades were in a downhill slide. It is ironic that in the same year the landmark case, Brown v. Board of Education, made it mandatory that African Americans receive the same quality of education as whites, schools were being desegregated every day, and the percentage of blacks achieving four or more years of college had skyrocketed to three percent. This advancement in education and in racial equality in general made me feel even worse that my personal academic career was being sacked. When I received my marks for the semester, it wasn't pretty: I had failed to pass more than half of my courses, and I was officially kicked out of school.

I was completely embarrassed. I felt like I had let down my family, my high school coach, my Penn State coaches, and everyone else who had encouraged me to go to college. I didn't know what to do or where to go. An article in *The Daily Collegian* quoted a spokesman for the University, who said that due to my poor academic performance, it would be highly improbable that I would be back for my senior year.

Rip, just like Coach Stopper before him, refused to give up on me. Sure, I was one of the best players on the team and it was in his best interest to get me back to academic eligibility, but that wasn't Rip's style. He cared about the person more than the player. He couldn't bear to watch me throw my whole career down the drain and talked the school into giving me a second chance. He soon came to me and I was given an offer: In essence, if I wanted to return to Penn State the next fall, I would have to retake much of my coursework from the fall and a full slate of spring courses and get passing grades over the spring semester and summer.

It was a tall task, but my options weren't many. I contemplated giving up completely and joining the service, which I was beginning to think I should have done in the first place. On my more optimistic days, I thought I might turn my back on Penn State and announce to the press my eligibility for the NFL draft (in those days, though, such an announcement would have caused barely a ripple of interest).

Finally, after talking with Coach Engle, I decided to give college my best effort. I stayed in Happy Valley and lived at the Kappa house and studied my heart out. Coach knew, and I knew, although we never said anything, that if I left school I probably would never go back. In retrospect, it was the best decision I could have made. I felt too ashamed to go back home anyway, with my tail between my legs. And what was there to do in Reading? Just mope around, bemoaning my fate? Coach Toretti got me a job at an asphalt factory to help cover rent, food, tuition, and books; and I settled down into my studies. I was determined to regain my eligibility to play football—which I could only do as a student in good standing.

A short time later, I received a draft notice in the mail. I was to report to New Cumberland, Pennsylvania. I didn't know what this was all about. I thought it may have had something to do with my enlistment in the Advanced Army ROTC. At that time, with the Korean War raging, a draft exemption was issued to those students who were both enrolled in an accredited university full time and a member of the Advance Army ROTC. What I had failed to realize in the tumultuous period following the season when I was expelled from Penn State was my attachment to the ROTC was voided, and through some clerical error I was not re-enrolled into the program when I agreed to follow Coach Engel's plan to get my grades up to par. I was open to the draft and I didn't even know it.

With nothing more than the clothes on my back, I reported to New Cumberland. When I arrived at the bus stop, I saw all these other boys with their bags packed as if they were going on a trip. I thought it was a little weird, because my notice didn't say anything about any travel. I was under the assumption that this was a routine ROTC gathering. I soon realized that I was sorely mistaken. What I found out was that New Cumberland was a regional draft post, and from my check-in there I was to be shipped with all the other inductees down to Fort Jackson, South Carolina.

I didn't know what to do, so I called Coach Engle for advice. I was scared. Although I had always given the military great consideration, I was caught off guard by the situation I found myself in. Coach got on the phone with the draft officer after I was done speaking with him. After a few minutes on the phone, I was told to stay put and wait for further orders.

The next thing I knew, I was sent to Geisinger hospital in Danville, Pennsylvania, and given an intense, three-day physical. After a preliminary interview, the doctors checked my kidneys, being suspicious about an injury I received during one of the games my sophomore year. Coincidentally, at the time I had blood in my urine. After the investigation, I was diagnosed with kidney problems and designated 4-F: not eligible for the draft. The whole experience was kept under wraps by Rip. All that was reported to the newspapers was that I was receiving treatment for a kidney ailment. The press would never find out how close I was to being drafted. By the grace of God and those who cared deeply about me on earth, I was saved from myself once again. Lord only knows how my life would've turned out had Rip not acted on my behalf. Yet another close call averted.

Another "ailment" I faced that spring was my second case of heartbreak. After Lorraine and I broke off our relationship, I began dating a young lady named Naomi Pelzer. She was a gorgeous young coed from Philadelphia, and we had a wonderful courtship. When I was kicked out of school after my junior year, she and I even talked seriously of eloping and starting a family as one of my options. This was another crossroads in my life that could have led me in a much different direction. But, after long heart-to-heart talks with her, we decided not to get married. She was an enormous help to me with my studies. She didn't want to see me fail either and did all she could for me. Unfortunately, our love wouldn't last. Naomi soon transferred from Penn State to Morgan State, where her sister was attending college, which left a hole in my heart. I knew that she was very close to her sister, but I didn't realize how serious she was about reuniting with her at Morgan State. I assumed that was the reason why she left, but I was never really sure.

It seemed as if my whole world was spinning out of control since the start of 1954.

That spring semester, I felt quite alone. I dearly missed the camaraderie I had enjoyed on the team. I was on the sidelines during every practice, in my street clothes, in support: I wanted them to know that my head and my heart were with them. It was during this observation of the team, from a distance, that I found my respect for Coach Engle growing. The amount of compassion that he and his coaching staff showed me was incredible, but I also learned to admire "Rip" for his integrity. A native Pennsylvanian from Salisbury, Pennsylvania, he had had tremendous success at Brown University, before he inherited quite a mess at Penn State. He had turned down head coaching jobs at Yale, Wisconsin, and Pittsburgh, and chose Penn State because his uncle had played there. Rip took on a tough job, though, because all of the schools in the region competed to recruit the same players, and at the point he accepted his position, Penn State's program was on the decline. In today's world, geography doesn't matter so much: kids from California might go to college in Kansas or Florida or Timbuktu; but back then, colleges tried to recruit homegrown kids—and there were almost more colleges in Pennsylvania than there were star players looking for football scholarships.

He never relented, though, because he truly believed that what he was offering was different than other schools. Although Joe Paterno would officially give the "Grand Experiment" its moniker, the idea was put in place by Rip when he arrived on campus in 1950. The "Grand Experiment" is simple: putting a winning football team on the field year after year by doing it the right way: no cheating, no under-the-table deals, only high integrity. It would mean that the athletes were true student-athletes in the eyes of everyone on campus and they would bring honor to the university. As I mentioned before, Rip truly cared about each one of us as people who played football for him. He didn't think of us as interchangeable parts. He cared that we completed our educations and wanted us to be as well versed in classic American literature as we were in the playbook. Being caught up in the day-to-day action of being on the team, I never really noticed all that Rip did for us, but those months away from the team really gave me a greater appreciation for the dedication that Rip showed to his players and to the university. I am proud to say that I was a part of it.

After sitting out the spring semester and hitting the books all summer long, as well, I rejoined the Nittany Lions for the 1955 season, as a senior in good standing. Everyone had high expectations: this was the 100th anniversary of the school and enrollment was at an all-time high. The football team was primed to make a move on a national level. We only had 11 returning lettermen, but some very talented sophomores were joining us. Nationally, Penn State was starting to receive some of the recognition it desperately wanted. I was named to the Captain's All-American Team, based on my performance in the 1954 season. Also, the team received coverage on a nationally syndicated television show, one of the many early forefathers to ESPN, when Norman Sper and his "Football Forecasts" announced that Penn State, and my performances, specifically, would be featured on his weekly broadcasts.

Even with all this hype and anticipation, my senior year was difficult for many reasons. In the middle of the season, a young black boy named Emmett Till was beaten to death in the South, shocking the whole population with the brutality of the crime. Then there was that notorious day when a Southern black matron named Rosa Parks refused to give up her seat in the front of a bus to a white passenger. Finally, a young black minister named Martin Luther King, Jr., was imprisoned for leading a boycott of the Mobile, Alabama, public transportation system. Racial tensions were mounting on a national scale, and black players at Penn State were not immune from the backlash.

The 1955 season was also a year of transition for the people to whom I was closest. Rosey and Jesse had moved on to play pro ball. Charlie suffered a string of injuries and was on the field with me less and less. Naomi had moved on by then. My support system that I had taken for granted through college was coming undone.

For the first time in my career, we opened the season at home, hosting the Terriers of Boston University. The coaching staff could not agree on a starting lineup until, literally, the day before the game. Being that I was the most talented and seasoned offensive player on the team, the Terriers stacked the line and dared me to run through it. But Boston just didn't have the manpower that we had, even without Rosey and Jesse and Charlie (who was injured almost immediately that season). Although the Terriers did a decent job of shutting me down (68 yards on 12 carries), a little known sparkplug of a running back was thrust into service for us Lions. He came out of nowhere to carry the ball five times and gain 52 yards, while scoring two touchdowns. Joe Sabol had the game of his life and paced the team as we thrashed the Terriers 35-13.

The team traveled to West Point for the next game, to take on a bruising Army team, led by their quarterback Don Hollender. We were truly outmanned this time and we were literally beaten up by the Cadets. I played 56 minutes and finished with 75 yards on 16 carries in the 35-6 loss. Ridge Riley was being generous when he reported:

"Moore, a truly great player, lost no stature in this game. He played a superb defensive game . . . returned three kickoffs for 60 yards . . . [and] made practically all his yardage through the tough Army forwards where it was worth your life to stick in your head. . . . He was a marked man on every play, took a severe physical beating and came back time and time again for more."

This was my first trip to West Point, and it was certainly intimidating. Playing on the same field as my hero Glenn Davis had,was very special. Unfortunately, the results could have been better for me and the team.

The next game was played at Richmond City Stadium against the Cavaliers of Virginia. It was dubbed the "Tobacco Festival," but it certainly wasn't very festive. It rained throughout the ballgame, but the team came back from an early 7-0 deficit to beat Virginia 26-7. The keys to this victory were the team's recovering two fumbles, and the 92 yards on 16 carries that I was able to gain. It was clear to us as a team, even just three games into the season, that we would be in for a long year.

The Midshipmen of Navy were the next opponents on the schedule. Navy had thrashed Mississippi in the 1955 Sugar Bowl, and they had 17 returning starters from that team. They also had the best defense in the country: unbeaten and unscored-upon, in their first three games. This was our Homecoming contest, but the weather didn't cooperate. Sheets of rain came down on State College in the 24 hours leading up to game time. The defense again focused on shutting me down, and the Middie offense, led by coach George Welsh, was just too much to overcome. I ended the game with just 37 yards on 18 carries, which was my lowest output since my first game on varsity.

At 2-2, we were a two-touchdown underdog going into our next game against West Virginia in Morgantown. The Mountaineers were undefeated and ranked eighth nationally. This game presented me with another opportunity to butt heads with my old nemesis, Sam Huff, for the third year in a row. West Virginia constantly substituted their players, which allowed them to stay fresh and made it difficult for us to keep up with them, especially late in the game. We put in a valiant effort, but without the deep talent that West Virginia had, we were defeated 21-7.

Our next game was at Penn. By this time, the Quaker program was in complete disarray, because the school's administration was moving away from an athletic emphasis, and the football program was a stripped-down carcass of its old self. We won easily, 20-0; and perhaps we were a little cocky going into our next game against the vaunted Syracuse Orangeman and their outstanding junior running back, Jim Brown.

Through the years, Syracuse and Penn State have had a long, intense, and bitter rivalry. Much of that had to do with the relatively close proximity of both schools, which meant they tried to recruit many of the same players. In the years that I played at State, the presence of Jim Brown on the Syracuse team made our contests with them even more intense.

The 1955 game mirrored most of the games our team had played over the last two years, in that we had a tendency to start out very slowly. By the time the second quarter was winding down, we found ourselves down 13-0, with Jim Brown responsible for all of the Syracuse points. Then the game finally broke our way. With mere seconds left in the half, Joe Sabol broke in front of an Ed Albright pass to Brown in the flats, and he rumbled down the field to the Syracuse 10 before being taken down with 15 seconds left in the half. Our quarterback, Milt Plum, stayed on the field and flipped a pass to Billy Kane at the two-yard line, then he scampered into the end zone to put us on the board going into the half. The momentum turned ever so slightly.

Re-energized by a pep talk from Rip and the quick score we enjoyed to close the second quarter, we came out of the locker room intent on slowing down Big Jim Brown. He had other ideas, though, as he took the kickoff and brought the ball to midfield to start the second half. Starting at the 47, it only took a half-dozen plays for the Orangemen to bring their lead back to 13 points. With 11 minutes left to play in the third quarter, we wouldn't give up. Plum took the kickoff and gave us good field position, so we marched through the Syracuse defense all the way down to the two-yard line. Then Plum handed me the ball and I plunged through the line to make it a six-point game once again. For the better part of the rest of the half, both teams attempted knockout blows, but nothing connected, and no scoring took place. Then a defining moment in this frustrating season: midway through the fourth quarter, our offense started deep in our own territory, but the offensive line was able to take over the line of scrimmage and open some holes. I was able to tic off runs of 22, 14, five, and four yards, to set up a touchdown on a quarterback sneak by Plum from the one-yard line. After Plum's point-after attempt barely snuck over the crossbar to give us a one-point lead, Syracuse drove back to midfield, with only minutes remaining. Yet, Sam Valentine forced and recovered a fumble at the Orangemen's 46, and we were able to run out the clock with the game ending on the Syracuse two-yard line. What a magnificent contest—easily the best of the year.

Some tremendous numbers defined the duel between Jim Brown and me that day. The future Hall of Famer for the Browns ended with 159 yards on 20 carries. He also caught two passes, scored three touchdowns and two extra points, had three kickoff returns for 95 yards, and intercepted one pass. The final stats on my performance were 146 yards on 22 carries, and one touchdown. Carl Hughes of *The Pittsburgh Press* wrote about my day in his game summary: "He came up with an old-time performance when it was needed the most. In Coach Rip Engle's jubilant words, 'Lenny never in his life was greater.'" This game foreshadowed so many epic battles between the two of us over the next decade in the NFL.

A less daunting opponent awaited us in the next contest against Rutgers. After facing Jim Brown, playing a depleted Scarlet Knights team was like slicing a hot knife through butter. This would be the last prolific game of my Penn State career. I finished with 179 yards on nine carries. I reached the end zone three times, including an 80-yard dash for the first touchdown. We won the game 34-13.

It would have been very satisfying to have finished my career, and a tough season for the team, with a victory against Pittsburgh. But the Panthers were revitalized this year and came into the contest having defeated another old nemesis, West Virginia. With a 5-3-3 defense that filled most of the running lanes available and a persistent snow that had started the night before in Pittsburgh, we found ourselves battling some icy conditions and difficult footing. Pitt managed to shut us out 20-0, and they held me to 13 yards on 10 carries.

That weekend was satisfying nonetheless. The Cleveland Browns and Marion Motley were in town to play the Steelers. I had started to follow pro ball after some of my teammates, especially Rosey, entered the draft. My first exposure to the pro game, in fact, was watching Rosey play for the New York Giants, earlier in my senior season. Seeing him out there with the Giants, I experienced my first desire to join the ranks of the NFL. When I met Marion Motley over that weekend, I was more inclined than ever to turn pro. After the game against Pitt, I learned that the Browns were staying in downtown Pittsburgh at the Schindley Hotel. On a lark, I went to the front desk and asked to have Marion's room buzzed. The clerk mentioned my name to him, and he came down from his room to greet me. I introduced myself, and he mentioned that he knew who I was and that he was very impressed with my record. He invited me up to his room, and he spent over two hours talking to me. I asked him what it was like to be a black man in the NFL, for I knew he had had some struggles.

Marion didn't pull any punches with me. His direct response to my question about the playing conditions in the NFL was simple: "Difficult," he said, "very difficult." He told me how he had to be physically tougher than any other man on the team, even to the point of getting into fisticuffs with his own teammates, to establish his place. He said that he was lucky with the fact that he wasn't doing it all by himself. Shortly after he joined the Browns, Bill Willis was signed as well. He said that it made it easier to have someone to talk with; someone he could trust. He told me how great a life it could be, even with all the racial tension that existed.

"What else would I be doing if I wasn't playing football?" he asked. The question hung in the air between the two of us. I knew what he meant, but he answered it anyway. "Pushing a mop. Digging a ditch. I don't have any other options. So I keep my mouth shut and I learn as much as I can, because as much abuse as I take off the field, I can take out my frustrations on the field."

He also told me how important it was to get on a team with a good coach. His coach at the time, the great Paul Brown, was very sensitive to Willis and Motley's plight, he tried very hard to make it easy on them. Individually, and as a team, death threats would be leveled at them constantly. Brown treated them each very seriously and constantly consulted with Motley and Willis regarding how they should address them, even to the point of offering to cancel trips to venues down South. Motley said that he never agreed to cancel a scheduled ballgame due to the threats, but he appreciated the input that Brown offered him to give.

Sitting with him gave me invaluable insight that I would use almost immediately upon entering the league.

Later that year, at an event in Atlanta, hosting some of the standout seniors from the 1955 season, I had a chance to meet another hero of mine, Ollie Matson. He made it a point to come up to me at the event and chatted with me briefly. He said that he had been following my career at Penn State and thought the league needed more players like me. He gave me great encouragement to enter the NFL. He would become a great confidant, as would Marion, throughout my time in the league. Both Ollie and Marion played a big part in providing incentive and encouragement for me to turn pro.

Years later, at one of the annual induction weekend banquets, held by the Hall of Famers, I stood up and publicly avowed my love for these two gentlemen. I frequently told Ollie and Marion in private how much I respected them; but I felt it was of utmost importance to let our peers know what a profound effect these men had had on me. At a gathering during one of the Induction weekends, I stood and toasted these two great men to let everyone know how much they meant to me and the other black ballplayers in the league.

All things being equal, now that Rosey was playing for the Giants, and then hearing Marion and Ollie's impressions of pro football, I became very intrigued with the idea of playing at the next level. In reality, I didn't have any idea what I was getting excited about, but I secretly prayed that I would be drafted by the Giants so I could play with Rosey. He would tell me how much fun it was to play football for a living, and how much he liked New York. I knew that the opportunity was out there, and I felt I was ready to explore it.

# FIVE

# Lenny Moore: NFL Running Back

I n midseason of my senior year at Penn State, I started wondering about what life would have in store for me next. Due to the spotty educational record I've described, I would fall ten credits short of my bachelor's degree; but, to be honest, I felt very satisfied with what I had accomplished, even without a diploma. Considering what long odds I faced, being born black in the pre-Civil Rights era, the fact that I completed four years of college was an achievement in my eyes. There would be many times in the future that I considered going back to school to get that degree. In fact, at one point, I enrolled at the University of Maryland, and I was all set to start classes in the off season after my first year with the Colts. But then life happened, and I never did get that elusive BA. In the end, I just couldn't convince myself that receiving that sheepskin would make a tremendous difference in my life. Attending Penn State for four years had opened doors for me that going into the army or working at American Chain and Cable, fresh out of high school, would not have opened. I was pleased with my life choices, and that was enough for me.

But—now what? Although it wasn't my goal when I enrolled at Penn State, I wanted to continue playing football, and I was determined to go pro. I bided my time that fall, waiting to hear from NFL recruiters. Drafting players in the 1950s was nothing like the hoopla that we see today. The draft consisted of team representatives meeting at a hotel for a day, picking players they had read about in the papers or heard about on the radio throughout that fall. Scouting departments, mock draft boards, draft combines, and individual workouts organized by high-powered agents were decades away from being introduced. In many ways, being solicited to play professional football was very similar to being recruited out of college to work in the business world.

In preparation for the draft, most of the seniors playing football across the country would receive a letter from the interested pro team's head coach or general manager inquiring if the player was interested in playing football professionally. One would also receive a generic application to complete and send back to the team. You have to remember that playing football for money was only recently deemed a viable career path. Only about 20 years earlier, the college presidents and legendary coaches such as Amos Alonzo Stagg, Pop Warner, and Fielding Yost begged a flashy running back from the University of Illinois named Red Grange not to shame the institution of major college football by becoming a professional. It was a national story that reached scandalous heights. In many ways, professional teams of my era still acted timidly when attempting to contact and gauge interest from college seniors of the day.

I still have notes from the different teams in the League that did contact me. For example, on November 17, 1955, George Halas sent me an impersonal note that was probably mass produced:

*"It is our understanding that you are completing your collegiate football career with the playing of the 1955 fall season and will be graduated in June, 1956. We would appreciate it if you would complete the enclosed Player Information Sheet and return it to us promptly in the enclosed return envelope.*
*With best wishes, I am Sincerely,*
*George Halas"*

The enclosed Player Information Sheet asked questions regarding my height, weight, position played on offense, position played on defense, and whether or not I intended to play professional football. An average college football fan of today knows more about the major college football players nationally than the decision makers of yesteryear.

On November 28, 1955 (consider the date of the note I discussed above), in the first round of that year's draft, the Baltimore Colts drafted me (ninth overall, according to the next day's newspaper). Shortly after the draft, the Colts sent word to my parents' home, asking what my intentions were for my post-collegiate life. It goes without saying that I signed with the Colts; but, in truth, I almost never made it. The experience of a little known black pioneer named Johnny Bright tempted me to shun the NFL altogether and head for Canada.

I'm sure the name Johnny Bright doesn't sound familiar to many football enthusiasts in the United States, but to any young black athlete in the 1950s, the name caused incredible debate. Johnny was a standout, all-around athlete from Fort Wayne, Indiana. By the end of his high school career, he had set 20 school records, not only in football, but in basketball and track as well. He had ended up embarking on his collegiate career in Iowa because he couldn't find any interest from the major universities in his own state. Indiana, Purdue, and Notre Dame did not court Johnny as a football player in the late 1940s, probably because Johnny was as talented as he was outspoken about breaking down the color barriers in the sporting world.

He was determined to prove all of them wrong. At Iowa's Drake University, Johnny led the NCAA in total offense, in 1949 and 1950; and he eventually set the record for total offense in a career with 5,983 yards. In 1951, as a senior at Drake, he was on his way again to leading the country in total offense, and he was leading the straw competition for the Heisman Trophy. Then his career was set back by a vicious hit in a game at Oklahoma A&M (now Oklahoma State): the tackle shattered his jaw. Photos of the hit were shown on front pages across the country, and there was no question that the blow was blatantly intentional. It didn't take a football fan to realize that this viciousness wasn't the result of Johnny being the most talented player on the field; it was an attack by someone who blatantly hated the color of Johnny's skin more than the color of the uniform he was wearing. The situation, which would become known as the "Johnny Bright Incident," resulted in the NCAA requiring all players to wear facemasks and mouth guards. But there was even more of a ripple effect from this event that almost killed the budding National Football League.

Johnny was drafted by the Philadelphia Eagles with their first pick in 1951. Still recovering mentally and physically from the hit he suffered in college, he had the guts to spurn the NFL, choosing instead to play in the Canadian Football League, where black athletes were far more accepted. In Canada, he went on to set numerous CFL records as a linebacker and running back. He was inducted into the Canadian Football and College Football Halls of Fame. Beyond changing the course of Johnny's life, his decision to reject the National Football League made an impression on many prominent black athletes from all sports. Canada benefited tremendously from the NFL's racism, as scores of black players migrated north to avoid the hostilities so evident in the pro ranks.

What happened to Johnny had repercussions for many, many years. It was another instance in which the black community stood up in caucus and asked, "Why do we put up with this?" It was one thing to deal with racism that was subtle and unspoken, but it was quite different when racists inflicted physical harm so openly. We did not mind, so much, having to be careful about the restaurants, shops, or hotels we entered. Boorish behavior of bigoted whites was usually something of an aberration, something that hurt us but did not endanger our lives. What happened to Johnny Bright, though, was so severe and sadistic that it alarmed the whole nation. There were many times we black football players sat around and asked each other what we would do if something like that happened to us or one of our teammates. We would say it was an impossibility: "Not on our field!" But thinking back on the lack of defense for Johnny on that fateful day, I don't think a damn thing would have happened to punish an attacker of one of us.

Society had us trained not to make a fuss. Furthermore, I don't think any of us were up to protesting or rocking the boat. The establishment knew that. Whites in the South had practiced intimidation for centuries. It was the classic, "Will he lynch me?" syndrome that controlled the slaves, through fear. As fellow slaves watched their family members being whipped, beaten, hanged, or burned to death, there were few among them who would speak out. In the America of the fifties, there were enough newspaper pictures of violent acts against blacks that this type of fear still reigned. It was suicidal to protest such acts; far better to remove oneself from the environment that condoned overt racism. For me, a young man who was still overwhelmed by the fact he had made it through college, the killing fields of the pros scared me so much that I almost went the way of Johnny Bright—straight to Canada.

Throughout the spring of 1956, white representatives for the Colts knocked at my parents' door, called, and sent letters, hoping they could persuade me to sign a contract, but to no avail. Eventually they sent John Steadman, who would go on to become the preeminent sports columnist for *The Baltimore News Spectator*. At that point John was a young administrator within the Colts organization who had a way with words. When he didn't get anywhere, Don Kellett, the Colts general manager, came out to discuss money with my parents, in a strategy to lure me financially. But it would take a lot more persuasion to shake my fears of playing professional football with the image of Johnny Bright still in my mind. What particularly made me leery was the possibility of moving to Baltimore, which was a model of segregationist boundaries at the time.

To make matters more complicated, a handful of Canadian teams knew of my talent and the trepidation I showed about signing with the Colts. Word spread quickly, and I was soon being actively pursued. I'll never forget a representative from the Toronto Argonauts who came down to visit my parents and me to convince me to play for them. After giving us a sales pitch of how good things were in Canada for black ballplayers and how successful the team was going to be, the man dipped into his coat pocket and took out an envelope with some cash in it. He took the stack of bills out of the envelope and slowly laid each one out on the kitchen table, in front of my father and me. When he was done, ten $100 bills lay there, luring us. The representative said, "If I can't convince you to play for us, maybe these can." My father and I were speechless. Never had either one of us seen so much money at one time, within our reach. It made both of us nervous, and I think it was that pressure that stopped us from signing that day. After much indecision on our part, the team rep picked up the money and put it in his pocket, saying that he'd be back. We never saw him again.

What finally tipped the scales in favor of the Colts was a visit one snowy spring day by future Hall of Famer Buddy Young. After a parade of white executives who all looked and dressed the same, this black man stood out from the crowd. His reputation preceded him. He had played football for the University of Illinois from 1947-1950. A performer who immediately reached All-America status in 1947, he led the Big Ten in rushing from the start. He was small in stature (5'4," 170 pounds) in his playing days; thus the nickname, "Mr. Five-by-Five," came quickly. But for all he lacked in height, he had stature and fortitude enough to help burst through the color barrier that was established, once the likes of Fritz Pollard and his contemporaries were forced out of the League in 1933. Buddy left college early, in 1950, because he had a wife and a child to support. He signed with the New York Yankees of the All-American Conference. Although that league eventually merged with the NFL, while it existed it did reopen the doors for black athletes in professional football, and Buddy lead the way.

From 1934 through 1946, there had been no black athletes in professional football. By the time Buddy signed with the Yankees, Marion Motley and Bill Willis were established with the Browns, but white players grossly outnumbered blacks. The first time Buddy played for the Yankees in Baltimore, he was mercilessly ridiculed and taunted by "fans" that appeared at the game in black face. Later, through a series of mergers, when a team was moved to Baltimore and became the Colts, Buddy faced the situation head on: instead of being uptight and guarded (with good reason), he instead became a goodwill ambassador for the team and for the League as a whole in his adopted city. His input on how the team was run was so far-reaching that he even persuaded team executives to sell tickets in northwest Baltimore so that black fans who wanted to attend the game could have easy access to buy tickets. He was a giant in Baltimore and around the country.

It was Buddy driving out to my parents' home in Reading, Pennsylvania, that allayed my fears about moving to Baltimore. His visit really impressed my parents and me. That someone of his stature would take the time to come to my home and personally sell me on coming to Baltimore was unbelievable. Furthermore, Buddy had an engaging personality and he mesmerized us. He assured us that Baltimore "wasn't that bad." He said the team was coming together, and Coach Weeb Ewbank, one of Paul Brown's former assistants, was a good man who tried to treat everyone on the team as equals. He painted such a positive picture of the Colts that I wanted to drive back with him and sign as soon as possible. I thought with someone like him on my side, everything was going to be all right.

Shortly thereafter, I agreed to sign with the team, and my professional career would soon be launched the following fall.

~ ~ ~

With my status as a first-round draft pick by the Colts, I was invited to a number of college All-Star games—all of them in the northern part of the United States. The South still wasn't a very inviting place for black players; it didn't matter how good you were, you just weren't invited to play. It was not that black players always received fair treatment in many games played in the North, but you had a better shot at showcasing your talents in places like Chicago than you did in Mobile, Alabama. Even with a friendlier environment, most of the plum starting jobs went to the white players anyway, but even a glimmer of hope was better than none.

As an example, at the East-West game in San Francisco, Hopalong Cassidy of Ohio State and I were both selected to play the left-halfback position. In our first practice, it was apparent to anyone who wanted to admit it that, physically, there was no comparison; I had the edge. I was bigger and faster than Cassidy, and that fact was borne out through the preparation for the game. But it wasn't long before Woody Hayes shipped me to the right side of the backfield, instead of keeping me on the more dominant left side. In the end, it didn't matter, since I played only in the final minutes of the game anyway. But what really hurt was that Rip Engle was an assistant on the team. I pleaded my case to him, but he was powerless. Woody made the rules and had the final say. This unfair treatment came to the forefront of national debate the next year, when Jim Brown made the rounds in all the All-Star games but barely received any playing time at all.

The trip to San Francisco wasn't a total loss, though, as I was able to meet Ella Fitzgerald for the first time. I was a big jazz fan, as was John Jenkins, my old friend from Reading, who had become a standout at Arizona State. John and I were excited to be in the same game together, which gave us a chance to hang out that we hadn't had since our high school days.

One day, as we meandered around downtown looking for something to do, we saw that Ella Fitzgerald was playing at one of the hotels. Later that day, we walked to the hotel with no illusions of being able to pay for a ticket—not these poor kids from Reading—we just wanted to be a part of the buzz and check things out. As we entered the hotel lobby, low and behold, who was sitting there, holding court over her fans, but Lady Ella herself? After gawking for a few minutes, we were thrilled to see her wave us over. Noticing our varsity jackets, she asked where we were from and what we were doing in town. We chatted for a while, and then she asked if we were planning on attending the concert later that evening. We said that we would love to, but we didn't have any money and that it was just a blessing for us to be able to sit and chat with her. Without saying another word, she motioned for her valet to come over. Ella arranged for us to sit at a private table and watch her performance that night. What a special evening!

Many years later I would see her at different functions around the country, and I would always recount the thrill I received at our first meeting. She would politely listen every time I told the story, but I knew she didn't remember the incident specifically, because she had done the same thing for many people, many times throughout her life. She was just a wonderful person whom I deeply admired.

Another All-Star game in which I appeared, before joining the Colts officially, was at Soldier Field in Chicago, playing against the NFL's champion from the year before, the mighty Cleveland Browns. We lost the game, 30-0, in front of 75,000 spectators; but it was a tremendous experience as I took the field for the first time against one of my idols, Marion Motley. Although it was an exhibition game, the contest was intense, as the Browns were in no mood to be upset by a bunch of college kids. The game was on national television, and I had told all of my friends and family to watch me play. The coach of the team was Curly Lambeau, and he assured me I'd get in; but by halftime, I hadn't played a second. The disappointment was too much for me and I broke down and cried in my locker stall. I was embarrassed about telling everyone back home to watch, only to disappoint them. After the good feelings that came out of my meeting with Buddy, I was quickly having second thoughts as to what I'd gotten myself into by joining this league that didn't seem too eager to see me play.

Luckily for me, I didn't have much time to dwell on this shame. I boarded a plane immediately after the game, bound for Hershey, Pennsylvania, to attend my first Colts game, an exhibition against the Philadelphia Eagles.

~ ~ ~

I was scared; I won't lie to you. Everything was moving so fast for me. Criss-crossing the country and experiencing so many highs and lows added a tension to some serious reservations that already were burning in my gut, as to whether I'd be able to make it in the NFL. Playing ball at Penn State had been a blessing, one that I enjoyed and tried to make the best of; but playing professionally was way beyond anything I could yet comprehend. Growing up, my greatest ambition, my definition of "making it," was merely to own my own house with a little grass around it. There were many days in Happy Valley when I used to walk the streets, dreaming about living in one of the picturesque little cottages that I'd pass around campus. But here I was, faced with a different form of success—one that I had not seriously contemplated until Buddy Young convinced me to play for the Colts. I felt for the first time in my life the pressure of real expectations. I hoped I would not fail, but I really wasn't sure.

In no time at all, I was rushed into a waiting car at the airport and taken straight to the stadium. Soon I found myself suited up and pacing on the sidelines, feeling quite small, among a team of hardened veterans. I'd heard through Rosey's experience with the New York Giants that seasoned players were generally suspicious of outsiders, so I tried to be inconspicuous. Assuming that I was there only to watch and learn, it was a big surprise when I learned that they had penciled me in to return kicks on special teams. Thank God they didn't put me out there on offense. Although I was petrified, I knew everything was going to be all right, because lined up next to me on the return was Buddy Young. He could sense I was nervous, and he took control. At kickoff, he literally coached the ball into my hands and yelled, "Follow me!" He blocked for me, all the way down the field. I though to myself, "Man, I need to stick with this cat!"

My comfort didn't last long, though. When I returned to the sidelines after the kickoff, I listened to the sounds of the game, in a way that I had never focused on them before. The players were hitting each other with such force that it sounded like a series of explosions. In college games, I'd faced many future pro players like Sam Huff, Jim Brown, J.C. Caroline, and Alan Ameche. But for every standout that I confronted, there had been a dozen players, fresh out of high school, who were still growing into their bodies and who had far less ability than even the least talented players on these NFL squads. If tackles and sacks in the current game that I was watching sounded like major car wrecks, those boys I had played in college were merely bumper cars. The Colts and the Eagles were out for blood, and it was only the preseason!

Although the NFL was still in its infancy compared to the spectacle that it is now, it was attracting some of the nation's top athletes. These were the best of the best in a sport that was decades away from the conditions of today, where there is unmitigated expansion and a watering down of talent. At that time, performance incentives, signing bonuses, and salary caps were ideas that no one had ever heard of; and there was no "job security" except in maintaining your strength, muscle, and determination to win. I took all this in from the sidelines, as I watched grown men, serious men, many of whom had seen battle in Korea, fighting for their jobs. Nothing could get in their way. These men played hard, as if their livelihood depended on it—which it did.

I was petrified, drowning in self-doubt. It wasn't long before I was looking for an exit. I noticed that a table that was covered with rolls of white tape separated the benches of the two teams. That tape caught my eye; I was "Spats," after all, known for the taped-ankles ritual that had fortified me before each Penn State game. Just then, the rough-and-tumble Alan Ameche, my former adversary from Wisconsin, came barreling out of the backfield, being forced out of bounds by two or three Eagles, who drove my new teammate into that table and landed on him. The table splintered under the force. The Eagles had landed. I said to myself, "Man, what is this game all about?"

What stunned me even more was the fact that no one was hurt. After the hit, Ameche got up, dusted himself off, and ran back into the huddle. For the life of me, I can't remember the final score of that game, but I always remember "The Horse" living up to his nickname. I was just thankful he was on our side.

Our second preseason game was against Pittsburgh and, after having a week of practice under my belt, I felt a little more comfortable. I actually notched two touchdowns, of which I was mighty proud. But even being a quick study to the team's game plans, I had to earn my position as the starting tailback and flanker. I soon found out that Weeb and Don Kellett had drafted me with the intent of using me as a defensive back. It was their thinking that, with Buddy at the running back and Raymond Berry on the outside, my skills would be better suited on the defensive side of the ball. Also, somewhere I had attracted the reputation for being slow to pick up an offense, and Weeb wasn't confident that I could remember all the plays. I would later find out that Andy Stopper, my old high school coach and guardian angel, and my Penn State coach, Rip Engle, came to many of our practices that summer, and had encouraged Weeb to use me in the backfield. With their endorsements and the eventual loss of my sea legs, it didn't take long for Weeb to see that my future with the Colts rested in the backfield. The starting halfback job was soon to be mine.

But let me set the record straight: contrary to popular belief, I did not beat out Buddy Young for his job. Nobody could beat Buddy. Even after a number of years in the League, he was still fast, still in great shape and, by far, the most technically sound player I had ever been around. Buddy was light years ahead of me. No, what actually happened was this: once Weeb made up his mind about me, he went to Buddy and asked that he accept a position in the Colts front office. Buddy would be the first black in such a capacity, something of an honor, Coach insisted. But Buddy was stunned. He was very taken aback and hurt. We never talked about it, but he must have felt betrayed by the team, seeing the position as a demotion. Months prior to this, he realized, he had been sent out to my home as a pawn to convince me to come to Baltimore—as his own replacement! I don't think he ever got over this abrupt ending to his playing career, which I can't blame him for. I know I would be devastated. Making the best of it, Buddy would excel as an executive with the team and was eventually recruited by the League office, in New York, to be a special assistant to Pete Rozelle (again, a first), a position he held for several years.

Personally, I was crestfallen when Weeb asked Buddy to retire so that he could give me Buddy's job. I knew that I could have learned so much from Buddy; I was sorry to see him go. Anytime a black player got cut, it hurt, because there weren't many of us. But in the NFL, I was quickly learning, it becomes a matter of worrying only about you and not concerning yourself with others. That is not an easy adjustment for me to make, since it is against my nature. It made it especially difficult because of Buddy's standing in the community, on the team, and in the League. To make matters more awkward, it wasn't as if Buddy was going anywhere, he stilled lived in Baltimore and I would keep running into Buddy around town.

Buddy was pretty much the big man in the Baltimore club circuit. I can remember hearing bar patrons telling Buddy, "Man, I can't believe you let that young boy beat you out and make you quit!" I always made sure to correct anyone who accused me of taking Buddy's job. Evidently, however, this constant misperception took its toll on our relationship, because Buddy never really took to me.

As a team executive, Buddy had everyone believing that he was some kind of "Den Daddy" to all the black players, some of whom would work at Buddy's house, doing various chores. For example, Jesse Thomas would cut his grass. It was a situation I wanted no part of. The "grunts" who worked for Buddy were allowed to go to his numerous parties, though: he would invite most of the guys, even the white players. He never invited me. I felt hurt when I would hear the guys say that they were partying at Buddy's house. It was silent payback, I suppose, for what Buddy considered my betrayal.

As years passed, I learned that Buddy represented everything that a black athlete should not be. He was very much an "Uncle Tom." When white people would make those "off-color" remarks," or use the term "black" (which wasn't accepted at the time), Buddy would laugh as hard as the white guy who slandered our race. And Buddy was always saying things like, "I don't want chocolate milk because I'm chocolate enough." He also used the word "nigger" when talking about other blacks, to white people. In time, I lost all respect for the man. My experiences with race at Penn State should have put me wise to him a lot earlier, but I learned the hard way.

The grudge that Buddy held against me not only hurt me emotionally, but it also started to affect my pocketbook and my standing in the community as well. Considering the meager salaries we earned as ballplayers at that time, any additional income we could make was very helpful. Buddy soon froze me out of any such side jobs through the Colts organization.

As the unofficial representative for all the black players on the team, Buddy had people in Baltimore thinking that all Colt appearances for black players had to go through him. I was not invited to attend many community functions in the black parts of town, because Buddy would tell them that I was too busy or that he couldn't get in touch with me. I found this out when, in the mid-1960s, the director of a YMCA branch that was a major centerpiece of the black community at the time, asked me if I would make an appearance at the David Hill "Y." I told him that I would be happy to come, and that brought a grin to his face. He said that he had invited me before, through Buddy of course, but he was always told I couldn't make it. He was shocked when I told him that Buddy had never mentioned it to me.

Another time, Bert Piggot, the head coach at North Carolina A&T, told me how disappointed he was that I wasn't in attendance at a function in Wilmington, Delaware, to meet his two star halfbacks. He told me that the only reason he brought them was to meet me. After hearing this, I apologized profusely to him but also told him that I never knew anything about the affair. Disgusted by this apparent double-cross, I later saw my name listed with the other honorees in an Afro-American newspaper. At the event, Bert said, Buddy had stood up and told everyone that I couldn't make it due to a prior engagement. That hurt me terribly.

When I found out what Buddy Young was doing to me—spreading a negative image of me in the black community, by making it appear that I was shunning my own people—I went to him and asked why. He just bullshitted me and continued his dirty tricks. Uncomfortable with fully confronting him, I let the situation go and just tried to mind my own business.

Monte Irvin, former Giant major leaguer and a Baseball Hall of Fame inductee in his own right, once advised me to watch out for Buddy Young. He said that he was at an event in New York with Buddy, and witnessed him blasting Jim Parker, Big Daddy Lipscomb, and me, calling us "back-alley winos." This was typical of Buddy, apparently, for Jackie Robinson also warned me about Buddy as well. He described Buddy as a "white man's nigger." Monte said that Buddy would tell his white friends anything they wanted to know about blacks. The more people to whom I talked about Buddy, the more information I was finding out—and the less I liked.

Every time the blacks on the Colts team wanted to take a stand against racism—protesting the inferior treatment we received from hotels in the South, for instance—Buddy would urge us to boycott or strike, or to generally raise hell. In one instance, Buddy had us really riled up over some injustice on the road. Of course, Buddy used this instance to warn team officials "the natives are restless." As a result, Buddy received a reputation around the League as someone to call when black athletes demonstrated that they didn't "know their place." Buddy was regarded as the special liaison between the white officials and the black players, for he had a way of playing both ends against each other.

The worst thing Buddy ever did to me personally was lower than low. I found out, after the fact, that Buddy was instrumental in my losing the sportscaster job at CBS, after I retired from the Colts. Buddy told CBS that the people in the black community didn't think I was any good. Fortunately, several black athletes in the League eventually became hip to him and told me what he had done. I paid a hell of a price, from the day he moved to the Colts' front office to the day he passed away.

There were times when I wanted to tell Buddy what I thought of him. I wanted to tell him, in a one-on-one conversation, how badly he had hurt me. I wanted to cite the betrayals, chapter and verse, for it was important to me that I get it all off my chest. One day, in the Gridiron Room in Memorial Stadium in the 1970s, before a game, I had a chance to sit down with Buddy and tell him everything I felt. I confronted him about all the missed opportunities I had forfeited; I complained about his choreographing the poor image I had in the community; and I let him know the pain he caused my family and me. I gave him example after example. Stunned, he sat there and had had nothing to say to defend himself, for there were no reasons, nor excuses, for his actions. He just sat at the table, hunched over, staring blankly into space. When I was finished with my litany of complaints, he quietly got up from the table. We wouldn't have any meaningful contact again. He died in 1983, from an auto accident, driving home from Joe Delaney's funeral.

The funny thing is, I never disliked Buddy. He had a magnetic personality that drew you closer and made you want to be around him. It just
makes me very sad how he had to prostitute himself to the white executives
he held in such high esteem, and how he was disingenuous with those
blacks who gave him their confidence. By playing both ends he didn't do
anything to improve racism; in fact, he perpetuated the bigotry that dominated the era.

All things being equal, Buddy Young could have been a true pioneer. He
could have used his influence and his contacts for better purposes than his
own financial gain through the manipulation of his post. What a shame and
what a waste.

# SIX

# ROOKIE OF THE YEAR

The city of Baltimore has a venerable history as a shipping community that has played an integral part in our nation's history. From the Revolutionary War to the Civil War, this town has a proud tradition. Unlike Pennsylvania, however, which was a major hub of the Underground Railroad and a safe haven for blacks during the Reconstruction Era, Maryland's multicultural co-inhabitants have long endured racial strife. Baltimore, in particular, has had a spotty track record of race relations, which torment the area even today.

During the Civil War, many Baltimore blacks fought on behalf of their slave owners. A reluctant member of the Union, Maryland held slavery to be legal for a longer period of time than many people care to remember. Frederick Douglass, the famous orator, abolitionist, and author, "belonged" to a slave owner in Baltimore. Douglass writes of watching the ships sail in Chesapeake Bay, wanting to experience their freedom himself. He worked at the same Fells Point docks that Harriet Tubman would use to transport blacks willing to risk their lives to escape slavery. Shortly after the first shot was fired in the Civil War, Abraham Lincoln put Maryland under martial law because he did not want Washington, D.C., the capital of the union, to be surrounded by Confederate states (with Virginia to the south). A large number of free blacks migrated to Baltimore, even under some of the most severe apartheid laws this side of the Atlantic. Baltimore thus had its share of "buffalo soldiers," former slaves who took arms in the struggle for inde-

pendence that they would have to wait for a century to officially enjoy
them.

In spite of the overt segregation that lingered in Baltimore for decades
after the Civil War, the fabric of the black community in Baltimore became
strong and self-sufficient. Numerous black churches sprouted up in the city
and became the anchors of the community. The Baltimore *Afro-American*
newspaper was founded, and it is still in circulation today. Another focal
point of the vibrant black community in Baltimore was Pennsylvania
Avenue, which became a hotbed of modern jazz where the likes of Billie
Holiday, Miles Davis, and Charlie "Bird" Parker became superstars. The city
would also give birth to Thurgood Marshall, the first black Supreme Court
justice. And the headquarters for the NAACP would be installed in
Baltimore. Nonetheless, white privilege ruled the day in the 1950s, when I
was forced to make Baltimore my adopted home city. A good majority of
the public school's population was black, but because of the mass migration
of the white population to the suburbs, funding to inner-city black schools
was drastically cut. The infrastructure of the city suffered, as did the education of black children, which is still a problem to this day. Even so, the area
around Baltimore boasts three noted black colleges: Morgan State, Coppin
State, and Sojourner-Douglas (the latter named for two former slaves whose
legacies of self-determination paved the way for freedom).

By the time I arrived in Baltimore, the city was alive with debate about
MLK's boycott of Montgomery Alabama's bus system, and Rosa Parks's
refusal to give up her seat on a Montgomery bus. Needless to say, these
events gave impetus to a domino effect. For the black population, there had
always been a dilemma: the fear of inciting physical harm at the expense of
abrogating our rights. For centuries, blacks have had to think carefully
about their every move. Given the bravery of MLK and Rosa Parks, though,
blacks were determined to keep the issue of racial injustice in the forefront
of society's collective mind—it was all about keeping the pot on the stove,
as it were. The Montgomery blacks were putting their lives on the line. They
had stuck their necks out to be agents of social change. Still, the order of the
day was nonviolence, even when violence was occurring everywhere, by
virtue of white policemen and their german shepherds, their billy clubs, and
their fire hoses.

What a time to enter big-city life. I was a fish out of water. To that point
in my life I thought I had experienced racism, but I would receive a baptism
by fire through my move to Baltimore! Between the headlines in the papers

and the debates on the street, I became more than a little nostalgic for the sleepy little town of Happy Valley, Pennsylvania, where people had a tendency to ignore anything that happened beyond their city's limits. The racism there was at least more subdued and covert. By contrast, in Baltimore, I felt like a magnet for all the hostility that white people wanted to express against blacks in the South.

Westminster, where the Colts' training camp was held, was even worse. It was a blatantly racist town where, outside of going to practice once or twice a day, there was nothing for a black person to do. We couldn't go to the movies or the restaurants; the only thing we could do was walk the streets. There was one food stand, way out on the outskirts of town, that wasn't afraid to serve the black players on the team. It wasn't a restaurant in the sense that there was no place to sit, but that didn't bother us. It was just a relief to get out of the dorm rooms we were relegated to and eat food that wasn't served cafeteria style for a change. Thinking back, it was dehumanizing, and we hated it, but we didn't have much of a choice. Most of us let the restrictions roll off of us like the rest of the treatment we received, but once in a while the pressure got to be unbearable for us each individually. As Milt Davis said once, "I cannot endure the mental punishment. Being black, there are so many pressures."

For the white players it was different. Many of them professed affection for this small community. But here is how the difference played out: The field at training camp was set in a hollow, and we had to trudge up the slope to get to the locker room. There, all of us would be besieged by autograph seekers of all ages, which we would gladly accommodate, but see one of these Townies on the street later that night, and the white players would be invited into the local tavern for a beer on the house while the rest of us received scowls. We were so unhappy with our experience in this town that, during one training camp, when Westminster threw its annual Welcome Banquet for the team, we black players boycotted it—with the encouragement of the NAACP. The boycott made the local papers and we received some publicity but, sadly, nothing changed. It got to the point that Weeb and Carroll Rosenbloom, the owner at the time, came to me, Jim Parker, and Big Daddy, and the rest of the black players on the team and asked us if we wanted him to move the site for training camp to Pennsylvania, or even to Canada. We each appreciated the show of respect we received from the team and contemplated the idea very seriously. After sitting around one night at dinner to talk about it, we decided to stay put. In the end, with its warts and all, Westminster was only a half hour from Baltimore, so we were close enough to see our families during the week, making it back to our Westminster dorms in time for bed check. We each agreed that the close proximity to our families outweighed the uneasiness we each felt during every training camp we attended at Westminster.

Things were better for me in Baltimore (but not much better), as my first season began. The end of 1956 seemed to be a haze to me, looking back. At times, I felt as though I was starring in a movie about a country bumpkin who steps off a bus and into the big city and is just overwhelmed with culture shock. Very early in my career in Baltimore, I was labeled as a "wild man," which I guess was true in some ways. But when you've lived like a hermit on Mount Nittany and in a matter of weeks you are dropped into the middle of a metropolis (with serious racial issues), without family or friends for support, you go a little crazy. Good friends like Alan Merkle, Coach Stopper, and Dorothy Robinson would occasionally drive to Baltimore just to see me play, which was very nice, but they would eventually leave; and then, BOOM, I'd realize I was all alone once again. The drinking and carousing in which I took part those first years in Baltimore were a way for me to cope. Drinking and listening to jazz at the various clubs in town dulled my senses enough to recharge for another day.

Eugene "Big Daddy" Lipscomb, one of the best linemen in the League and a black player for the Colts, was the first person I could call "friend." The two of us found we had a lot in common, and we soon became buddies. Big Daddy loved the movies, as did I; and he had even done a bit of acting. Watch the 1954 movie, *Kismet*, and you can actually see Big Daddy for approximately four minutes, playing a litter bearer, carrying a Chinese girl. Big Daddy also had a love for jazz and the nightlife, and for VO and women. He eventually took a job at a local brewery for two nights a week, acting as a greeter. He loved being around people. He played Santa Claus every year at Douglas Memorial Community Church. He became known for giving money to children all over Baltimore.

Big Daddy had not had a chance to go to college as I had, but that didn't make any difference to me. He had joined the military right out of high school and had played football in the army, at Camp Pendleton, against rivals at army bases all around the West Coast. His size and his ability to dominate a game drew interest from two of the local teams, the Los Angeles Rams and the San Francisco 49ers, and eventually Big Daddy signed with Sid Gilman and the Los Angeles Rams. Gilman helped secure

Big Daddy's release from the military in time for him to play the last game of the 1953 season against the Baltimore Colts.

Sadly, his Rams teammates looked down on Big Daddy because he had not played college football. From a technical standpoint, the other players on the team were far superior to Big Daddy, who had spent most of his high school and semi-pro career bullying the smaller opponents he played against. He was also very sensitive about his lack of education. Although he never let it show publicly, his academic deficiencies were far more embarrassing to him than any deficiency in his football technique. He was such a monstrous individual that his raw talent could overcome any blocker. He felt, though, it was his academic failings that were his true Achilles' heel. The friction between the Rams' "college boys" and Big Daddy led to numerous fights with teammates, as well as with his opponents on the field. He earned the nickname "Fifteen-Yard Daddy" for all the roughing penalties he would receive during the game. Eventually the Rams ran out of patience and gave up on Big Daddy and released him.

The Colts' coach, Weeb Ewbank, scouring the waiver wire, saw the opportunity to bring Big Daddy into the Colts camp. He vividly remembered the '53 game that Big Daddy had played against Baltimore, and he thought it would be worth the $100 claim fee to give Big Daddy an opportunity to make the Colts squad. Weeb and the other coaches did their best to mold and coach Big Daddy into a player who could leverage his size to dominate opponents. Treating Big Daddy the same way he would treat his own son, he would use innocent little motivational tools to help Big Daddy reach some of his potential. As an example, Weeb offered to buy Big Daddy a new hat every time he blocked a kick. Being a notorious fashion hound and well known for the different hats and suits he would wear around town, Big Daddy responded to the offer of new hats with a vigor. He started to feel more at home with the Colts, for he felt Weeb understood and respected him.

Big Daddy lived with Sherman Plunkett (another very close friend of mine) and saw Buddy Young a lot during his time in Baltimore. He fell in love with Buddy's kids. He was a big kid himself. He literally became part of the family. Since it was Buddy who recruited me, I met Big Daddy through Buddy shortly after I joined the Colts in 1956. After every game or practice, we would take a cab down to Pennsylvania Avenue, to catch some jazz. One night I would pick up the food and he would get the drinks, then the next night we would switch. I never really fancied myself as a big drinker, so I was happiest when it was my turn to buy the food. Most of the time the reason I would go out drinking after games was to relieve the tension I was feeling from trying to prove myself to my teammates and coaches, as well as to cope with the stress of living in a racial pressure cooker.

Another person whom I met soon after moving to Baltimore was Francis (Frankie) Martin. We were introduced by an acquaintance I had made at one of the local taverns. We started dating in September of 1956 and were married by Christmas that same year. She was stunning in her ice-blue satin dress. Looking back, though, I wonder if the color of her bridal dress was a perfect match for the "blues" I was feeling. If you think courting a woman for three months and then marrying her is ludicrous, you are probably right. I don't think I was aware of what I was doing at the time and, to be honest, no one really asked. Big Daddy was angry with me, but I think he was less concerned about my welfare than he was sorry to be losing his drinking buddy. My parents did not question my decision to marry; they just told me that I was grown and out of the house, so I could make my own choices. Mom and Dad came to the wedding, but I could tell they were uneasy about how fast things were moving for me.

Frankie and I went to New York City for a short honeymoon, and then we immediately found an apartment in Baltimore. Since I first moved there, I had lived in a spare bedroom of my cousin's house, just off Poplar Grove and Brighton. The apartment where Frankie and I began our lives together was four blocks up the street. It was nice and cozy, and I presumed I was happy. Sadly, for both of us, we had a lot to learn about marriage. I wonder, sometimes, whether our marriage would have been better if we'd met in the '60s when I was older and wiser, instead of the '50s, but this was the situation we were in and we attempted to make the best of it.

~ ~ ~

One only has to take a brief glance at the NFL's history to see how the decade of the 1950s altered the course of the league permanently. The League as we know it now is very different from the NFL into which I was drafted. To start with, America's favorite game in the '50s was baseball. In the professional sports pantheon, the NFL, the NHL, and the NBA were all a distant second behind Major League Baseball. In just one decade, though, the NFL would be nipping at the heels of America's Pastime, well ahead of both basketball and hockey. The Colts played a major role in this evolution that cannot be mistaken.

The Colts themselves evolved over the 1950s. The first game played by the Baltimore Colts was against the Brooklyn Dodgers on September 7, 1947, with a 16-7 victory. Soon thereafter, due to mismanagement, the team would fold in 1951 after a 1-11 season. The city was definitely football hungry and had proved that it could support professional football (residents of Baltimore felt strongly that it was the ownership that needed improving); but the city was passed over multiple times for an expansion franchise (which would happen once again to the city four decades later), and went without a team in 1951 and 1952. It wasn't until the fall of 1952, when the Dallas Texans were struggling mightily at the box office in their hometown and became a traveling sideshow for the bulk of the season to try to draw interest to the team. It also allowed the League to test out other cities to see where this vagabond franchise would land, for it was crystal clear that Dallas was not ready to support the NFL. At the risk of nearly missing out for a third time in trying to land a team, the city of Baltimore put together an attractive financial package that guaranteed the city would purchase at least 15,000 season tickets before the season started. This aggressive strategy persuaded Commissioner Bert Bell to take a chance on Baltimore and soon awarded the city the franchise. Thus the Colts (aka "Texans") were reincarnated.

I remember that I was just entering my sophomore year at Penn State, when the St. Louis Browns baseball team moved to Baltimore and borrowed the local minor league team's nickname "the Orioles." That same year, 1953, I remember reading how Baltimore caught lightning in a bottle a second time, when the city engineered the first two professional sports franchise moves of the decade, and the Texans became the Colts. It was soon thereafter that the franchise would start a new winning tradition as they won their first game, 13-9, against the Bears, on September 27, 1953.

My first game as a Colt was a win against the Bears as well. At that time, Johnny Unitas was not *the Johnny Unitas*. He started out on the bench, behind a very capable quarterback, George Shaw. But we beat the mighty Bears anyway, 28-21.

I wish I could tell you I knew Johnny better. As with the other white players on the team, we never mingled. One thing I can say about him is that I never saw him use the race card. From Day One, Johnny was always consistent in the way he treated people, white or black. Another thing I liked about him: he was a true leader in every sense of the word. All he wanted to do was win ballgames, and he didn't care who got the ball or how it was done. He was the ultimate bottom-line competitor. Johnny was head and shoulders above the rest, but he would be the first to tell you it was because he had the benefit of working with an absolute craftsman like Weeb. Everything trickled down through Weeb; he was always so prepared. Although Johnny would become famous for calling plays in the huddle and utilizing the audible like no other, it was Weeb who painstakingly drilled those options into the team in every practice. As Johnny became a master at the two-minute drill, it was like having another coach out there on the field with us. These two geniuses would form the greatest coach/quarterback combo until Bill Walsh and Joe Montana would revolutionize offensive football again three decades later.

Johnny and I would eventually form a great team on offense, but he had to establish himself first. During the first part of the 1956 season, Johnny was firmly entrenched as a back up to the talented Shaw, who was both more mobile than Johnny and was a much sharper passer at the time. After we beat the Bears, we went up against a major juggernaut at the time, the Detroit Lions. This team had many fantastic players, and the incomparable Bobby Layne led them. With the team still trying to find its footing, the Lions showed that they were a far superior team and dominated us early, leaving with a 31-14 win. Next we traveled to Milwaukee to play Vince Lombardi's Packers. Green Bay came into the game winless, but didn't leave that way. It wasn't a total loss for me, though, as I scored my first two touchdowns for the Colts in that game. We found ourselves sitting at 1-2, with little hope of catching the streaking and undefeated Lions. Weeb encouraged us to keep working and preparing for each game as if it were our last. He was a firm believer in making our own luck. Remarkably, it would be a monumental stroke of bad luck that would change the course of our season, the franchise, and the history of professional football as we knew it.

Halfway through our next game against the Bears, Weeb wasn't thinking about the future of the NFL, he was just trying to hold his team together. The team would suffer three fumbles that all resulted in scoring drives for the Bears. J.C. Caroline, my nemesis from my college days a few years before, stuck a dagger in our hearts by rumbling for a 54-yard touchdown.

You would think that very little good could come from a dismal 58-27 loss to the mighty Monsters of the Midway, but something did. After being crushed by the Bears on a broken play that had George Shaw scrambling for his life, he was slow to get up, and it was apparent that some damage had been done to his knee. Unable to walk back to the huddle, he was carried off the field by two of his teammates. Without anything to lose, Weeb told Unitas to jump in there to see what he could do in this lost cause. Johnny replaced Shaw that game and never looked back.

Johnny always had confidence in himself, but the rest of the team thought we were doomed. Up to that point, everything we did on offense was dependent on George Shaw. He was a running and passing quarterback who brought a great dynamic to Weeb's offense; but he just couldn't recover from the hit that blew out his knee. Everyone liked George and rallied around him, but his body just broke down and was never able to regain his speed and agility.

Out of desperation, Johnny's first career start came at just the right time. Our losing streak ended with the next game, against Green Bay. With 22 seconds to go in the first half, I took a reverse around the end and ran 72 yards for a touchdown. In the fourth quarter, I had another long run, this time for 79 yards, that turned out to be the decisive touchdown. Unitas had two touchdown tosses. He was in complete control and looked as if he were a ten-year veteran. Needless to say, he was settling into the offense very nicely.

The greatest thrill of that first season was our next game against the Cleveland Browns, where I would play against Marion Motley for the second straight year, this time as his peer. The fact that the Browns were the defending champs made it all the more special. I played as if my life depended on it. For the third time in the last two games, I had a touchdown run of at least 70 yards that came off the first play from scrimmage. I rumbled down the sideline carrying two defenders over the goal line. With a hard-fought 21-7 victory, our once dormant team now had some momentum heading into our rematch with Layne's Lions.

Our return trip to Detroit was a disappointing setback to our developing team. The Lions had just come off of their first loss of the season and were tied with the Bears for first place; they were in no mood to lose another game. Our passing game was clicking (we racked up over 300 yards in passing offense), but we could only muster up one field goal by Bert Rechicar. We lost, 27-3, before a standing-room-only crowd of 55,788.

On a wet and gray day in late November, the Rams left Memorial Stadium not knowing what had hit them. We rebounded and really felt the team coming together after being dominated just the week before. Our eight-touchdown affair would be the highest scoring total in the NFL for the season. Billy Vessels played most of the game for me due to a nagging injury and had a career day with three touchdowns. Alan Ameche ran for 162 yards and a touchdown. The team was hitting everybody that game; Bert Reichicar even flattened the field umpire and sent him to a local hospital and the Rams went back west after a 56-21 thrashing.

We really thought we had some momentum going into our final game against the 49ers. Winning this game would have squared the season and allowed us the chance to finish the year on a high note by winning two in a row and three out of the last four. The San Francisco 11 had other thoughts, though, and would squeak out a 20-17 victory. The clincher was a pass to Joe Perry, who shook off Bert Reichicar and Don Shula, to score. The loss spoiled the two-touchdown effort from Alan Ameche, but more importantly left a sour taste in our mouth that would stay with us throughout the off season.

For a scared kid who didn't know if he belonged on the team in August, I didn't do too badly. My first year in the League came to an end and I was voted Rookie of the Year. My award would be the second straight for the team, as Ameche had won the honor in 1955. For the first time I felt like I belonged, which gave me even more motivation to follow up this award-winning season to prove to myself that it wasn't a fluke.

~ ~ ~

By my second year with the Colts, I knew what a genius we had in Weeb. Although he wasn't the first choice of Carroll Rosenbloom, this graduate of Miami of Ohio turned out to be a fantastic head coach. In my mind, he has to be rated as one of the best coaches the League has ever seen. Weeb had coached with the Browns since 1953, adding his own spin to the structure that made Paul Brown's namesake so successful. He brought the same creativity and structure to the Colts.

Up until I met Weeb, I had thought Andy Stopper and Rip Engle were very precise coaches, but Weeb took precision to the extreme. We had classroom sessions before every on-field practice, and he gave us grades of 1 through 5 after every game. He was meticulous. He would take everyone's meal order before the game, going from player to player, like a waiter. He was also very superstitious and a perfectionist to a fault, which allowed him to mesh with Don Kellett, the general manager, who was a stickler for organization.

Weeb also had a way of using psychology to keep everyone on the team happy. Every club has internal problems, and the trick is to handle the problems without causing chaos among the group. There were times, for instance, when the players wanted to get out of the hotel and go have some fun, which meant a late night and the potential for a sluggish game the next day. Weeb would slyly call a meeting the night before and use up all of our free time reviewing some missing detail we hadn't covered previously, leaving us nothing but minutes before bed check at 10 p.m. Often, his last-minute meetings were about nothing more serious than the options for breakfast. He would go into a long, crazy oratory about the next morning's breakfast. "Who wants eggs?" he would ask. "Who wants eggs light? Who wants eggs over easy?" He was never our warden, keeping us in lock down; but he controlled our time and managed our routines as if he were Svengali. We were well taught a routine, and he trained us to eliminate stupid mistakes and cut down on mental errors. The older I become, and with the distance that many, many years away from pro ball affords, I finally understand his coaching methods. He not only made us a better team but better individual players.

As a black athlete under his tutelage, I noticed early on that Weeb tried his best to ignore the fact that he had black and white players on his team, which didn't encourage much change in the racial situations the team would encounter during my time there. It is not that Weeb wanted to see us suffer; he just didn't want to deal with it. His strategy was merely to avoid any uncomfortable conflicts. He knew that we blacks counted on him to provide an equal opportunity, but with all of his ability to diffuse most racial tensions, the practice of stacking black players in the usual positions was clearly in effect. Essentially, the theory behind "stacking" is to control the number of black players on the team by making them compete for the same position, which was primarily the position farthest from the ball. Blacks were therefore named as wide receivers, running backs, or defensive backs. White players, meanwhile, were awarded those positions closest to the ball: quarterback, center, and linebacker. By implementing this practice, it was easy to cut black players without disturbing the team's cohesiveness to any great degree.

Black athletes would have to wait decades to receive the opportunity to play any of the "thinking" positions, such as quarterback, middle linebacker, pulling guard, or center. If a young black athlete managed to come into the League as a quarterback, he would soon be shuffled to receiver or defensive back, where he could be pitted against other black athletes. Future Hall of Fame performers like Roosevelt Brown, Emlen Tunnell, Dick ("Night Train") Lane, Jim Parker, Len Ford, and Joe Perry paved the way for the future of the League by proving that they could withstand the increased competition among teams when black players vied against each other for a roster spot. By the 1950s, most every team had blacks on it, although rarely did that number exceed a total of seven. What the black player did bring to the League was an athleticism that had never been seen before, and the mark that was left on the League was indelible.

Whether that athleticism was a source of envy or distaste to white players and white management, there was a palpable racial tension that permeated the League. Many of the coaches, general managers, and owners liked the fact that black players had dramatically increased the athleticism on their teams (which resulted, of course, in an increased number of victories every year); but what the coaches, managers, and owners did not like were the many logistical problems that integrated teams confronted when they traveled to different cities, especially those in the South. It was into this racial tug-of-war that I started my professional career.

What many people fail to point out were the intellectual strengths that many black athletes brought to the game. Perhaps this escaped the notice of the white owners and managers of the League, because black players were forced to be tricksters, forced to talk in code sometimes, so as to confound any whites who might be eavesdropping. We often literally changed our language to communicate with each other when Weeb or Unitas were around, so we could talk freely. This code language has roots going back to the slave days, when blacks would sing as they worked in the fields, making the overseer think they were just happy while, in reality, they were communicating information about how to escape from the plantation. The language of the songs was in code, but there was also a nuance of tone and pitch in the songs that they sang.

In our case, we black Colts were not planning an escape, nor were we sharing secret gossip, or "playing the dozens" against the Coach or the white players. We were just reminding ourselves that we were a unit unto ourselves, a community of blacks, and we could only count on each other to survive in this brutal game.

Here I am as a happy ten-year-old, sporting one of my brother's army caps.
*Photo courtesy of Lenny Moore*

My dad, Jack, and mom, Virginia.
*Photo courtesy of Lenny Moore*

I played some basketball at Northeast Junior High School. That's me on the lower right. Number six in the second row was Alan Merkle, my best friend as a child. *Photo courtesy of Lenny Moore*

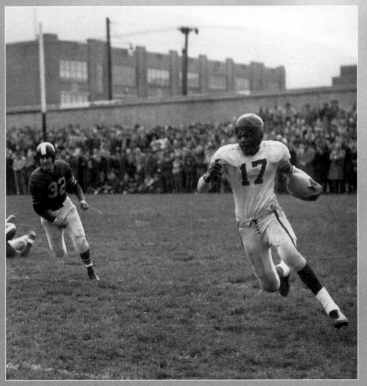

Turning the corner as a lanky junior running back for Reading High School. *Photo courtesy of Lenny Moore*

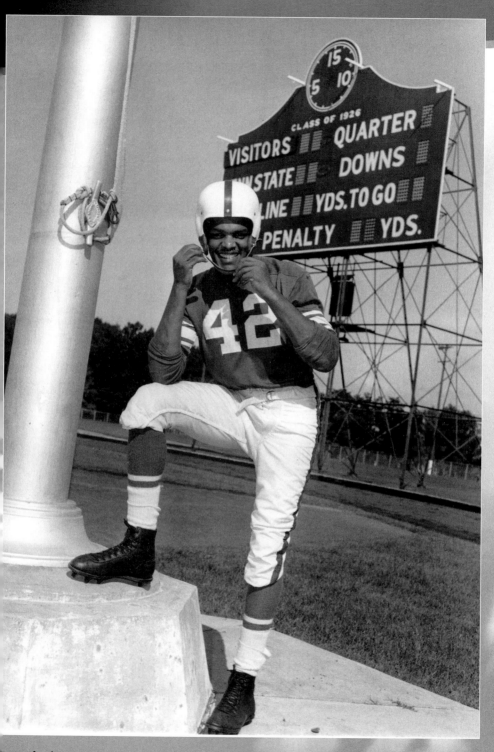

Posing for the camera at University Park on the Penn State campus in 1955. *AP/WWP*

Sharing a moment with Penn State legend Eugene "Shorty" Miller. I broke many of his records while playing at Penn State. *Photo courtesy of Lenny Moore*

This wasn't the only time that Coach Rip Engle gave his advice to me. This picture was taken shortly after I worked hard to regain academic eligibility between my junior and senior years at Penn State. *Photo courtesy of Lenny Moore*

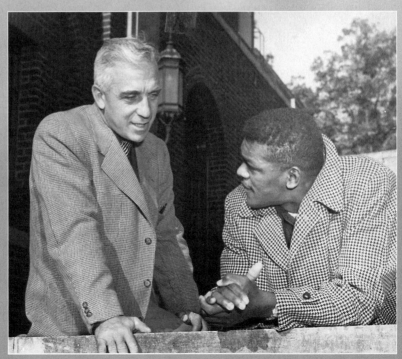

Johnny Unitas looks on as I head upfield with the ball. Johnny and I played together for 12 seasons starting in 1956 until I retired after the 1967 season. *Pro Football Hall of Fame/WireImage.com*

My son, Les, and my first wife, Frankie, and me. *Photo courtesy of Lenny Moore*

Left to right: my son, Les, a neighborhood friend, my daughter, Carol, and me. The kids were fascinated with the cast I earned in a game against the Steelers. *Photo courtesy of Lenny Moore*

I'm glad they were on my team: (left to right) Jim Parker, my good friend "Big Daddy" Lipscomb, and Art Donovan walk off the field together. *Photo courtesy of Lenny Moore*

Being inducted into the Pro Football Hall of Fame in 1975 was such an honor. I'm glad that my old high school coach, Andy Stopper, could be there to share it with me. *Photo courtesy of Lenny Moore*

My lovely wife, Edith. We've been happily married for more than a quarter century. She's my rock.
*Photo courtesy of Lenny Moore*

My family sharing a moment with me during the Hall of Fame induction banquet. Left to right: My oldest son, Leonard Jenkins, my brother, Sonny (standing), my daughter, Toni, my daughter, Terri, me, my son, Les (standing behind me), my second wife, Erma, and my daughter, Carol. *Photo courtesy of Lenny Moore*

My friend Rosey Grier (left), Joe Paterno (center) and I spend some time together at the funeral of Rip Engle.
*Photo courtesy of Lenny Moore*

# SEVEN

# A Championship Foundation

G oing into the 1957 season, I thought I deserved a raise from my rookie salary of $10,000 per year. After clinching the franchise's second consecutive Rookie of the Year award and proving my worth to the team (and myself) it seemed fair to me. I made my request to Weeb and Don Kellet during the summer of 1957, shortly before the start of training camp, to avoid disrupting the team, I didn't want to miss any time, but I also wanted to make my point clear. The team didn't see it my way, though. The story blew out of proportion, as my request soon became the holdout I was dreading. I found out that Ameche hadn't received a raise after his Rookie of the Year award, either, so we both held out in an effort to correct this oversight by the team. Eventually the Colts capitulated and gave us each small raises to get us back into camp. I would enter camp earning the princely sum of $11,500 annually. Soon I found out that this wouldn't be the only struggle of the preseason.

Coming off a promising 1957 season, the coaches made some changes, enhancing the roster by adding some great talent. We welcomed a great, all-around, All-American in Johnny Sample from Maryland State on Eastern Shore. Johnny's future was to become a phenomenal defensive back even though he was a great running back, not only with the Colts, but with the Steelers and the New York Jets. We also added the late, great Sherman

Plunkett, who could block almost as well as Jim Parker and who would become one of my dearest friends. Lenny Lyles was another newcomer: he was a great offensive runner, and he also played defensive back for us. Lyles could run a 9.4 in the 100-yard dash, and was one of the few players who could keep up with me in practice. We also added Leo Sanford from the Cardinals.

After two years in the pros, it was apparent that there was a quota for black players on each team in the League. Remarkably, with all the pick-ups we made, the number of black athletes on the team never really changed. The quota for us was seven. An eighth black would be shipped out; it didn't matter who he was—a mediocre talent or a future all-star—he was gone. It was ruthless. Many times a player would be awakened out of a sound sleep and get cut at two o'clock in the morning. There were days when we'd go to a team meeting, and find a seat or two empty; explanations were not offered. To be fair, cutting players from the team was one practice that cut across all color lines: if the coaches didn't like you or thought you didn't fit, they would tell you to pack your bags without a moment's notice. But many players were cut just because they were black.

~ ~ ~

One might wonder why I lump the 1957 and 1958 seasons into one in this chapter. Logically, most football historians combine the back-to-back championship season of 1958 and 1959 in any discussion of the Colts' past, but I don't buy that. Although the 1957 season would end in disappointment, this was the season we truly came together as a team. All the major pieces were in place, and it was in this campaign that we learned to compete as a unit. The 1959 season was icing on the cake. Our track was truly laid this fateful fall on the gridiron.

Even though we'd had a tumultuous training camp, the team regrouped and began the season with confidence. We opened the season in front of a capacity crowd. I'd never been so happy to be back in Baltimore. We were excited to host Detroit and exact some revenge from the previous season. Johnny was on fire and passed for four touchdowns; the highlight came when L.G. Du Pre made a one-handed catch on Johnny's last toss—the second of Du Pre's catches for the day. The defense was stout as Big Daddy and

Art Donovan plugged the line and held the Lions to only 23 yards rushing that day. It was sweet revenge.

Trying to keep the momentum going, we next hosted the Bears. It was a tight game until the middle of the third quarter. We were losing 10-7 and, since Johnny had hurt his leg in the first half, he was hobbling. When we were at fourth down, the Bears expected us to kick for the tie; but Johnny threw a jump pass to Jim Mutscheller, for the score. Leading 14-10, Ameche took a nine-yard plunge for the final tally in our victory.

Our first road game of the year took us to Milwaukee to face the Packers. Trailing 10-7 at the half, we scored a full 17 points in the first six minutes of the third quarter. In the fourth quarter we added 21 more points to blow out the Packers 45-17. Ameche had three touchdowns, and even old George Shaw saw some action and tossed a touchdown. For the first time in my professional career I was playing for a first-place team!

We wouldn't hold the division lead outright for long, though, as our first loss of the year came in our return trip to Detroit to play the Lions. The hot commodity in the league, Hopalong Cassidy, the Heisman Trophy winner from Ohio State the year before, caught a 39-yard pass from Bobby Layne with 50 seconds left. This was a very tough loss to swallow because we were up 27-3 in the third quarter. Although Mutscheller and I had two touchdowns each, it was my fumble on a Statue of Liberty play at the 39 in the last minute of the game that led to the Lions' final touchdown. That fumble hurt bad. We had the game sewn up, and the loss was solely on my shoulders. For the first time in my life, I had to find a way to cope with the fact that I had lost a game for my team.

The truth be told, that error on my part almost ruined my career for good. I had never been responsible for losing a game in my brief football-playing life. I had grown so confident in my abilities that I never even considered this type of failure. The next day's headlines screamed, "Moore's Fumble Lost Game." This public criticism was new to me as well. After being the darling of Reading High and Penn State, this was the first time I had been blamed for anything but success. In practice all the next week, I worked on drills to hold onto the ball. The miscue in the Lions game was all I could think about as we prepared to meet the Packers. Weeb could see the anguish on my face for days. He was concerned with how I would bounce back—and I was, too.

Luckily, my confidence was somewhat restored, but the team's momentum was lost as Green Bay beat us in a heartbreaker in front of 45,000 screaming fans at Memorial Stadium. I concentrated on where the ball was the whole game. I refused to be embarrassed again. The Packers weren't embarrassed at all as they scored all of their touchdowns in the fourth quarter. Trailing 17-14, and the crowd on our side, we dominated the line of scrimmage and marched downfield. As the clock wound down, we were sure that we would score to take the lead and at the same time not leave enough time for Green Bay to respond. Inside the ten-yard line, I took a pitch from Johnny, shook off a defender and scampered in for a six-yard score. But it wasn't meant to be: we lost, 24-21. In fact, we did leave enough time on the clock and the Packers scored the winning touchdown as time expired. It was a heartbreaking loss for the team and our fans. To make matters worse for the faithful, the Colts instituted a "dry law" at this home game—we were the first team in the league to prohibit fans from bringing any alcoholic beverages into the stadium. It resulted in the expulsion of 1,000 fans at that game, which meant we disappointed "only" 44,000 fans. After this heartbreaker, the whole town needed a drink!

The slide continued as we met Pittsburgh and a future Colt, Earl Morrall, who hung us with yet another loss at home. The defense allowed the Steelers their best passing game of the year with a 270-yard effort. By contrast, we slid backwards to a 3-3 standing, second place behind the 49ers. This was a pivotal point in the making of our mini-dynasty. Although there were rumblings in the press over the poor play of the defense, the lack of creativity of the play calling, and Weeb's effectiveness as a leader, he kept the team together and stuck with his plan. He believed in us and our ability to execute. Without Weeb's steady leadership, all might have been lost. Instead he would lead us to greatness.

Traveling to Washington the next week, the team was able to stop the slide. It was the quietest player on the team who stood tall and led us with his actions. Raymond Berry refused to let us lose. Catching 12 passes for over 200 yards and two touchdowns, it was his fourth-quarter touchdown off a 55-yard pass from Johnny as time expired with the deficit at 17-14, that halted our losing streak and righted the ship. It was a masterful performance by the best wide receiver in the game.

Raymond's never-say-die attitude was contagious, and our hero of the day in our next game, against the Bears, was Milt Davis, who sealed our victory with a 47-yard scoring interception, one of five team interceptions for the defense that day. The 29-14 win put us into first place, in a three-way tie with the Lions and the 49ers.

The biggest game of many of our young careers was against the 49ers the following week. This was for the division lead, and with our future in our own hands, we prevailed with a 27-21 victory. Since the Lions had lost to the Bears earlier that day, we now sat alone at the top of the division. Things had not looked very good in the fourth quarter, though, when San Fran had the lead, 21-20. But the lead changed hands four times in that game, one of which was due to my 41-yard run. I also had a 32-yard catch on a "flea-flicker." The defining part of the game, though, was in the fourth quarter, as Berry keyed an 82-yard drive with a 31-yard pass reception.

The biggest crowd in the Colts' short history in Baltimore was made up of fans gathered to watch the Rams come to slaughter. We didn't disappoint: the final score was 31-14. It was one of my best performances that year, as I ran for three touchdowns, the last of which came after a 16-yard pass from Unitas. I also made a 34-yard run after I broke a tackle by Don Burroughs. My fumble against the Lions earlier in the year was nothing but a distant memory for me now.

With the Division championship now firmly in our sights, we were re-matched with the 49ers in San Francisco, on a cold, gloomy day. The difference between an outright conference championship and a three-way tie for first place was a rookie quarterback named John Brodie. He was just a back-up then, but he would play a major role in our demise. The starter that year for the 49ers was a slightly more seasoned quarterback named Y.A. Tittle, who was having a tremendous game, but he suffered a leg injury that sent him to the sidelines. Brodie entered the game with less than a minute left and with San Francisco trailing 13-10. We thought the game was ours when a no-call from the refs changed history. Desperate for the victory, Hugh McIlhenny went deep for the decisive play of the game. Brodie hoist-ed a long pass that looked as if it would be intercepted. Out of nowhere, McIlhenny shoved Milt Davis out of the way in time to make the catch and score the winning touchdown. The ref was standing right there, but he never made a move to his flag. He couldn't: he would not have been able to leave the stadium alive. I scored two touchdowns, but it just wasn't enough; my butterfingers returned as I suffered another key fumble, and the title slipped through our grasp.

Going into the season finale against the Rams, we still had an outside shot at the division title. We would need the Lions and the 49ers to lose and we would need to notch a victory ourselves to make it happen, despite the long odds we were optimistic. For whatever reason, we just came out flat. Losing 20-7 at the half, we made it competitive in the second half only to lose 37-21. Sadly, if we would've won the title would've been ours, but our stars just weren't aligned. It was out of the ashes of this disappointing finish that one of the greatest teams in history would be born.

~ ~ ~

Throughout the off season, our sights were set on 1958. After our late-season collapse, the anticipation that we each felt was palpable. Unfortunately, our preparation was sidetracked by some awkward trips down south. With the NFL continuing to seek expansion, each team had to play a slate of preseason games in some of the Southern states that were ripe for an expansion team in the eyes of the league. By scheduling preseason games in Dixie, the NFL could gauge fan response.

Now, as I've said, black players weren't particularly welcome in the South at that time. The night before we were to play the Chicago Cardinals, in Austin, Texas, a few of us wanted to go out to get a bite to eat and maybe have some drinks. We intended to go to the black section of town, so as not to cause a commotion among any unfriendly whites. Weeb asked Ken Jackson, a white player who was an Austin native on our squad at the time, if this was a good idea. Ken told Weeb that the Negro area was rough and we could be stabbed, mugged or get into all kinds of trouble. As a result, Weeb wouldn't let us leave the hotel. It didn't irritate us that Weeb was trying to protect us from danger, but it did make us mad that he had asked a white player about a part of town that he probably had never been in. Furthermore, Weeb didn't even discuss it with us; he just made up his mind and kept us in the hotel, as though we were caged animals.

We went to Weeb and he heard us out. He understood our complaints and sympathized. In order to allay any fears he had for our safety, and to allow us a chance to blow off some steam, he hired some taxis to take us down to the most popular black bar on the outskirts of town. He rode with us. When we arrived, Weeb asked to speak to the owner of the bar. After introducing himself, he told the man who we were and that he would like him to take care of us. The man looked up and said that it wouldn't be a problem. He'd show us a good time and keep us out of trouble. With that, Weeb left. He certainly wasn't a perfect man, but gestures such as these always made me play that much harder for him on Sundays.

Our first game in the 1958 regular season was at home against the Detroit Lions. I lined up as both a running back and a wide receiver this game. I preferred to run with the ball, but Weeb wanted to utilize my speed and decided to line me up at split end and in the backfield. The new look added a little wrinkle to the game plan and seemed to work out well. We came from behind to beat the defending champion, who gave it their best effort. Losing 15-14 in the fourth quarter, the Lions found that the combination of Raymond Berry and Johnny Unitas was just too much. Berry had ten catches for 149 yards, and I scored a touchdown on an eight-yarder. We were off and running with a 28-15 victory.

The next game, against the Bears, was a rout—a 51-39 win. We led 27-3, after the first quarter. I had three of the touchdowns that helped build the lead, and I scored again in the fourth quarter. Lennie Lyles was a standout performer as well. He had a 103-yard kick return that was timed by our coaches on the sideline at 10 seconds from the time he caught the ball. The 52,000 fans at the game (which set a new attendance record) went crazy with pride. It was the most complete performance our team had shown yet.

Another of our greatest moments that season was playing in Milwaukee against Green Bay. We were down 17-0 in the second quarter; but by game's end, Johnny snuck in for a touchdown and passed to Jim Mutscheller, to set up the win, 24-17.

Next we met the Lions and essentially knocked them out of contention for the season. Unitas's touchdown to Mutscheller in the fourth quarter put him within reach of Cecil Isbell's record of 23 straight games with a touchdown. In four games against the Lions in two seasons, Johnny had racked up 951 yards and 11 touchdowns.

Trying to keep the roll going, we played the Redskins next. We were losing in the first quarter, 7-0; but that didn't last long. Lenny Lyles had a 101-yard kick return for a touchdown. The defense stifled the Redskins by allowing only four completions.

I moved into place as the third-leading ground gainer that season in our game against Green Bay. Our 56-0 thrashing was an embarrassment of riches. Johnny passed for two touchdowns with deadly precision. Not even Johnny's cracked ribs could slow us down. Although he was taken to Union Memorial Hospital before the end of the game, George Shaw came in and led the team to three more touchdowns. Lenny Lyles caught a two-yard pass for a touchdown, and followed that up with a 63-yard completion that led to an Ameche touchdown. It was the highest scoring tally in team history, and the first ever shutout for the franchise.

It was clear that we were a team to be reckoned with as we were undefeated and dominant going into our clash with the New York Giants. In front of a capacity crowd of 71,163 at Yankee Stadium, the Giants came out on top, 24-21, with a fourth-quarter field goal. With Unitas out for the first time in his two years on the team at that point, George Shaw stepped in very capably. He passed to Lennie Lyles to tie the score in the first quarter. Lennie tied it again on a 47-yard pass that set up a four-yard pass. Although losing by three points was heartbreaking, it gave us an opportunity to see up close the kind of support we had from the city of Baltimore. On the train ride back to town, we were able to commiserate with many visitors from Baltimore who had made the trip to New York. As they gathered in Union Station on their way home, the crowd chanted, "C-O-L-T-S!" and disrupted the flow of traffic for hours. It was this kind of support from the town that wouldn't allow us to hang our heads.

We quickly rebounded with a 17-0 victory at Chicago. It was the second shutout in team history, and the first time the Bears had been shut out in 12 years. But it didn't come easily. George Shaw missed on his first six pass attempts. He connected on the next nine passes, though, for 131 yards. It was Chicago's biggest crowd of the season, something we would soon grow accustomed to—as we consistently drew a big crowd both home and away.

By the time we met the Rams, Johnny had come back from his rib injury. The defense gave up a total of 344 yards but had five fumble recoveries to boast of, and we came out of it with a 34-7 victory. As important as it was to start a new winning streak, it was equally as important to get Johnny back out onto the field. He played flawlessly, passing for two touchdowns to pace the victory.

With only the loss to the Giants to date, and the rest of the league suffering from parity, we would have the opportunity to clinch the Western Conference title with a win over the 49ers. It wasn't going to be easy. Probably our greatest game—yes, even better than the Championship game to be played weeks later—we trailed by 20 points, going into halftime: 27-7. Weeb then gave us his best halftime speech. In a calm, yet forceful tone, he told us that we would march out onto that field in the third quarter and physically dominate the 49ers en route to victory. The resolve and determination he showed were contagious, and we would do exactly what he described at the half. We walked back out onto the field as if we were up 20 points and dismantled the 49ers for the next 30 minutes of play. Everyone chipped in. I scored on a 73-yard run down the sideline to tie it, and Berry caught a seven-yard pass from Unitas to put us ahead for good. Once the clock ran out, the hometown faithful stormed the field. We had met and conquered a San Francisco backfield that was studded with future Hall of Famers—Y.A. Tittle, Joe "The Jet" Perry, and Hugh McElhenny. Our defense, consisting of Big Daddy, Donovan, Marchetti, and Ordell Braase, had played impeccably well in the second half and we were champions!

There is an urban legend about that game that I would like to clarify. The story that Art Donovan tells is that after Johnny gave me the ball in the 49ers game on six straight possessions, I came back to the huddle and told Johnny to take it easy, that I was getting tired. Then it is claimed, Johnny responded, "Don't tell me to cool it! I'll run your ass until you die."

This is a prime example of the rift between the two races on the team. As I mentioned before, the team was never as tight knit as you might think. After a game, the white players went home to their white suburban neighborhoods, and the black players went home to our black urban neighborhoods. Without a sense of off-field unity or camaraderie, many stories and anecdotes get distorted. First of all, Johnny had too much respect for his teammates to use such language. He certainly was no pushover and wanted to win more than anything else, but he never said any such thing to me. It is true that when a player comes back to the huddle, he communicates to the quarterback his status; this happens all the time. In this case, I may have said that I needed a breather after six runs, and Johnny may have said something like, "That's not going to happen." But the way the story was told, time after time, it sought to depict me as a "lazy nigger," a flunky to John. It was not only inaccurate, but it wounded me whenever I heard the incident being spun way out of proportion to the truth.

It just goes to show that, when two sets of people live in segregation, realities become exaggerated. I'm sure the tale originated over a few beers one innocent night, but later built up into a ridiculous version of the truth. The distortion was an insult, both to me and to Johnny. It is just one example of many rumors that ran rampant in our day.

Johnny was playing at a high level in the years leading up to 1958, and he would set numerous team and NFL records afterward. But it was in 1958 and 1959 that he operated at the highest level I ever remember. It should be said, though, that no small factor of his career success was the benefit he received from the teamwork that Berry, Ameche, Unitas, Parker, and I had perfected after playing together for years. The five of us became a cohesive and well-choreographed unit that supported Johnny, time after time. This back-up pentad was second to none in the League.

Of course Johnny called most of his own plays. There were times when Weeb would call a play off the bench, but if Johnny didn't want it because he had a feeling for something else, he would put it in the back of his mind to be used later. Since I spent some time as a receiver, I'd often call to him, "Hey John, I've got a little seam here," or, "I've got this open to me." He may not have done anything right then, but he would come back a series or two later and say to me, "Is it still there?" I'd respond, "Oh, yeah, any time you're ready." Even then, he might or might not act on this cue; but that's the way he operated. He called it when it was comfortable for him, and it usually worked. Johnny had a give and take with all the players in the huddle, and it was beneficial to everyone involved.

In late 1958, Johnny's broken ribs had healed nicely, and all of us were bursting with pride, since the Division was clinched after the 49ers win. When we left for the West Coast to play the Rams and the 49ers again, our confidence level was high, but we were not reckless: we didn't want to incur any serious injury before the big game, so we played these two games at less than full throttle. We actually lost the first game on the road trip, in front of over 100,000 fans, the third largest NFL crowd in history. Unitas contributed three touchdowns but also had two fumbles and we were intercepted five times. Then we fell to the 49ers, 21-12. Nonetheless, we finished the season with a 9-3 standing, and we were in good shape to take on the Giants in Baltimore's very first championship game.

Even though the team stayed in a Palo Alto motel, 40 miles outside of San Francisco prior to the 49er game, it was almost impossible to sneak out and have fun without being mobbed by fans. So with time on our hands, we sat around discussing ways to divide the winning (or losing) shares of the championship money. Should we include the trainers' shares? Who should get a half share? Who should get a full share? You never saw such arguing and bickering in your life! We finally made a list of potential shareholders, but that caused more debate:

"If we include all these guys, that will be less for us!"

"The hell with them!"

"Hey, he didn't contribute!"

Alex Sandusky was one guy who was completely livid about who should or shouldn't get shares. In the end, though, we decided to include all of the coaches, players, and trainers, and everyone would have full shares. That was probably the hardest part of our team preparation for the game!

~ ~ ~

The Colts played the Giants at Yankee Stadium on December 28, 1958. NFL commissioner Bert Bell called it "the greatest game ever played," and that moniker has held fast for more than 45 years.

In the capacity crowd of some 64,000, there were more than 15,000 loyal fans that had come from Baltimore. Bill Hughes, recalling the game from a 40-year vantage point, wrote the following for *The Baltimore Chronicle*, in December, 1998:

"[I]n the late '50s, Baltimore was considered a hick town. . . . There was no Harbor Place, National Aquarium, Meyerhof Symphony Hall, Morris Mechanic Theatre, Center Stage, or $800 million dollar subway system to be found. . . . [In 1958, Baltimore] was a rundown neighborhood featuring decaying warehouses and pot-hole-filled streets, drunks and sleazy pubs that even Elvis wouldn't be found dead in. Although the city had just gotten a new major league baseball franchise . . . the no-name Orioles were pathetic jokes. In short, in 1958, Baltimore City was a 'loser.'"

". . . When we would stand to cheer for the Colts, the locals would invariably yell at us in a loud mocking voice, "Sit down, you farmers!"

". . . The train ride back to Baltimore was a special trip unto itself. The happy Baltimore fans were at a "Mach-3" level of unbridled celebration. Some of them were carrying parts of the goal post with them, others could barely walk to their seats from having one beer too many. It was a party train like no other. It lasted right through to our landing at Penn Station and spilled out into the joyful night onto Charles Street."

If the 1958 championship game was the "greatest ever," it was also football's longest game and the first title to be settled in sudden-death overtime. It was a fantastic time, a thrill I could have never imagined when I signed on in 1956.

After having one of the most dominating regular seasons of my career, my main contribution to the championship game, after I was injured in the second quarter in the chest and ribs, was to occupy space so that Raymond Berry had an open path. He made 12 catches and gathered a total of 178 yards. I played the entire second half of the game with injuries. We kept it quiet because we didn't want the Giants to know and make defensive adjustments. In fact, I never talked about my limitations in that game until many years later. But there were times in that game when I was doubled over in pain. I also had trouble raising my arms. Of course, playing injured was not uncommon, especially in a game of this magnitude. Many players have taken painkillers to manage, which is what I did. Even so, I couldn't do half of what I wanted to do, and I did not figure in the running game.

The highlights for me were when Frank Gifford tied the game at the half, and when Unitas got the ball at the 14-yard line, with a minute and 56 seconds to play. Then, in the sudden-death overtime battle, the Giants had the ball, but they gave it up after four plays and wouldn't ever get it back. Our stats told the story: we drove 80 yards on 20 plays, with Johnny going four of five.

Each of us received $4,718.77, and each Giant teammate received $3,111.33. More rewarding, though, was the place we will forever have in the fans' hearts. None of us would ever appear at any event, or even walk down the street in Baltimore, without being recognized. It is flattering to be forever remembered by such great people. To know we touched so many hearts and souls is overwhelming.

When the team returned home in the middle of the night, it received an ovation from 30,000 fans at the Baltimore airport. I stayed on in New York for a family reunion: One of my sisters was living in New Jersey at the time, and my family had traveled from Reading for the game. We celebrated of course, but we were all missing the most important person in our lives: sadly, my mother had passed away in June of 1958. She died of cancer.

My mother had attended so many of my games, and I loved to see her in the stands along with my Dad. When she died, I felt my whole world falling apart. I almost had a nervous breakdown at training camp in July. The trainers, especially Ed Block, sensed my pain and watched me closely. I had problems sleeping, so I was taking heavy doses of Equinol.

What pained me most was that I had been looking forward to the opportunity to contribute financially to the family so that Mom wouldn't have to work anymore. True, football players didn't make much money in those days, but I hoped to help ease her life in some way. I will never forget seeing her on her hands and knees scrubbing floors for several white women in town. I made a vow to provide money whenever I could so that she would never have to scrub another floor. She died before I could completely fulfill that vow, and that fact haunts me to this day.

It is a tragedy how my mother's life turned out, for she was very bright. At that time, though, because she was not only black, but female as well, her intelligence went unrecognized. My mother's family were very successful members of the middle class. My grandmother were definitely a debutante; she always dressed in the latest fashions. My uncle was a deacon in York, Pennsylvania, and my mother's father was a small business owner who ran the dance hall where my parents met. Family members would show up at our home every weekend, with food that lasted us through the week. Their generosity never seemed to be a handout; it was just family taking care of each other. We always had a fresh meal on the table after my grandparents had visited, although I never saw them give my parents any money.

My mother lost a sister the day before I was born. She also had two brothers who played baseball in the Negro Leagues for a while, in Baltimore. I never had a chance to meet them and didn't really know about them until I was much older, but my family attributes much of my athleticism to my mother's side of the family.

For Mom, though, life consisted of scrubbing floors, earning just enough to put an extra quart of milk in the icebox or a fresh loaf of bread on the table. Yet she had a quiet strength and a spiritual love that is beyond description. Despite the fact that what she was doing was hard, thankless work, she was always calm and loving. Not once did I hear her complain. She accepted this lot in life, I believe, because of her children. That was all she cared about. I so wished that my mother could have been there to see the Colts win the championship.

To keep myself busy, so as not to miss my mother so much, after the season was finished, I took two jobs. I started working community relations with National Brewing Company, and I also got a Saturday job as disc jockey, with WSID, a radio station in town. I loved both jobs because they allowed me contact with the public. It was also fun to play all the Top 40s hits that were on WSID's program (and I also got to sneak in some of my favorite jazz artists as well). I would eventually be named sports director at the radio station, and I gave a five-minute report every weekday.

Another memorable event in the days immediately following our championship title occurred when Marvin Mervis, who was a high-profile person in Baltimore at the time, invited me to a Baltimore country club one night for a banquet honoring Barney Ross, the former prizefighter and war hero. I was looking forward to being on the dais with Barney and talking with him. When I arrived at the country club, I was told I couldn't park my car on the main lot but had to go around to the back and use the kitchen entrance. Being naïve and still riding high on fan adulation after the championship game, I thought, "Maybe the VIPs use a special entrance for crowd-control purposes." Then it dawned on me that white people probably expected a black person at the country club to be a server from the kitchen, not a guest!

Even fame can't crack racial prejudice, apparently. I was incredulous but determined to attend the banquet. I parked my car down in the lower lot, and then I went in the front entrance. I showed my invitation to the man inside the door. A club representitive told me to stand to the side while he checked for my name on his list. It seemed like I had to wait an eternity, as he scrolled up and down the names. It got to the point where I was creating a spectacle, just by being the only black person there. Marvin Mervis finally saw me and came over right away. He told the man at the door that it was okay; I was an invited guest.

Embarrassed, I went straight to the bar because by then, I needed a drink to relax. The bartenders refused to serve me. Then, as I glanced around the room, I saw my teammates, Art Donovan and Jim Mutscheller; but they didn't seem too eager to speak to me. I saw other people I had met before, and they refused to talk to me as well. That's when I said to myself, "Three strikes and you're out!" I left the country club immediately, disgusted with the whole scene. This was only one of many similar incidents that I faced as a black man in Baltimore. I figured, all things being equal, it would be different, being a member of the celebrated Colts. I guess some things never change.

# EIGHT

# SOLIDIFYING OUR PLACE IN HISTORY

Before the 1959 season was to begin, the Colts went to Chicago as the defending champs to play the College All-Stars. I'll never forget how, in that game, Unitas found himself trapped behind the line of scrimmage. I heard this voice yell, "Hey John-John!" That was the team's signal for, "Give me the ball!" Well, linemen are not supposed to touch the football; but here is big Jim Parker, hollering for the ball. Johnny flipped it to him, but before Parker could move, the whole All-Star team jumped on him and hit him everywhere but Sunday. He didn't fumble it, but the team got a laugh out of that story for years to come! Big Jim never wanted to touch the ball again!

The preseason wasn't all fun and games, though. We met the Giants in an exhibition game in Dallas, as the League continued to spark an interest in professional football in Texas. When we arrived at Love Field, the plane wouldn't taxi to the gate, because the airport didn't allow black people. What a farce it was to see a special bus sent out onto the tarmac, to relieve the airplane of blacks, so that the white players could be delivered to the terminal. The black players on both teams were also forced to stay at an all-black motel outside of town, called the Peter Lane Motel. Peter Lane himself checked us in and assured team officials that he would take care of us and keep us out of trouble. Mr. Lane even offered to be our tour guide that night, and he took us to a bar so we could have some drinks. Even with his hospitality, though, every black Colt was livid. We voted on whether we should boycott the game in response to the treatment we'd received in this town. Each of us sat there wondering what Jackie Robinson would do in a case like this. The answer was eventually evident to all of us: we didn't boycott. Some of us had second thoughts, though, as we black players were herded onto yet another "for blacks only" bus, to get to the stadium.

In the locker room, everyone was completely silent. Each player had his head down, taking care of his own business. Raymond Berry was the only man to show any empathy, as he came up to each of us and apologized for the treatment we were enduring in Dallas. Later, on the field, Ameche came up to me and just shrugged his shoulders, without saying a word. Some ten years later, in the late 1970s, Ameche would share his feelings about that experience in Dallas, and other instances, as well, by talking to me privately during a get together at Donovan's Club in Baltimore. Ameche told me then that there were many times he had wanted to go to management and complain over the way we were treated, but he never did. He said he felt ashamed about that. I told him that I had always known where he stood by his actions, and that I appreciated his concern even after a decade had passed. I don't recall any other player ever mentioning what was, for us blacks, a depersonalizing experience.

As we opened the 1959 season against the Detroit Lions, the offense struggled—we were losing 3-0 at the half and 9-0 early in the third quarter. The combination of Ameche, L.G. Dupre, and I got the team down to the 1-yard line and on to an eventual score. The offense got the ball back and led another charge, which was capped off by a Raymond Berry touchdown. Soon, Unitas popped a 40-yard touchdown to Mutscheller, and we were well on our way to the 24-9 victory.

In the next game, the Bears exacted some revenge on us for beating them in the previous season, and we lost by five points: 26-21. Unitas had three interceptions in the first half, but to make up for those he made three touchdowns, all in the fourth quarter. This game lengthened Johnny's touchdown streak to 27 consecutive games.

The game in Detroit the next week was bittersweet, as we heard that long-time commissioner Bert Bell died of a heart attack while attending the Pittsburgh and Philadelphia game at Franklin Field. We were trailing 14-3, but Berry and Unitas would team up to score the clinching touchdown, which secured the victory.

Back in Baltimore, the Green Bay Packers came to town, only to witness three touchdowns by Johnny. Bill Quinlan, a big, mean defensive lineman, gave Unitas a shot to the ribs and sent him to the hospital. We won the game anyway and tied for the lead of the Western Conference once again.

Next we hosted Cleveland, one of my favorite teams as a collegiate, and always a special treat for me. Jim Brown scored all the touchdowns for the Browns. Jerry Richardson, the future owner of the Carolina Panthers, scored a touchdown, and I had a three-yard touchdown catch; but we lost, 38-31, in the end.

We traveled to the Redskins the following week. I tied the score at 17 in the third quarter on a 66-yard pass play and a halfback option to Jerry Richardson. But it was Sam Baker's 46-yard field goal, with 11 seconds left, that helped seal our fate: we lost our second straight.

In Milwaukee we won a close one, with three touchdowns from Johnny and the team scoring 21 points in the second half. The team climbed within two yards of first, but Bart Starr led the Packers to good things in his first year as starting quarterback. As for the Colts, many on the team felt we were playing well below our potential. A rumor of infighting erupted, with the absurd claim that I blamed Alex Sandusky for missing a block. That couldn't have been further from the truth; the offensive linemen and the backfield had a very strong relationship. Alex, or any of the others, would be the last people I'd pick on. Without the efforts of the linemen, there would be no "me"!

Our team rebounded by the time the San Francisco 49ers came to town. Our 45-14 win served to tie us with the 49ers for the lead in the Western Conference. It was another Memorial Stadium sellout, and the crowd saw us unveil a 6-1-4 defense. We also employed the "hook and go" strategy with the halfbacks. This play sent me in the slot, Ameche up the middle, and Berry and Mutscheller on the ends. Abe Woodson, my old friend from Illinois, was playing defensive back for the 49ers, and he had a busy day chasing us down the field.

We remained tied for first place by beating the Rams. There was another capacity crowd at Memorial Stadium to watch the Colts jump out to a 14-0 lead. Unitas again passed for another two touchdowns, and I had a 17-yard reception in the third. The final score was 35-21.

Just like in 1958, a big win against the 49ers in San Francisco played a key part in our qualifying for our second championship game. Johnny had three touchdown passes and one running. The defense intercepted John Brodie four times in the first half; then, the old warrior, Y.A. Tittle, led a second-half comeback. San Francisco went through a stretch where they had only four offensive plays in 14 minutes. Milt Davis had a 57-yard interception. The final Colt touchdown was a 64-yard pass from Unitas to me. Johnny used that score to break Sid Luckman's single-season record for touchdown passes.

A 45-26 victory over the Rams finished the season and set up a rematch between us and the New York Giants for the 1959 championship game.

This time the game was held in Baltimore, on a balmy, 51-degree Sunday afternoon. Vice-president Richard Nixon arrived, looking quite relaxed, having sewn up the Republican nod for the presidential election. The Giants were leading until Johnny Sample had two interceptions of Giants quarterback Charlie Connerly. In the third quarter, Pat Summerall booted a field goal with 7:21 left. That triggered a scoring drought for the Giants until 2:42 in the fourth quarter. I fought through a big block from the Giants' Cliff Livingston, to help trigger a Unitas score. The prettiest play of the game was when Johnny faked a handoff to Alan Ameche, with me split wide right at the 38-yard line. I juked Lindon Crowe and hooked around him to score the first touchdown of the game.

The League had not had back-to-back champions since the Browns in 1954 and 1955, and the crowd was ecstatic. We felt as if we were in the prime of our careers, we believed we couldn't be beat. Unfortunately, the magic wouldn't last.

~ ~ ~

As the defending champions, we again started the 1960 preseason with a victory over the College All-Stars. Then we traveled to Dallas for a rematch with the Giants. This time, though, the whole team stayed together at a Ramada Inn on the outskirts of town. In later years, the Sheraton Dallas would change its segregation policy, and we stayed in town when we played the Cowboys. In 1960, though, the "Big D" was not a model of desegregation.

It was not much better for the game against the Cardinals in Charleston, South Carolina. Our team stayed together at one motel, but black players on the Cardinals were at another place, far from where we stayed, while their white players enjoyed a downtown hotel. I can remember that Jimmy Hill and Dick "Night Train" Lane were incensed over the

situation. We had a meeting with Weeb at the hotel to discuss the inequalities we were facing in this town. But in typical fashion, Weeb tried to quell
the situation. He obviously wasn't going to act on our complaints, so we
dropped the subject of racism for the time being.

Bigger problems awaited us in Miami the very next week. Someone had
booked the team into the McAllister Hotel in downtown Miami, where we
unknowingly broke the color line—at least, at the front desk. Miami was
highly segregated at the time, and even though we had rooms in the hotel,
we could not go anywhere else, within either the hotel or the city. We could-
n't even grab a cab that would take us to the black part of town. The black
players on the team, including Big Daddy, Jim Parker, Milt Davis, Johnny
Sample, Sherman Plunkett, and me, had a meeting with owner Carroll
Rosenbloom and Weeb. After we expressed our displeasure (that is a mild
term for what we were feeling), Carroll told us that he sympathized, because
he often faced discrimination as a Jew.

Big Daddy chimed in and said, "Yeah, I understand that; but you are
still white! If someone says you can't go somewhere, then you Jews will just
buy them out and take over!"

This brought a big laugh from Rosenbloom. He made some calls, found
us a driver to take us out for the evening, and he picked up the tab. Carroll
was always understanding; but we continued to be subjected to embarrassing situations and involuntary "lock downs," knowing full well that the
white players could do their own thing, whenever and wherever they
pleased. The tensions mounted over the 1960 season, to the extent that this
turned out to be the last year Big Daddy and Johnny Sample would play for
the Colts.

Johnny and Weeb were at odds after Johnny was fined over a scuffle he
had with a white player on the team. Johnny said that if he was fined and
the other player wasn't, that he'd walk out of camp. At the next team meeting, as Weeb was reading the fines, the white player's name was missing,
while Johnny's name was the last one read. He slowly got up, gathered his
things, and walked out, just as he threatened. Weeb kept him on the team
for the 1960 season but would eventually trade him to Pittsburgh.

Big Daddy was also traded to Pittsburgh after the 1960 season. There
was really no reason given. I think it was because of the management was
afraid they couldn't control Big Daddy anymore, who wouldn't tolerate any
more mistreatment of the blacks on the team. Also, many coaches thought
that Big Daddy's drinking had caught up to him and that he'd lost a step.

Either way, I was devastated to see my best friend leave the team. I really thought Weeb was cutting off his nose to spite his face, but it was his call to make.

While Johnny Sample and Big Daddy were still part of the team for one more season, though, we felt optimistic about 1960. We fully expected to make it three in a row. We started off with a fantastic victory over the Washington Redskins, winning 20-0, in front of a capacity crowd of 53,818. It was strictly a defensive game, as the Redskins decided to double team Raymond and me. I nevertheless scored on a four-yard plunge at the half, and on a 38-yard touchdown pass from Unitas.

We had quite a defensive team at the time. Gino Marchetti, one of the greatest to have ever played the game was at defensive end. Don Joyce, "Mr. Mean," was also a defense cornerstone; he became nationally known when he hit Les Richter of the Rams across the face with his helmet and inflicted quite a wound. And of course, Big Daddy played defense: he had the greatest lateral movement of any lineman, and he could catch running backs from behind. It was Daddy's fumble recovery in the 1960 Redskins game that paved the way for our victory.

The 1960 season kept rolling with a huge win against Chicago, at Baltimore. Johnny Unitas tied his own record with four touchdown passes. We intercepted seven passes ourselves. Johnny Sample ran a kickoff for 94 yards, and Johnny hit me for catches that earned us 66 and 18 yards. We led by as much as 35-0 in a 42-7 rout.

There was a hiccup at midseason, though. At Green Bay, our 35-21 loss reminded us that we were only human. Green Bay scored on two fumbles and two interceptions. From there, our game went downhill after a 7-7 half-time score. The Packers really squashed us. One good thing: Unitas notched his 40th game for touchdown passes.

The team rebounded as the LA Rams made their annual trip to Baltimore. I ran for three touchdowns and caught a fourth from Unitas—a 57-yard bomb—as the second period started. I dashed for another touchdown five minutes later. Unitas ran for 34 yards in the third quarter.

Next we traveled to Detroit. A highlight for the Lions was Jim Martin's 51-yard boot, in a two-of-three performance, breaking a 17-all tie. He set up his second field goal by tackling Unitas for a fumble at the 33-yard line. Dick "Night Train" Lane had an 80-yard interception for touchdown.

Our 45-7 win against the Dallas Cowboys was a cakewalk. Unitas had four touchdowns on 270 yards. Raymond Berry (who had starred at SMU, in Dallas) had a fantastic day, with 190 yards and three touchdowns. I had a 20-yard touchdown catch with three minutes left.

The roll continued: we played Green Bay again at Baltimore. Two late touchdowns in the fourth kept the Colts in title contention, and our win moved us into first place. Unitas had two first-half strikes to Berry that were sandwiched around a pass from Alex Hawkins to Johnny for a touchdown.

Another home game, this time against Chicago, ended in a 24-20 victory. With nicks and scrapes all over his face, and blood streaming down his jersey, Unitas hurled a 39-yard pass to me in the final 41 seconds, which ended the battle and put us atop the Division. This was truly a bloody game. George Halas claimed that I pushed J.C. Caroline on the clinching touchdown; but the truth is that I had J.C. beat by a step and a half and I was on his outside, going down the sideline. Unitas threw the ball perfectly over J.C., who was trying to close in on me when he discovered the ball was already out of reach. I caught it over the shoulder for six points. If I had pushed Caroline, I would have had to turn around and shove him, but I was too busy concentrating on the ball.

A loss to San Francisco preceded another devastating loss to Detroit. In the latter game, we all thought we had won, thanks to a 65-yard pass play in the final 14 seconds remaining. But while we were on the Lions' 38-yard line, I couldn't shake "Night Train" Lane. I dove to catch the ball, tumbling six feet in the air and rolling into the end zone. I looked up to see the ref signal a touchdown and Big Daddy doing a jig. We figured the ball game was over. The fans rushed onto the field with such fervor I thought I was going to get killed. Then the officials yelled that there were still seven seconds left on the clock. The fans were cleared from the field, as the Lions got the ball and returned to the 35-yard line. But instead of restarting the game, the Lions started a fight. This stopped all play and allowed the Lions to regroup. Earl Morrall came in and drew a play in the dirt, with Jim Gibbons looking on. When the clock began again, Morrall lofted the ball to Gibbons and he ran under for a touchdown. Ian Webb brutally flattened Johnny Sample. We could do little more than shake our heads in bewilderment.

The team was deflated after that loss and proceeded to lose to the Rams, 10-3. The 47-straight touchdown streak that Unitas had going was shattered. To make matters worse, the final game with the 49ers was another loss. Ameche injured his Achilles' tendon in that game, prematurely ending his career. Although Unitas set a number of records, including total passing yards for the season, our win-loss record was a disappointing 6-6.

1960 was a devastating season for the franchise, coming off of two championship seasons, when the team was truly clicking on all cylinders. Things may have gotten too easy for us. With our hopes of being champions for a third straight season ruined, we had to find some way to recapture the magic.

# NINE

# TRAGEDY STRIKES

With a disappointing 1961 season in the rearview mirror, the team experienced some very significant turnovers. Part of those had to do with personal decisions by the players, and part were due to decisions made by Weeb and GM Kellett in an attempt to rejuvenate the team.

First, a key member of the offensive line, Art Spinney, retired. An underrated guard who consistently did an excellent job, he was one of the many unsung heroes of the two championship years. He led me into the end zone on more than one occasion.

Then Milt Davis left. He was a highly educated individual, a tremendous team leader, an excellent safety, and a fierce competitor. Milt was even our locker-room diplomat, helping many players overcome their differences in troubled times. He entered the League later in life than most, and he was older and well tutored when we got him. I'm happy to say that, to this day, he is a dear friend, and I don't use that term loosely.

Another change in the team was due to Ameche's injury to his Achilles' tendon. Weeb went looking for a replacement and finally made a trade for Joe Perry. I admired Joe from his days with the 49ers: he was one of the first players to keep himself in shape all year long. I got to know Joe quite well, as he and I roomed together on the road. Before that I had always roomed with Big Daddy.

We lost Big Daddy, as well as Johnny Sample, before the start of the 1961 season. As I related earlier, Weeb traded both of these fine players to the Steelers in order to infuse some new talent on the team and, in my opinion, because Big Daddy and Sample never felt bashful in expressing themselves. Without a word being said, I believe these moves were done to reestablish the front office's control over the blacks on the team.

The final change made, very near the beginning of the season, was to trade Sherman Plunkett to the San Diego Chargers. In spite of Sherman's large size, he was agile and could outrun most halfbacks in a flat race. But Weeb was anxious to trade him for Lenny Lyles. Our former Colts teammate, Lenny had been traded away after the 1958 season, and now Weeb wanted him back. Weeb actually asked me what I thought of bringing Lyles back to the Colts, and I agreed that it was a great move: Lyles was a good, hard-nosed ballplayer, one of the most solid cornerbacks in the League.

Given all these turnovers, it was predictable, I suppose, that the 1961 season would be challenging. As always, there was a sampling of racial tensions that would be dramatically added to the mix. To start with, there were more encounters with prejudicial treatment in the preseason games in the South. This time the setting was Roanoke, Virginia. A telegram from R.R. Wilkenson, president of the Roanoke NAACP, was sent to Joe Perry and me at training camp, asking that the blacks on the team boycott the upcoming game unless the seating arrangements were corrected. At the time, Roanoke Stadium was owned by the citizens of Roanoke, but the seats were sold on a segregated basis: black patrons were strictly confined to seats in the end zone, behind a chain-link fence that obstructed their view of the game by rounding them up like cattle.

This was an outrage. To imagine the black patrons at the game caged like animals in the end zone, while the rest of the white audience was comfortably seated along the sidelines was appalling. At times it was tiring for all the black players in the league to continue to make these stands. Many times we just wanted to show up and play football and not have to constantly take a stand against injustice. It would have been easy to turn our backs, but the question always came back to, "What would Jackie do?" and the discussion ended right there. He wouldn't turn his back. He wouldn't take the easy way out. He never did.

Joe and I talked this over with Weeb, Kellet and Rosenbloom. We were serious in our intention to boycott, and each of them knew it. Although they didn't make the rules, they were man enough to see to it the change was made: the best seats would go to the first fans who bought them. We decided to play in the game.

But when I went onto the field in the pregame warmup, I looked around the stands and it was obvious that black fans were still sitting in pre-determined blocks of seats. I walked down the field, to the end zone, to meet some of the black kids. They were fenced in, like pigs in a pen. I had to reach through the chain-link fence in order to shake their hands. No image had ever made me realize, with such force, just what blacks have been up against all through American history: we have always been on the out-side looking in. We are isolated by the spaces we have been allotted, watch-ing society from a distance, given only a partial view of reality. "All things being equal," some might have said, "blacks are lucky to be allowed in the stadium at all." Well, all things are not, and never have been, equal. The teams are integrated, finally; so why not the stands?

The 1961 season started out on a determined note: After the disap-pointing follow-up to our back-to-back championships, the team was look-ing to re-establish its dominance in the League. Opening against the Rams at Memorial Stadium was a good start. The Rams gave us a run for our money, but our defense was stout, and we held them scoreless up to the sec-ond half. I had a good start to the season myself, with a 38-yard touchdown pass reception and, with the help of a Marchetti fumble recovery, I also scored on a two-yard reception for a touchdown.

Next we met the Lions in front of a sellout crowd of 54,259. We led the game by a touchdown with seven minutes left on an eight-yard reception I caught from Unitas. Unfortunately, Mike Smolinski fumbled in the fourth quarter, which was recovered by the great Alex Karras. It led to the clinch-ing score by the Lions in a 16-15 defeat.

In the following game, a ghost from the Colts' past came back to haunt us: George Shaw had hooked on with an expansion team, the Minnesota Vikings. In what would become a pattern throughout this season, Steve Myhra made a long field goal, a 52-yarder, on the last play of the game. It was his second field goal in the final two minutes. I had two touchdown receptions from Unitas, and one from Lamar McHan. Johnny wasn't used to sharing the spotlight on the field, but he and McHan were becoming a team unto themselves.

The Green Bay Packers were next. In 1961 they were beginning their dynasty in the League. Vince Lombardi had assembled an amazing array of talent, such as Paul Hornung, Jim Taylor, Bart Starr, and Herb Adderley. In this game, Hornung broke the single-game record for points scored, with 33 points on four touchdowns and a field goal. The tandem of McHan and Unitas was an uneasy platoon: between them, they had five interceptions. The only score was a touchdown that I notched. The ugly result was 45-7.

Then we traveled to Chicago, only to be shut down by the mighty Bears. Willie Galimore took a screen pass 84 yards to put the Bears permanently ahead in the fourth quarter. They never looked back. With two straight losses under our belt and a 2-3 record out of the chute, the hopes of starting the season strong were dead. It would take a tremendous effort for us to salvage the season and still make a run.

Our game with Detroit ended on a better note, with a 17-14 victory. Again, a 45-yard field goal from the team's most valuable player at that point, Steve Myhra, was converted, with only eight seconds left on the clock. I was responsible for both touchdowns with two scoring runs.

Unfortunately, the team by this point was dancing: one step forward and two steps back. The Bears visited Memorial Stadium and would sweep the season series with a 21-20 victory. The Bears capitalized on a pass-interference call in the fourth quarter that resulted in a touchdown. I was able to contribute with a 68-yard pass reception for a touchdown. Bill George, the mighty Midway linebacker, proved to be our nemesis, as he blocked Myhra's last extra-point attempt of the game to seal the victory. The refs seemed to have it in for us as three blatant pass interferences were not called.

We exacted some revenge on the Green Bay Packers with a 24-point victory over Lombardi and company. I put the team ahead for good with a 38-yard touchdown run. Johnny, feeling frustration over the tandem quarterback system that Weeb had put into place, waved off the field-goal unit twice. Both times he was successful and reaped touchdown receptions. The point wasn't lost on Weeb. With the inconsistency that the team was displaying, Johnny wanted to capitalize on all the opportunities that were available. In today's game, a move such as that would be grounds for a fine and/or a benching, but everyone knew Johnny was different. Furthermore, he rarely disappointed.

In our game against Minnesota, we learned that a young rookie named Fran Tarkenton had taken over for George Shaw. This was very reminiscent of Johnny's usurping George for the quarterback position five seasons earlier. Fran ran and passed for a touchdown and clinched his first of many victories for the Vikings.

The loss to the expansion Vikings certainly hurt, and we wouldn't soon forget it. To finish out the season, we would take the final four out of five, starting with a tilt in St. Louis against the Cardinals that ended in a 16-0 thrashing of the home team.

Remarkably, in our first meeting against the Redskins in 1961, they still hadn't employed a black ballplayer in their franchise's history. As the country was continually pressing the issue of equality through the election of John F. Kennedy as our 35th president and the efforts of Martin Luther King Jr. in the South, they were the last NFL team to succumb to the trend of integration, as the famously racist George Preston Marshall sternly refused to see a black player on the team. It wasn't until after the 1961 season that the team finally traded for Bobby Mitchell, who was a standout at Illinois in his collegiate career, and a prized Cleveland running back, but had the great misfortune of playing behind Jim Brown in his prime. Beating the Redskins 27-6 was always a sweet victory. Subconsciously I always seemed to play harder against the Redskins, knowing their racist ways. With a keen focus, I helped set up the first touchdown for the team with a 45-yard run from scrimmage and also contributed a 54-yard run from scrimmage for a touchdown.

At 6-5 and mathematically out of any conference championship race. We then split the annual West Coast trip through Los Angeles and San Francisco to cap another subpar season for the franchise.

~ ~ ~

There were many rumors as to why the team had continued its struggles for two full seasons. No one was able to escape the blame: Weeb had lost the team, Johnny didn't have his magic touch anymore, there were too many off-season distractions for the team as the player-owned restaurants opened up all over town, and, finally, whispers that there was dissension amongst the players on the team. I certainly won't deny any of these points weren't true. The group had changed, and we didn't seem to have the same spark. Early on in 1962 we began accumulating too many defeats for us to be holding personal grudges, much less thinking about title contention. This would be the year that marked the end of the Weeb Ewbank era in

Baltimore. It was also the year in which, for the first time in my career, my body failed me.

It happened during the exhibition game against the Steelers, in Pittsburgh's Forbes Field. I was actually giddy with excitement, for this would be my first chance to play against Big Daddy since he'd been traded. But when I was tackled out of bounds on a tail-end run, I hit the ground hard, and my knee slid over an exposed spike used to anchor first base during Pittsburgh's baseball season. The spike cracked my kneecap in two.

At first I didn't realize how severe the injury was. But as I tried to run back onto the field and join the huddle after the tackle, I was bewildered by the inability to bend my knee. It would only flex so far, and then it would lock up. I limped off the field and had the trainer and our orthopedic man, Dr. Edmond McDonnell, check it out.

"It's only a severe bruise," said the doctor.

But either I wasn't checked out thoroughly enough or the doctor had made the wrong diagnosis and treated the injury inadequately. All he did was put ice on my knee and send me back into the game.

Assuming the doctor knew what he was doing, I made the mistake of going back in, despite the pain and lack of flexibility. We were trained to play with pain, and no one wants to sit out with an injury. It is a team thing—and I prided myself on being a team man.

On the next play from scrimmage, Big Daddy and a few other Steelers tackled me. Immediately sensing that I was in pain, Big Daddy yelled at his teammates, "Get the hell off of him. He's hurt." As I limped back to the huddle, I heard Big Daddy shouting to me, "Get the hell out of the game, Spats. Don't get yourself messed up in this exhibition game with the season coming up next week!"

I appreciated his concern, but I thought I could gut it out another play. My knee couldn't be too bad, since Dr. McDonnell had said it was fine. On the next play, I managed to lead the fullback around the left end, but it was clear that my knee still wouldn't bend. It kinked and locked when it should have flexed. I left the field and I could hear Big Daddy hollering after me, "Man, get your ass out of here. The hell with them!"

I put ice on my knee, and watched the rest of the game from the sidelines. When we got back to Baltimore, I went to Union Memorial Hospital, where X-rays showed that my kneecap was broken in two. Dr. McDonnell himself applied the cast on my leg, from my ankle past my knee. This would put me out for half the season, and I missed seven games.

It was the first major injury I had suffered in my life. Up to that point I thought I was indestructible—that I would be able to play forever. This was also the first time since my academic ineligibility at Penn State that I wasn't an active participant on my football team. Watching from the sidelines was more painful than the crack in my knee.

What made matters worse was the performance by the team. For the third straight year it was evident that we just didn't have the magic that we took for granted just three seasons ago. The team was only able to notch three victories in those first seven games, and Weeb seemed to be out of answers. It got so bad for the team that Weeb did the unthinkable; he benched Johnny in the third game of the year, which was a loss against the 49ers. In the second period of that game, Johnny was only two for six passing for five yards. Weeb had seen enough and sat Johnny until the fourth when he connected on two touchdown passes to Alex Hawkins in an effort to come back, but the damage was done.

By the last game I had to sit out, a hard-fought battle with the Packers, the team was in its death throes. Like a prizefighter just trying to hang on, we battled the eventual Western Conference winners to a 17-6 loss. The writing was clearly on the wall, and a change of some kind was imminent.

Weeb must have been wracking his brain trying to come up with a plan for a more effective Colts team. I was still recovering from the broken knee when Weeb told me he was changing my position on the team. He wanted to take me off the split end/flanker position so that I could concentrate only on being a running back. I wasn't sure whether or not I wanted to do this, but it was put to me in such a way that I had no choice. Weeb pushed the right button when he told me that this would be "best for the team." That was all it took. I didn't care how I was used; I just wanted to play.

I returned to the field in time to witness our team finally clicking on offense. We traveled to the West Coast and completed a sweep. We had a 22-3 victory over San Francisco and a 14-2 victory over the Rams. I got back into the swing of things and turned a six-yard reception into a touchdown in the first game and an 11-yard scoring run in the second. I was clearly rusty, but it felt great to get back out there and contribute. If my return provided some small spark for the team, that was all I could ask for from myself.

Unfortunately the spark I provided was short-lived. The Green Bay juggernaut was just too much. Herb Adderley ran a kick return back 103 yards to clinch a 17-13 victory for the Pack. Attempting to regroup as we returned home, the Monsters of the Midway thrashed us 57-0. It was the worst loss in our team's history, and the first shutout the franchise had suffered in eight seasons. The Lions finished off a Midwestern thumping with a 21-14 victory in Detroit. A win to cap the year off against Minnesota at home was a small consolation. The team was beaten soundly throughout the season, and it was clear a change had to be made.

If our 1961 season had been disappointing, the 1962 season left us even more disheartened, as we ended with a pitiful 7-7 record. It had been a rough couple of seasons. In this last year, though, I felt something peculiar had happened. In the first few games, I had felt something of a rejection, as though I were being left out of the team's efforts. Then, having to miss half the season due to injury, I felt abandoned. It didn't help that most of my support system was now gone: Big Daddy, Sherman, and Milt were no longer around to pick up my spirits.

My depression was only to worsen, though, as the biggest loss yet was lurking around the corner.

~ ~ ~

Eugene "Big Daddy" Lipscomb was by far the most intimidating football player of his generation. At 6'6" and 300 pounds, he towered over and outweighed most offensive and defensive linemen of his era. Those measurements may not sound big today, but many linemen of the era weighed 50 pounds less than Big Daddy. Inside this mountain of a man, though, was a small child looking for acceptance and security. He was always very self-conscious about his size and his lack of schooling. Rooming with him on road trips, I was often astounded to hear him cry himself to sleep at night.

Big Daddy was a victim of the same self-loathing that many blacks have been taught, growing up in a world that privileges white skin. For Big Daddy, though, the internalized hatred was self-annihilating.

Growing up in the ghettos on the east side of Detroit in the 1930s, Big Daddy never really knew his father, who had died while working for the Civilian Conservation Corps when Big Daddy was very young. So the little boy who would become Big Daddy was left to be raised by his mother, a ne'er-do-well with a seedy reputation and suspect friends. One morning, when he was 11, after his mother had gone to her job at a nearby laundry, Big Daddy was preparing breakfast for himself. A stranger knocked at the door, and asked if this was the residence of Mrs. Lipscomb. When this was confirmed, the man put his hand on Big Daddy's shoulder, sat him down, and told him that his mother had been murdered. She had been waiting at the bus stop, and a man had walked up to her and stabbed her 47 times.

Big Daddy grew up very quickly in that moment. He was sent to live with his grandfather, whose idea of raising a child was to use strict discipline reinforced by the belt. The boy had a checkered high school career at Miller High School in Detroit. Barely making acceptable grades, he was sent to jail twice: once for breaking into a building with some other kids, and once for getting into a racial altercation with some local police.

The only time the young man felt happy was when he was playing sports. He participated in high school football, basketball, and track. To support himself and to pay his grandfather for room and board, he worked at a steel-pickling plant from midnight to 8:30 a.m.; then he would go to school until 3:00 p.m.; and finally, he would play whatever sport he was involved in after school. While still in high school, he was recruited to play semi-professional basketball for the Joe Louis Brown Bombers, who toured Michigan. This lasted until his senior year, when a rival high school coach recognized him at a Bombers game and reported him to the Michigan High School Sports Association, for accepting money to play sports. This revelation made him ineligible for high school sports his senior year, a fact that devastated him.

Without many choices, he did what most young black men do, they join the military. With his size, the marines quickly assigned him to their football team. It was there that the great Sid Gilman spotted him and signed him on the spot to play with the LA Rams. After a short and undisciplined stint with the Rams, Weeb signed him off the waiver wire for a few hundred dollars, and Big Daddy finally found stability in his life for the first time.

With a support system of friends like me, Johnny Sample, Milt Davis and Sherman Plunkett and a coach who believed in him, the sky was the limit for Big Daddy.

He was an athletic marvel. Once he joined the Colts, during the off season he would tour the Midwest and California with the United States Professional Wrestling Association, under the name "Waffle Ear." He and another Colt, Don Joyce, wrestled in tag-team matches against the likes of other NFL players Leo Nomellini and Tom Rice. Big Daddy also maintained his love of basketball and signed on with the Eastern Basketball League in January of 1961. This resulted in a legal mess. Commissioner Pete

Rozelle reminded Big Daddy that NFL players couldn't sign professional contracts with other leagues, especially ones that were rife with gambling scandals, as was the EBL at the time. As a result, EBL president Harry Rudolph sued Pete Rozelle in a $1 million defamation case. All this trouble swirled around Big Daddy and most likely contributed to him being traded to Pittsburgh after the 1960 season.

Big Daddy and I kept in contact after he joined the Steelers, for he continued to make his permanent home in Baltimore. Although Big Daddy and I married our wives just a few short weeks apart from each other, Big Daddy just wasn't the marrying type. He continued to date other women, drink a lot of liquor, and live the good life. He also continued to carouse, and his carefree lifestyle would eventually catch up to him.

One Tuesday in May 1963, Big Daddy and I talked about our plans for the weekend. We were at the home of our friend, Clyde Mills, who lived across the street from me. Daddy said that he was going to play some softball on Friday, but after that game we could drive to New York to see jazz organist Jimmy Smith at the Village Gate. Daddy also mentioned that after our trip he was going to go to Pittsburgh to sign his season contract with the Steelers. We coordinated our schedules for the week, and our plans were set to meet on Thursday. But that Tuesday would be the last time I saw Big Daddy alive.

On Thursday, after pitching a softball doubleheader in Baltimore, Big Daddy went out on the town. Somewhere along the way, he hooked up with a man named Timothy Nathaniel Black, whom I had never met; nor had I ever heard Big Daddy mention him. Later, we would learn more about Mr. Black: he was a slightly built, 27-year-old black man who had a leg that was previously ravaged by polio. He worked at a local bottling company and had a history of drug trouble.

According to Timothy Black's testimony, Big Daddy came by his apartment on Brice Street in his yellow Cadillac. The two men had plans to go cruising. After a few hours, they returned to Timothy Black's apartment with two female friends and some malt liquor. Eventually, Robert Douglas Waters, whose sister Big Daddy had previously dated, came by. The group partied until the early morning hours. When everyone left, according to Timothy Black, he and Big Daddy drove down to Pennsylvania Avenue, where Black bought some heroin.

According to Black, the two men returned to the apartment. Big Daddy sat at the kitchen table and shot up with a homemade syringe. Then he immediately fell to the floor, unconscious. Waters, who either lived in the neighborhood or had driven by, noticed that Big Daddy's car was still parked outside Black's apartment; so he went up to see if the party had been revived. Waters testified that when he returned to the apartment, he saw Big Daddy on the floor and Timothy Black attempting to revive him by rubbing ice cubes on his skin and injecting him with salt water—all to no avail. After momentarily arguing over whether they should call an ambulance, they finally dialed the hospital. But it was too late: Big Daddy's body lay motionless on the floor. He was dead at age 34 of an apparent overdose.

The subsequent autopsy confirmed portions of Black's story: there was morphine in Big Daddy's bile and urine, his lungs were filled with salt water, and there was alcohol in his blood. What doesn't add up, though, is that I, as well as everyone who ever came in contact with him, knew Big Daddy was deathly afraid of needles. In training camp, when the team doctor would administer mandatory flu shots, Big Daddy would be hiding in the corner of the locker room. It literally took six men to hold him down for the doctor to administer the shot. Yet Timothy Black asserted that Big Daddy was a consistent user. If so, why did no one in the Colts' locker room ever notice any track marks on Big Daddy's arms? Another thing that I find troubling about Timothy Black's story is this: Big Daddy was right-handed, yet the heroin was administered to his right arm. Now how can a man shoot himself up using his weak hand if he was terrified by needles and had had no practice (that I knew of) in shooting heroin?

I learned of Big Daddy's death when I heard a flash on the radio, around 7:00 a.m. Friday—the day we were set to drive to New York. I refused to believe what I had heard until it was repeated on the radio. I called Sherman Plunkett's house, because Daddy and he were living together at the time; but the phone was busy. That scared me into reality: was it true what they were saying on the radio? Frantic, I called Jim Parker, but his phone was also busy. Then I called Buddy Young's house, only to hear the busy signal again.

I was crazy for information: How could it happen that this larger-than-life, happy-go-lucky, fun-loving guy was gone! The radio had said "heroin overdose." That was absurd; if Daddy were using drugs, we would have noticed a behavioral change. Plus, he always wore T-shirts with the arms cut off at the shoulders, so we would have seen track marks if there were any. How could I, or Sherman, or Jim, or Buddy not have known? Furthermore, the coroner told me that Big Daddy had three fresh needle marks in his right arm with no previous needle marks. If that was the case, the three needle marks account for two saline shots and one herion shot. It just doesn't make sense.

The five of us were like fingers on the same hand—nothing like heroin use would have escaped our notice. Big Daddy left behind four bewildered friends who always believed there was foul play involved in his death, but we could never piece things together. To this day it remains a mystery.

Once the news was out, the whole town was devastated. Sherman and I helped arrange a public viewing: it lasted 12 hours and consistently had a two-block-long line of fans waiting to pay their respects. Someone estimated that nearly 30,000 people came to honor this man. Then we transported the body back to Detroit, his hometown. At the funeral there, the pallbearers included Sherman, Johnny Sample, Night Train Lane, Jim Parker, Eli Barnes, and me.

Another mystery emerged when Big Daddy's grandfather, who had raised him since his mother was murdered, was trying to collect Big Daddy's estate. There was no estate, no money or property, nothing at all. Now how does a man who was making almost $1,000 a night at wrestling and who played professional football, die without having a penny to his name? It was finally determined that Big Daddy was signing over all of his checks to Buddy Young, trusting him to manage his finances. Sherman told me that whenever Big Daddy wanted any money, he would just ask Buddy to cut him a check.

There are so many things about Big Daddy's death that don't add up. We'll probably never know the truth. All I know is that I miss this man terribly. Whenever I'm in Detroit, I make it a point to go out to his grave and pay my respects. I have no doubt that if it were me who had died Big Daddy would make regular visits to my gravesite. When my mother died, in 1958, Big Daddy cried as much as my family did. His heart was bigger than anyone's.

Big Daddy's life was another in a long line of tragic figures in my life. All things being equal, he should have lived a long, jovial life and been voted into the NFL Hall of Fame to live in perpetuity with the other Giants of the game. But, like many other blacks of the day, the self-loathing and low self-esteem led to a destructive and morbid end. At that point, other than my mother dying a few years earlier, it was the most devastating period of time in my life. I was shaken to my core and didn't know if I could recover in time for the 1963 season that would be starting soon.

# TEN

# SEASON OF DOUBT

C arrying a heavy heart, I reported to training camp in 1963. With Weeb fired shortly after the 1962 season, Don Shula was named the new head coach. In addition to a new coach, the Colts picked up five new recruits. Foremost was John Mackey, who was destined to become the best tight end in the game. The team also picked up J.W. Lockett from the Dallas Cowboys. Bob Vogel, also destined to become a top offensive tackle and an All-Pro, was one of the great technicians at his position. Fred Miller at defensive tackle was probably one of the fastest at his position. Finally we added Jerry Logan at safety and Willie Richardson for help at flanker. To further shake things up, Shula decided to move Jim Parker to offensive guard instead of the position he was used to playing as an All-Pro, tackle. For Big Jim, it didn't really make a difference, because he was an All-Pro wherever you put him. He would eventually lead me through my greatest year, in 1964. In spite of all the changes, there was a spring in everyone's step as we had a new coach with fresh ideas and a lot of great new blood coming in at the same time.

Shula was a guy who liked to holler and scream on the sidelines. At times it seemed as if he went too far. Although the tension would never manifest itself physically, I knew many guys on the team wanted to take a shot at him. We hated to lose as much as he did, but he didn't seem to think so. Looking back, it was as big an adjustment for him as it was for us, which most likely accounted for much of the tension. We felt that maybe since he played the game so recently (as a teammate of ours) that he would have an understanding of a player's point of view and our problems. I felt confident that we'd finally have a players' coach on our side, but that didn't last long. He took to the title of head coach instantly, but with this new sensibility, many on the team felt he was very difficult to communicate with when problems arose. It would take time for both sides to find common ground.

Furthermore, many on the team still had strong feelings for Weeb. For many of us, he was the only professional head coach we'd ever had. He taught us how to play the game his way. His quirks and eccentricities were tough to adjust to at first, but with his stewardship the team reached unprecedented heights. His leadership was comfortable—like a well-worn glove—which ultimately led to his dismissal and replacement with a coach who had a completely different personality.

Going into the exhibition season, we played the Steelers in Atlanta. Even in the mid-1960s, it wasn't an easy time to be playing pro football in the South. I didn't play this game due to a hip pointer, but I made the trip anyway. We stayed at the Dinkler Plaza in Atlanta. After we left we found out that the management had received death threats for having blacks stay in the hotel. This made sense to me after the fact, because I'd felt a palpable tension throughout our whole stay. I could tell something was going on, because the wait staff was a little stiff. During the game, I was on the sideline when John Henry Johnson came by. John Henry was really taking a pounding during the game and I shared a laugh with him. When he went back in the game, he yelled at me, "Get out here and get some of this ass-beating, too, you son of a bitch!"

The last exhibition game was in New Orleans against the Bears. The night before the game, Jim Parker and I wanted to go to the black section of town to get some food due to the segregation policies in downtown New Orleans, but we couldn't even grab a cab—they just went by us. Finally we found a black cab company that gave us a ride. Coming back to the hotel, Parker and I had to damn near walk all the way. The black players in the League often had problems whenever exhibitions were held in New Orleans, even up to the year before they brought in the Saints, so our treatment wasn't a surprise. At the hotel, I had a chance to speak with some of the League and city officials who played an integral part in getting a franchise granted to the area. I relayed my most recent experience with Parker and some other stories I'd heard from other players in the League. I made it clear that they had better make it a priority to clean up the city, because in its current condition, black ball players would not want to subject their families to this type of racial injustice, which would in turn hurt the franchise's chances at success. It was hard enough just playing the game without having to worry about how your kids are being treated in school or what kinds of looks your wives get at the supermarket. I don't know if those slick corporate salesmen were really listening to me or not, but I do know the Saints played their first season in 1967. They didn't have a winning record until 1987.

In our first game of the season, we opened up at Memorial Stadium against our old nemesis, the New York Giants. In front of a sellout home crowd, the two teams battled in a titanic struggle. Fifteen years before, Y.A. Tittle took the field as a 21-year-old in his debut as a young Giant quarterback against the first incarnation of the Colts. Now, as an old man, many felt he was on the downside of his career. I don't think anyone told Y.A., though. On that day, he would equal Johnny Unitas in a duel of genius quarterbacks until Tittle was knocked out of the game late in the second half, but not before passing for three touchdowns.

Johnny put us ahead 21-3 early in the second half when Tittle took control and led the G-Men back. This seesaw game would be a microcosm of the season as a whole. With a heroic comeback that resulted in a 37-28 victory for the Giants, it was the first time that the Giants beat us with Johnny at quarterback.

Personally, it was the start of a tough season as well. I didn't play in this first game because of an emergency appendectomy the Friday before the game. Not knowing how long it might take me to recover, the team didn't disclose this information until many days after the Giants game. Nonetheless, I refused to let my team down before the season had even really started. I pushed myself hard to get back early, and in only ten days I was practicing in time for the annual trip to the West Coast.

Wearing a pad over the incision, I started in Raymond Berry's front-end spot because he was hurt as well. Although I was in immense pain, I didn't have much time to think about it because Johnny continued his hot play by throwing for 288 yards. Even though we trailed by four points, 14-10, in the fourth quarter, JW Lockett led the team on the ground to a 20-14 victory.

The sweet taste of victory didn't last long as we lost the next two games to Green Bay and Chicago, which was becoming a trend that irritated everyone on the team. What I would soon find out was the team's rocky start and my ailing midsection weren't the only problems rearing their ugly head.

After being whipped by the Packers 31-20, we traveled to Chicago to take the Bears on in Wrigley Field, which is where my relationship with Shula started to get rocky. The night before the game, I was having a little bit too much fun barhopping the famous Chicago blues and jazz clubs and I lost track of the time. It was a totally innocent mistake that I knew I would have to own up to. As a result, I was late for check-in at the hotel and it didn't take very long for Shula to find out. I barely made it into my room when I heard a knock at the door. Sure enough, it was Shula and Gino Marcheti, who was serving the team as an unofficial player-coach at the time. I knew this could get tense, so I spoke up first and told them both that I was sorry for my tardiness and I knew I was to be fined and hoped it would be left at that. I felt that since I was one of the veterans on the team that we could talk man to man in the privacy of my room. I should've stopped there, but this private moment presented me with a perfect opportunity to broach some of the double standards that were becoming all too common. I told Shula, "If Jimmy Orr misses a block it seems to be a big joke, but if I do, I get cussed out." As I continued talking, I got more worked up. It seemed to be the same old bullshit that was going down and I wanted to let my feelings known to my new boss before it went too far. I wanted some feedback. I wanted to nip some of these issues in the bud, but I seemed to be the only one in the room who thought that this matter was important enough to waste my breath on. I was very disappointed to see Shula turn around and leave without saying a word. I could tell I was in hot water from that point on.

In an effort to show Shula that I was a team player and I held no hard feelings, I played hard and had a good game against the Bears. Although it would be a tough, hard-fought battle that was tied at three for the most of the game, we just couldn't seem to get over the hump. After knocking out the Bears' starting quarterback, Billy Wade, Rudy Buckich came in and led the team on an 80-yard drive that would seal the deal and put us on a 1-3 start.

With the offense still not in sync, we hosted the 49ers at Memorial Stadium. They couldn't have come at a better time. The 49ers hadn't won in 11 games and we would make it 12. Johnny threw a scoring strike on the first possession and I would add my first touchdown of the year on an 11-yard pass reception and lead the team to a 20-3 victory.

Prior to taking over the Colts, Shula had spent some time under the tutelage of George Wilson, the coach of the Lions, as their defensive coordinator. To add another angle to our next game, Jim Martin, our MVP so far this year, was picked up in a trade by the team prior to the season's beginning. There were many angles that presented themselves when we traveled to Detroit to face the Lions, but the best angle of all was that we would leave town on a modest two-game winning streak. It would be a great game and a great win for the team. Although the defense would give up three touchdowns in the first half, the unit regrouped in time to stop the Lions offense, which allowed Johnny to lead the team to a 25-21 victory.

Of course, just when things were looking up, we faced the Packers and the Bears in consecutive Sundays once again. True to form, the Midwestern Goliaths throttled us. Riding a two-game losing streak, we hosted the Lions. Although it wouldn't be a pivotal game in the franchise's history, it would have a dramatic effect on my own career.

The coaching staff did all it could to focus the team on the task at hand as the Lions rolled into town. In the week of practice before the game, Shula and the staff preached consistency and execution—two hallmarks that carried him through a Hall of Fame career. He believed the season could be salvaged and felt he had a plan to get the team back on track. His defiance in the face of adversity rubbed off on the team. We would come out smelling blood. With scores on our first four possessions, we were able to hold off Detroit 24-21. Johnny had a monster game, passing for 376 yards and two touchdowns. I would score the clinching touchdown on a four-yard run in the second quarter.

On a later possession, after being squashed in a pile, my helmet came off and I was inadvertently kicked in the head. I instantly became disoriented as my vision became blurry. I barely made it to the sideline and was finished for the day—little did I know that it would actually mean the season. I immediately went to the hospital for X-rays and it was agreed that I had a severe concussion and I was ordered out of practice the following week.

Having the concussion was a very odd sensation for me. I could walk around and function, but if I moved too slowly or quickly, I would become nauseated with vertigo. Without a cast or a scar to show for my injury, I was soon sensing that the team was leery of my injury. In the middle of the week, I remember the general manager, Don Kellett, calling the house early one morning to check if I was home—or out carousing. Although I had said or done nothing wrong that week, the rumors started circulating that I really wasn't injured. I was accused of quitting on the team, which upset me greatly.

With all I had given for the team, I assumed that I would be above such innuendo. Over the last two seasons, I had attempted to play through a cracked kneecap, an appendectomy, and now a concussion. While the white players would be ordered to sit out practice if they were feeling under the weather, the black players, including me, were asked to play through it. Never once did I publicly raise an issue. I certainly tried to talk about it privately with the front office and the coaching staff, but publicly I believed that we were a unified front. It was apparent that I was one of the few who felt this way.

In the midst of my own controversy, the world would be shocked by the assassination of JFK as he drove down Daley Parkway in Dallas. Pete Rozelle ordered the games to be played as we traveled to Minnesota for a 37-34 win to again square our record. Many football historians place great significance on this weekend in NFL history. They argue the fact that by suiting up shortly after such a world-changing event, the fledgling League was given a black eye. Commissioner Pete Rozelle himself was even on record as saying it was the worst decision he had made in his tenure. I can understand their sentiment, but from a player's perspective, it was just another Sunday. If you'll remember, that weekend the world didn't stand still. The mail was still delivered, banks were open, and water still ran out of everyone's faucets. It was the same for us. These contests are fun and games to everyone else, but to the players in the League, especially at that time, it was our job. That's not to say we weren't lucky playing a game for a living, but we all took our jobs very seriously. If the League thought we should play, then we did. In all honesty, as I was collecting my thoughts for this season in writing this book, I didn't have any distinct memories about this weekend. It may have been because I was still suffering from the concussion and I was under verbal attack from both my organization and the media alike, but from a historic standpoint, I don't have strong feelings over how the assassination affected the team.

In retrospect, I was actually happy we were traveling to Minnesota to play the game. It gave me a chance to get out of town and away from the spotlight surrounding my injury. As I watched the contest from the sidelines, my mind wasn't on the game, it was on my health. To me, the worst thing in the world is to sit out of any game. I wanted nothing more to put on the uniform again. I made sure the team knew what I was feeling. I wanted them to know how badly I wanted to be out there. Unfortunately, talk is cheap, but it was all I had to give.

Despite my constant communication with the team regarding my status, things continued to get tense. It was apparent that the organization was buying into the rumors, and as the days passed with me in street clothes on the sidelines, I could feel my teammates now ostracizing me. No matter how hard I tried to be a part of what was going on, fewer and fewer of my teammates would talk to me.

Even though I was a pariah on the team and just wanted the season to end, I still traveled to LA with the team for a tilt against the Rams. Playing only for pride at this point, the team gave it a valiant effort, but it wasn't meant to be. Danny Villanueva kicked a game-winning field goal to beat us 17-16.

Being on the sideline watching the action makes you die twice as hard when a play goes south. I couldn't help but think that things would be different if I were out there. The team wanted me out there, too. Anxious to find out what was wrong with me, Kellett sent me to a specialist in Los Angeles to get me checked out once again. After a thorough examination, the doctor echoed the sentiments of the other physicians in Detroit—it wasn't worth risking another blow to the head, which could affect me permanently. The doctor said in no uncertain terms that, without proper healing through rest, my career was in danger. He said that if he were me, he'd would've packed it in for the year as well. I told him how much I wanted to return to the lineup, and he said no chance. I said, "You're the Doc." Uncertain that Kellet would believe me, I asked him write down what he said to me so I could go back to Kellet and Dr. McDonnell. The doctor told me not worry about it, that he'd call Dr. McDonnell himself.

Feeling vindicated, I rushed back to the team hotel to find Dr. McDonnell, Kellett, and Shula standing in the lobby. I asked if they had spoken with the doctor, and they said they had, and that they were happy to hear that I had a clean bill of health. I was surprised and shocked by what I heard. Clean bill of health? I told them that the doctor told me the exact opposite and that I should pack it in for the year. I told them to get the doctor on the phone and to clear it up right now. They declined and said that we would pick the matter up when we returned to Baltimore.

I was pissed. I felt like a piece of meat, like all they wanted was for me to suit up and play, my health be damned. We returned to Baltimore in preparation for the Redskins game, and I refused to suit up even for practice, although I continued to attend all team meetings and practices. I was beginning to feel as if because I was black, I was expected to suit up no matter what. I was ashamed at my own organization for not giving me, a perennial Pro Bowler and veteran of the team, the benefit of the doubt. To be honest, if Carroll Rosenbloom himself had come to me and told me to suit up, I would have, in spite of the injury, but Shula and Kellet were clearly shielding me from him. Out of all of them, Carroll was the one I would run through a brick wall for. It killed me not to be out there for him. I just wasn't physically able to perform. I knew my conscience was clear in spite of the bad press I was receiving.

The team would finish up 8-6 as we ended the season with a road trip to Washington and a pair of home games. Johnny kept the Redskins guessing with a variety of play calls and we thrashed them 36-20.

Hosting the Vikings the next week, it would be another runaway. Looking to build some momentum going into next season, Johnny set a career record for passing totals in a season. He had two touchdown passes to John Mackey to seal the deal.

Hosting the Rams in our final game of the year, Johnny set another record, this time for total pass completions for the season at 237, which outpaced Sonny Jurgensen as he set the mark with the Colts in 1961. The Rams were leading 16-13 in the fourth quarter. After a fumble by Johnny in the end zone, Bobby Boyd forced a fumble and recovered the ball for Johnny to lead a four-play drive that was clinched on a winner to Tom Matte, who would finish the season at halfback in my place.

Despite the team's strong finish, a storm of doubt surrounded me to the end of the season and into the off season. I should have had the support of the team behind me in this time of trouble. Not only was my integrity questioned, but my place on the team as well. Although my life was in Baltimore, I was so fed up that I was prepared for anything. All things being equal, maybe it was time for a change of scenery.

# ELEVEN

# COMEBACK PLAYER OF THE YEAR? I NEVER LEFT

Ninteen-sixty-three was a disappointing year for both the team and me. Compounding the controversy over my concussion at the end of the year was the fact that I'd missed time from the appendicitis, cracked my kneecap into two pieces in 1962 and also missed a few games in 1961. Considering I was entering my ninth year in a league where the average career of a running back is four years, there were whispers that my body was breaking down. In addition, because having a concussion is something that can't be visibly seen by others, my credibility was being questioned regarding the extent of my injury. There was a heavy shroud of misinformation that enveloped me.

Unless you're an athlete, it is impossible to know the daggers you feel when you read about the fact that you might be traded to another city. Unlike many of today's athletes who can demand access to private jets and can afford homes in multiple cities, the NFL was a much different animal in the 1950s. It would be the equivalent of working in a factory for eight years and then waking up in the morning one day to see that you were being considered for a new position across the country at any time. At that point, you have to worry about selling your house, moving your family, becoming acclimated to a new part of the country, enrolling your kids into new schools, etc. It was completely overwhelming.

Based on the rumors I read about in the papers, it looked like I was going to be traded to New York for Sam Huff, but as the story has it, the

Giants backed out because they were unsure of my health, both physically and mentally. Weeks later, I would read about a quote from Vince Lombardi. He mentioned that he considered bringing me to Green Bay that off season as well, but he didn't because he was concerned when he heard that I wasn't "behaving." What an insult. To talk about me as if I were a child really burned me. I know that he wasn't the only one thinking that, he was just one of the few who was actually quoted saying it. In all, between the end of the 1963 season and the beginning of training camp in 1964, the Colts discussed trading me to six different teams, with no takers. Not only did the rest of the League have their doubts about me, but I was starting to wonder myself.

In the end, the one person chiefly responsible for keeping me in Colt Blue was the owner, Carroll Rosenbloom. Since the start of my career with the franchise, we had developed a great affection for each other. It was widely known throughout the organization that I was his favorite, which probably prevented my outright release at the end of the 1963 season. He had very little interest in seeing me leave but knew that this tension between the organization and me had to be dealt with. Considering the animosity that had developed, he was the only one powerful enough to make things right.

In April of 1964, Rosenbloom called a meeting in his office with Kellett, Shula and me. There was no small talk, no pleasantries, just a very simple question and a very simple answer. Carroll looked me straight in the eye and asked, "Lenny, do you want to play for the Colts in 1964?" I answered yes. He replied, "Fine, I just wanted to hear it from you directly. This meeting's over." That was it. The gathering literally lasted about two minutes.

With my future no longer in doubt, I could finally relax knowing that I would be a Colt for the foreseeable future. Now that my future was settled, I put all my energy into getting in shape and regaining my starting position in the backfield and the respect I had lost amongst my teammates. I knew that it wasn't going to be easy, but I was confident that I still had it in me.

There was only one strategy I could use; I had to keep my mouth shut and work like I'd never worked before. I made a vow to myself that I wouldn't give Shula or any of the other coaches a reason to say a word to me the whole year. If we were scrimmaging and I broke free from a tackle, I wouldn't jog another 15 yards and then turn around and come back. I would continue running at full speed until I reached the end zone and turn around and sprint back. When there was a moment of transition during practice and the guys were getting some water and taking a break, I didn't stand around and laugh with them. I stayed by myself, off to the side. I wanted to blend into the landscape. If keeping my mouth shut and my head down was what they wanted from this black athlete, then that was what they were going to get.

At the start of camp, Shula told me point blank that the starting job was Tom Matte's to lose. He told me that if I wanted any playing time that I would have to earn it. That was fine with me. I respected that he told me exactly where I stood with him. With the tone set and the ground rules in place, I went to work. I had total confidence in myself. I knew I could beat out Matte, or whomever else they threw out at me.

That year we also picked up Tony Lorick, who was a hard-nosed full-back from Arizona State and Alvin Haymond, who would ignite the Baltimore fans every time he touched the ball with his exciting punt and kick-off returns. We also brought in Neil Petties, from San Diego State, for spot receiving duties and special teams. Each of these new players would be in direct competition with me for playing time on special teams, flanker, and running back—but I didn't care. I encouraged the competition, because it would just drive home the point I was trying to make. When I beat them out, I could look the whole team in the eye knowing that it was my talent and my drive that got me back into the line-up.

Throughout camp, not just in practice, I literally didn't say anything to anybody. It was very difficult not to sit around the training table and shoot the breeze about the day's practice. When a meal was done, I would immediately return to my room in solitude. During the half-days or off days, I would hop in my car and drive home to Baltimore from Westminster to spend time with my family. In the spare hours of downtime, I would go to this little duck pond across the street from campus and just sit and meditate. Sometimes it would be for five minutes and other times I would be there for hours, but it was my special place that no one knew about where I could go and blow off steam. I just sat and watched those ducks. I laugh about the time I spent there now, but then it literally saved my life and my career in Baltimore. Sitting there allowed me to reenergize myself for the next battle of the day. I was able to get my mind and my attitude straight so that I could focus on what I wanted to do—prove everyone wrong. I sat there visualizing my return to glory and how my talent and desire were greater than anyone who tried to tear me down.

By the end of camp, Shula and the staff held a team meeting to formally announce the starting lineup for the opener at Minnesota. As soon as he started reading the lineup, position by position, a pit developed in my stomach. I hadn't been this nervous about making the first team since high school. I knew I had done everything asked of me. I worked harder than everyone else. I behaved better than everyone else. But I truly didn't know if it would be enough. If Shula didn't want to start me, it was his prerogative. He was the man in charge. I soon realized, though, he was a man of his word. Without skipping a beat, he read my name off as the starting tailback. It was as if a load had been lifted off my back. I had never felt so vindicated in my life. From that point forward, I had a new and profound respect for Shula as a man of his word. I wouldn't let him down.

~ ~ ~

In 1964, we began the season at Minnesota, against the quickly ascending Fran Tarkenton and his Vikings. The triple threat of Tarkenton in the air with Billy Brown and Tommy Mason on the ground proved to be too much for our defense. I had an excellent start to the season, though, as I scored twice: once on a two-yard plunge and once on a 70-yard pass reception.

The following game was in our nemesis's hometown—Green Bay—and it was nip and tuck throughout the whole contest. I opened the scoring with a 52-yard touchdown reception and then added a four-yard touchdown run to get us on the board quickly. After allowing Paul Hornung to score on a 20-yard romp that knotted up the ballgame, the defense held firm. We made two interceptions in the fourth quarter, which stopped two deep drives by the Pack. When it was all said and done, our defense recorded six sacks. This was a huge victory for the team. As I had mentioned before, through those rough seasons from 1960-1963, the Packers and the Bears constantly manhandled us—but this season was different. This contest was the start of an 11-game winning streak.

Next we hosted the mighty Chicago Bears. Johnny had a fantastic game, passing for three touchdowns. I contributed with a three-yard touchdown run, and then the defense pitched a shutout that would result in the most lopsided defeat in the history of the Chicago franchise. The 52-0 final score humiliated those Monsters of the Midway. Our dominance would continue through games against the Rams and the Cardinals, winning easily in both of those contests. This set up a return match against Green Bay—another huge test for the team.

Sensing some magic from this season, general manager Don Kellet tried to increase the size of the audience by showing the game on closed circuit in three Baltimore theaters. Everyone knew the magnitude of this game, as Memorial Stadium and the three theaters were instantly sold out. Thus, a huge fan base witnessed the tortuous, successive hits I took from the Green Bay defense. The Packers had been playing us close for the whole game, but we finally broke through in the third quarter as I scored on a 20-yard run. Many have said this was the greatest run of my pro career. As I began the run, triggered by a pitchout from Johnny, I darted to my left and cut back, then bulled through a pair of tacklers, and finally, there stood Ray Nitzschke, the big middle linebacker, at the five-yard line. It was the "immovable object" against the "irresistible force." Unfortunately for me, the "immovable object" outweighed me by at least 30 pounds. Somehow I shook him but, man, did I feel the impact when he connected with me. I kept my balance long enough to fall into the end zone for the score.

Squeaking out that 21-20 victory was easily the biggest win of the year. Beating Green Bay twice solidified our standing as a true contender. The last time we won six games in a row was in 1958. But the even better result of our victory was that we were in the Western Conference lead.

The next four games saw us roll over the competition. In successive weeks we beat the Lions, the 49ers, and the Bears by an average of 26 points. This streak set up a rematch with the Vikings, who handed us our only loss of the season. We were out for blood.

The Vikings visited Memorial Stadium for this round, but our record didn't intimidate them. Although we jumped ahead, 10-0, in the third with a 35-yard field goal by Lou Michaels and a 74-yard pass reception that I turned into a touchdown, the Vikings wouldn't give up, and they turned the score around to read 14-10. This time we would not be denied. With time running out, Johnny drove the offense 74 yards down the field and sealed the victory by tossing a pass to Alex Hawkins, who made an acrobatic grab for the victory, when he dove to catch the ball in the end zone. We enjoyed our revenge with a final score of 17-14.

In Los Angeles for the next game, we were intent on putting away the Western Conference title before Thanksgiving. The gate for this game was 72,137, making it the largest crowd to see any game, since the 75,461 who had witnessed our game against the Rams in 1960. Late in the first period, I put us on the board with an 18-yard burst from the right side of the line. The defense shut down Roman Gabriel by recording an amazing 11 sacks. Our 24-7 victory clinched the earliest division title ever in League play.

With the Conference lead sewn up, we coasted the rest of the season in an attempt to get everyone healthy for the season-ending championship game. We sandwiched a meaningless loss to the Lions around victories over the 49ers and the Redskins to end the season. For more than a month the team was scoreboard watching to see whom we would be matched up against. We wanted the League crown so bad, we could taste the champagne already.

All season long, the team was buoyed as, win after win, our roll had continued. We were all thinking "Championship!" so I wasn't too mindful of the numbers I was putting up in overall game stats. As I read our reviews, though, I was surprised to learn that I was working on a consecutive scoring streak that rivaled Jim Taylor's single-season record of 19 touchdowns.

It looked like my streak might end, though, with the arrival of the Detroit Lions, whose defense was by far the most physical we'd played all season. In fact, the Lions not only gave Marchetti a concussion, they whipped us 31-14. For my part, a freak play kept my scoring record alive. Unitas hit Orr with a pass at the 35, and he was running everywhere trying to shake loose. He was a man on a mission and refused to be denied: he broke four tackles to get to the five-yard line. Then he fumbled. I had been tracking the play all the way downfield in an attempt to throw a block to protect Jimmy. In the confusion, Berry saw the ball pop loose and lunged to pick up the fumble, but he kicked the ball into the end zone instead, where our offensive tackle, George Preas, had a shot at it. It got away from him as well. Remarkably, I recovered it for the score and kept my streak of games with a touchdown alive.

To finish the season, the Redskins came to Baltimore and it would prove to be a landmark game in my career. I scored twice on runs of one and three yards, which was all I needed to break Jim Taylor's record, set in 1962. It was also my 18th straight game with a touchdown, another record.

We finished the season 12-2, and we prepared for our championship rival, the Cleveland Browns. We worked extra hard in practice after practice until we felt we were ready for them. I can remember the scene in the locker room after practice: you could sense in the air how anxious we were to get at them. We knew we had a better record than the Browns going in; and since the Browns' defense had been maligned all season, we were the heavy favorites. The press predicted that our offense would run all over the field. Our defense was keyed in on the Browns' notorious Jim Brown: he was so big and strong that whenever our defense hit him hard enough to knock other backs out of the game, he would just get up and calmly return to the huddle. We weren't alone in witnessing his brute strength.

Sadly, it wasn't meant to be. How disappointed we were to lose this championship game! In the first half, we had many opportunities to score, but we failed. By halftime, the teams were tied at zero. In the locker room, we talked about taking it to them in the second half but, unfortunately, it never came to pass. A 24-year-old flanker named Gary Collins had the game of his life, scoring all three touchdowns for the Browns. Frank Ryan, their quarterback, was in control all during the second half, completing 11 of 18 passes on this cold and windy Ohio afternoon. It seemed all we had accomplished all season had gone down the drain in just one game.

I have no explanation for why we lost other than it just wasn't our day. We couldn't have prepared better. Shula was a stickler for detail, and we prepared for every angle that the Browns could run at us. In the end we were flat, and the combination of Jim Brown and Gary Collins was just too much. Considering the team was filled with veterans like Unitas, Marchetti, Donovan, and me, we knew that these opportunities couldn't be squandered. We were all devastated.

~ ~ ~

In spite of our defeat, I was voted by the players in the League as the Jim Thorpe award winner (NFL's Most Valuable Player), which is the highest single award that any ball player could win. It meant so much to me knowing that it was my peers who had voted me in. At the banquet where I received my award, I expressed appreciation for my late mother and for my high school coach, Andy Stopper.

I also received the "Comeback Player of the Year" award, of which I was proud as well—but I was a little chapped. Comeback? From what? I had never left. I was with the team the whole time. In fact, I felt it was they who did not always welcome me.

Another unexpected honor was making the All-Pro squad, which meant I had another chance to play in the Pro Bowl.

All this attention, perhaps, made me a little arrogant: I was expecting endorsement offers to come rolling in. I had seen it happen to all the white MVPs and All-Pro players; it seemed like there was a white quarterback or lineman hawking a product in a TV commercial every night. Having a contract to endorse tennis shoes or sausages or deodorant, or even pantyhose, meant good money for an athlete in the off season. But no offers from product sponsors, either from Baltimore or national companies, ever came my way. It really made me bitter to be overlooked because I was black. To be proactive, rather than sit around waiting for the phone to ring, I made some inquiries of some local and national firms; but I always received the same response: "Thanks for calling. We'll be in touch."

One of the black athletes you see constantly in TV commercials these days is George Foreman. But back in the '60s it was Cassius Clay who attracted the media and, thus, the public at large. In 1964, I was fortunate to meet both Cassius and the great Jackie Robinson at the same function. It was in Canada, after I won the "Comeback Player of the Year" award and I was attending a banquet to honor a number of Canadian sports stars. When I introduced myself to Jackie, he was as humble as ever and insisted that I take his card and call him if I ever needed anything. I was in awe of him, but he was comfortable to be around. While mingling at the banquet before the festivities got started, we both happened to spot a lonesome figure sitting by himself at one of the tables.

Jackie turned to me and said, "Isn't that Cassius Clay?" We wandered over and, sure enough, it was him. We made the introductions and had a very nice conversation, exchanging pleasantries. Soon the emcee of the event asked everyone to take their seats, and Jackie and I said our goodbyes to Cassius, then we took our seats on the dais. Each of us was introduced to the crowd and instantly the music started blaring and the spotlight snapped onto the curtains of the stage. To deafening applause, Cassius Clay appeared. That shy, quiet, polite young man we had met a few minutes earlier had metamorphosed into someone full of bluster and audacity. Jackie Robinson and I just looked at each other and shook our heads in amazement. Cassius took the whole ballroom by storm.

The point of this anecdote is this: Cassius had the ability to adopt a public persona that belied his gentle inner being. Like flipping a switch, he could instantaneously play the clown, the minstrel, the entertainer; and the white folks—especially those in the media—loved his antics. Unlike Cassius, I wanted to be admired for my athletic talent, which was equal to any white man's. Jackie Robinson felt the same way, I believe: he would never prostitute himself as a minstrel just to earn some publicity or pick up a few endorsements.

All the same, maybe Cassius had the better method of coping as a black in a world run by whites. Every time I had seen Jackie, by contrast, it seemed he had aged another ten years. It was as though the stress of living in two worlds—one black, one white—had begun to show on his body. His mind was always sharp, but the mental toll that he endured in his life took a toll on his appearance. He was, after all, the only person of color in base-ball in his time. By comparison, Bobby Mitchell, Rosie Grier, Herb Adderley, and many other black football players through the years have always known that they shared the field of play with other blacks. But Jackie had no one. Reflecting on the prejudice and unequal treatment that I have gone through—in Baltimore, Dallas, New Orleans, and elsewhere—it bog-gles my mind to think of what Jackie had to endure as the token black in the '40s and '50s.

Jackie once told me as we were discussing the reality that my career was nearing its end that it was not going to get any easier when I retired. All things being equal, he told me, I could very easily rest on the accomplish-ments of my career when I retired, but he told me that it would be a trav-esty. He emphasized that with my notoriety, I was obligated to still knock down doors and open bigots' minds. Man, I had no idea how right he was.

# TWELVE

# A CAREER
# WINDS DOWN

As early as 1965, I could feel my career winding down. Without knowing it at the time, the 1964 season was my one last push for glory. By training camp the following year I could see in the game film preparation in training camp that I was losing a step. I didn't feel threatened by any of the other players I was competing against for playing time, such as Tom Matte and Jimmy Orr. Even at 80 percent of my peak, I could still beat out those guys. But occasionally on the field I found myself thinking more than reacting on impulse, which usually signals the beginning of the end—especially for such a demanding position as tailback.

Although I never did much preseason training up to this point in my career, outside of the comeback preparation for the 1964 season, I made it a point to be in pretty good shape by the time training camp began in 1965. With regard to my place on the team, I wasn't as vocal as in years past. To be honest, I really didn't need to be. Sure, there were still inequalities on our team, and throughout the League, for that matter. But by the mid-1960s, the influx of black players was undeniable. With the percentage of black athletes increasing year by year, things were slowly getting better.

Personally, my relationship with Don Shula would be at an all-time high. With my triumphant return in 1964, I had proved to Coach Shula that I still had something left in the tank. I was still an asset to the team. As a result, I was treated with the type of respect that I deserve as a grizzled veteran. We still had our differences, but the mutual respect we had for each other superseded most disagreements we had.

With high expectations for another great season after the surprise year the team had in 1964, we began the season with a game against the Vikings. It was a viciously balmy day, with the temperature hovering in the mid-90s throughout the contest. Our team was feeling a little lethargic. Falling behind 10-0 early in the game, it took real perseverance for the team to rally and capture a 35-16 victory. I scored one of the five touchdowns for the team. Although Shula was feeling pretty good, since this was the first time we actually opened the season with a victory under his stewardship, the good feelings didn't last long.

We traveled to Milwaukee to take on the Green Bay Packers. On game day there was a stiff wind and 43-degree temperatures. Our problem wasn't the weatherman, though, but the four fumbles we lost. The defense did its part by knocking out Bart Starr at the end of this close game. But out of nowhere, Zeke Bratkowski came off the bench to complete a pass to Max McGee for a Green Bay victory.

A lot has been made of the rivalry between the Colts and the Packers during this time, but these teams had mutual respect for each other, although we felt confident that we could beat anyone who lined up against us. Certainly, the Packers had Nitzschke, Taylor, Starr, Adderley; but they didn't intimidate us. Speaking for myself, I enjoyed every encounter. For a true competitor there is nothing like playing against the best, and Lombardi's Packers never disappointed.

The team would get back on a roll with wins against the Lions and the 49ers in successive weeks, but my body continued to give me problems. Shortly after scoring another touchdown against the 49ers, I was kicked in the head again, the second time in three seasons. As a precaution, the team held me out for the rest of the game. While I watched on the sidelines, we held on to celebrate a 27-24 victory, and even though I didn't finish the game, this was a milestone in my career: I had scored the 100th touchdown of my career.

Detroit visited us at Memorial Stadium next. They came in with an undefeated record, but they didn't leave that way—we beat them 31-7. Until they met us, the Lions had the best defense in the League; but Johnny turned that around by leading scoring drives of 55, 80, 53, and 47 yards. Even in defeat the Lions were as rough as the Packers in those days, and I ended up with the worst of it once again: I had to leave the game for X-rays for cracked ribs.

Due to the cracked ribs I suffered the week before, I wasn't able to compete in our next game with the Redskins. Instead of risking further injury, Coach Shula inserted Matte into the lineup in my place for the 38-7 win against the Redskins, as well as victories against the Rams and the 49ers over the next two weeks. Logging so much bench time really frustrated me. I accepted the fact that my body had a lot of miles on it, but these nagging injuries were starting to get to me. I could feel the grip I had on my starting job slipping away, and I couldn't do anything about it.

With a solid grip on first place, the team doctors cleared the way for me to rejoin the team in time for a match up against the Bears at Memorial Stadium. Like the Packers, I always enjoyed lining up against the Chicago 11. It meant even more since Gale Sayers joined the Bears. Gale and I had socialized at a number of postseason awards ceremonies and soon became fast friends. Considering his short-lived career, the opportunity to share the field of battle with him was always a pleasure. Although I only rushed for 35 yards that day, the team rallied around me and we came out ahead 26-21 with Berry and Mackey both scoring touchdowns despite Johnny being knocked out in the third quarter with a back injury.

With Gary Cuozzo in to replace Johnny while he was recovering from his back injury, I took it upon myself to take more responsibility with the offense so that Gary wouldn't feel so much pressure. I was finally feeling like myself again, which allowed me to contribute a 29-yard touchdown pass reception in a 41-21 victory over Minnesota. Luckily, Gary was a consummate pro and, as a result, we didn't miss a beat with Johnny on the sidelines. Gary quickly settled into his role as the starting quarterback and he kept us in the Western Conference lead by throwing for another four touchdowns. The team was so effective we drove a legend out of the League for good. The loss resulted in Norm Van Brocklin's resignation. "The Flying Dutchmen" would never coach again.

On the heels of the Vikings win, I would put together the best performance of my career against the Eagles. I gained 217 yards of total offense and scored the winning touchdown. Even with this performance, I was eclipsed as the story of the day as Jimmy Orr had to leave the stadium in the third quarter to get X-rays on his leg, but he actually made it back in time to score a touchdown in the fourth quarter. Our eighth straight victory would come in a 34-24 triumph.

The MASH Unit we were running throughout the season didn't slow down for a Thanksgiving matchup against the Lions. Johnny recovered from his back injury and returned to the lineup. Meanwhile, I had contracted a viral infection prior to the game. I was in the starting lineup and was featured on the first drive, picking up 11, 15, and 24 yards on runs from scrimmage, which lead to our first touchdown, but I just couldn't continue. I was replaced once again due to fatigue and took Johnny's place on the sideline watching him throw for three touchdowns—two to Mackey—in the fourth quarter, which resulted in a 24-24 tie. Despite the setback, we still had a share of first-place status, which was our focus this late in the season.

The fatigue I suffered in the Lions game stayed with me over the next two weeks and I wouldn't see much action in losses to the Bears and the Packers. To make matters worse for the team, Johnny was knocked out for good in the Bears game and wouldn't return for the rest of the season. Unfortunately, the Packers would knock Cuozzo out the next week. This left the team with Tom Matte, my replacement at tailback, as our only quarterback.

Before traveling to Los Angeles for a pivotal game to decide the Western Conference, Shula and Kellett went out and signed Ed Brown off the waiver wires for $100 to fill in for Unitas and his own injured replacement, Gary Cuozzo. With Brown and Matte sharing the quarterbacking duties, we felt we could handle the Rams. We did well: I returned to the lineup to score the game's first touchdown with a 28-yard run and Mackey scored a 68-yard touchdown. To force a one-game playoff, though, we needed Green Bay to lose later that day. Luckily the Packers obliged.

You would think that a Packers-Colts one-game playoff to see who would go on to play the championship would be a star-studded affair. This couldn't be further from the truth. Before and throughout the game, we played with our third-string quarterback, the great Bart Starr was knocked out of the game on the first play from scrimmage, and I was rendered useless in only gaining five yards on the ground. The result was an ugly football game won by the Packers as Lou Michaels missed a 47-yard field goal with five minutes left. There was no honor lost in falling to the mighty Packers 13-10, but for the second year in a row we would have to swallow a hard loss and miss the brass ring once again.

The Consolation Bowl against the Cowboys in Miami was a bittersweet victory. The 35-3 victory was a total team effort. I started the scoring with a six-yard run, and Matte added two touchdowns passes. Maybe it was the lopsided, ho-hum victory, or maybe it was just the postseason blues; but all of us felt unfulfilled and wondered what could have been. We should have looked back on the season and been thankful for getting as far as we did without Johnny and Gary, but our standard was excellence, not second place.

Completing my tenth season, in which I had had such high expectations for myself, I had a vague sense that there was something yet unaccomplished. I felt more disappointed than I'd ever been after any season in my career.

~ ~ ~

In April, well before the 1966 season was to begin, I started working out. It was one way to overcome my personal disappointment over the '65 season. I circled September 10, 1966, on my calendar: Opening Day against the Packers. I vowed to myself that I would review where I stood at the end of the season and only then make a decision whether I would continue my career or end it. Although I still loved to compete, I refused to hang on too long. This was the first time that I seriously considered retiring. I knew that I wasn't the player that I used to be physically, but I was so much smarter than the younger players I was competing against that I could outplay many of them with my diminishing physical talent. Nonetheless, I had to take a serious look at my future.

Once again the core of our team consisted of Marchetti, Berry, Parker, Unitas and me. Johnny and I had been together for the better part of a decade. We'd been to the mountaintop twice, and we each knew that time wasn't on our side. At the start of this new season we were anxious to prove we still belonged.

After a strong training camp, we arrived in Milwaukee's County Stadium to play in front of a record crowd of 48,650. It wasn't a good sign that we had a whole off season to prepare for this contest yet we still came out flat. Unitas threw three interceptions, two of which turned into touchdowns for the Pack. Part of the reason Johnny had such a bad day was the fact that we didn't have much of a running game. We were held for less than 100 yards rushing as Green Bay controlled the offensive line. In the end, the Packers dominated 24-3. Unfortunately, this game would be a portent of things to come.

For our next stop on the 1966 tour, we traveled to Minnesota to take out our frustrations on Bud Grant and the Minnesota Vikings. Parker and Orr each got into fights during this contest, one of which led to Orr's being kicked completely out of the game.

But after trailing 16-0 in the first half, the second half was all ours. Johnny managed to set the career mark for touchdown completions with four total, breaking Y.A. Tittle's record of 212.

We would split the next two games, beating the 49ers and losing to the Bears to start the season squared at 2-2. If we wanted any chance to compete for a championship game birth, the team needed to start winning some games in order to keep up with the Packers. We started to click on all cylinders and proceeded to reel off four wins in a row against the Lions, Vikings, Rams, and Redskins. Going into the Falcons game, our record was 6-2, and we were in the thick of things. We were confident that if we could hang around in the standings long enough, we could catch front-running Green Bay. Traveling to Atlanta was just what we needed to tie for the division lead.

A record crowd of 58,850 turned out in Atlanta, even though the Falcons were a pathetic team. Nitschke and Butkus get most of the credit for revolutionizing the middle linebacker position in the 1960s; but for my money, Tommy Nobis, the middle linebacker for the Falcons, was the hardest hitter of them all. Unfortunately, playing for a consistently miserable Atlanta franchise kept him in the shadows for most of his career. To our surprise, the Falcons actually led at half time, but it wouldn't last. Lou Michaels had four field goals, and I scored on a one-yard plunge in the third quarter to take the lead for good in a 19-7 victory.

With a share of first place and riding a five-game winning streak, we looked forward to meeting the Lions—a team that we had already beaten once this year. But it was a different team that we faced this time around: Rookie Karl Sweetan had better control of the team, and the Lions' defense actually showed up. Sweetan teamed up with Gary Yepremian, who had two field goals. Five interceptions by Unitas didn't help at all. I scored the last touchdown of the game on a six-yard run to make it 17-14, but we lost the game and our share of first place by a 20-14 score.

The next contest against the Rams was a low point of the season, for we only gained 33 yards on the ground. Unitas's shoulder, which had been bothering him all year, was still tender from the Lions game; he was unable to start. Unfortunately, Garry Cuozzo was so inept that Unitas had to come in for the third quarter to try to spark the team. Nothing seemed to work, as the offensive line provided little protection. This was a pivotal game in the race for the division lead: the Rams moved to within a half-game of our second-place standing. A touchdown by Matte, with two and a half minutes left, was all we could muster in the 23-7 loss.

With the way this race was shaping up, we needed to win our next three (Chicago, Green Bay, and San Fran) to have a chance at the championship game. We received a boost when Johnny returned to the lineup in the contest against the Bears. This good news helped our offense get untracked. In a tight game, Johnny led us on a last-minute, 68-yard drive to win the game. The clinching touchdown came on a catch by Berry at the 10, as he broke multiple tackles to get into the end zone with 38 seconds left. It was a struggle all day long: Lou Michaels missed a 52-yarder, and two more were blocked. We pulled it out, nonetheless, at 21-16.

The win was energizing, but to stay in the race we needed to beat the Packers at home. It wasn't meant to be, though. An intermittent rain fell throughout the day, as 60,000 spectators watched Lombardi and company win the West in our own backyard. The score was 14-10, with one minute to go, when Unitas fumbled at the 9-yard line. The Packers' Willie Davis recovered the fumble to set up Bart Starr's 80-yard drive for the winning touchdown.

Disappointed by the loss, but thankful that we were nevertheless headed for another Consolation Bowl appearance, we were eager to meet the 49ers—a sure remedy for whatever ailed us. We had beaten San Fran the last eight times we had played them, but we couldn't be too cocky, for our offense was still weak. As an example of the uneven offense we had exhibited all year, Johnny had had only one touchdown pass in the previous five games. However, in this contest Unitas passed for four touchdowns and paced our 30-14 victory. It was our ninth straight win against San Fran.

For the third straight year we missed another chance to compete for the crown. For the second straight year we'd be traveling down to Miami to play for third place in the League. Like a college team that goes to the same Bowl game two straight years, we were unimpressed by our invitation to Miami to play the Eagles, and we played like it. Tom Matte scored the winning touchdown with just 14 seconds left. Jerry Logan, one of our standout defensive backs, had set up the touchdown with an interception of Jack Concannon. Along with our win, at 20-14, the team netted $1,200 each. It wasn't the Super Bowl, but it did provide us a little extra cash to enjoy sunny Miami in the middle of January.

~ ~ ~

As I promised myself at the beginning of the 1966, I took the summer of 1967 to determine whether or not I wanted to go through the grind once again. Sometimes I think that Miami sun got to my head, but after mulling it over for a while, I decided to stick with the Colts for the 1967 season. I had accepted the fact that Shula wanted to use Matte and Orr more extensively, and I didn't mind serving in a more limited capacity. Actually I had become more of a specialist, being counted on whenever we needed to score on short yardage or as another receiver at third and long. In name only I was still the starter, but I had been used less and less as the focal point of the offense, and I was fine with that.

Mentally though, I wasn't ready to give up the game. I didn't have any idea what I wanted to do after football, and I wasn't ready to find out. Then, too, the salaries were starting to increase pretty dramatically in the late 1960s; after playing for very small wages at the start my career, I had grown fond of the salary increases over the years. As an aging but relatively healthy running back, I wasn't getting Unitas or Namath-type money; but it definitely provided a very comfortable lifestyle that my family and I were accustomed to. So, yes, I would have a go at it for another year.

The important thing was that we were still a very good team. To complement our traditional core of players, Matte had established himself as jack of all trades, able to fill in at just about any skill position when needed. Mackey had established himself as the best tight end in the League—on his way to becoming the greatest tight end to play the game, in fact. For decades, Mike Ditka was put on that pedestal, but even he will tell you that John Mackey was better than them all. In terms of blocking, he had as good a technique as any offensive lineman. He had the hands and the speed of a wide out and the body of a linebacker. He was the total package.

Opening the 1967 season against the Falcons should have been an easy start, but the game wasn't a cakewalk as it had been in previous seasons. Unitas had 401 yards passing, but with each team scoring on an interception, it was a close battle—until the offense exploded for 21 points, midway through the second quarter to secure a 38-31 victory.

Then in Philly, Unitas topped the 30,000 mark in career passing yards with two touchdown passes to Willie Richardson. I chipped in a three-yard touchdown of my own to contribute to the 38-6 victory.

We enjoyed our third straight victory when we played San Francisco next. Unitas had two touchdowns and then turned the reins of the team over to rookie Jim Ward. Ward threw a touchdown to future Buccaneers head coach, Ray Perkins, who replaced an injured Ray Berry. Matte scored two touchdowns and I chipped in a three-yard run for a third touchdown on the ground.

With the team on a roll that we would enjoy all year, we then traveled to Chicago. Following the pattern of a new standout player featured in every game, one of our star rookies from Michigan, Rick Volk, took an interception back for 94 yards and a touchdown—the longest TD run in team history. That interception of Volk's was also important because it killed a 74-yard drive by Rudy Bukich. It was a sloppy passing game all around, as each team had three interceptions in the first half alone. But beating the Bears 24-3 was a key victory, it put us at 4-0.

For readers who don't remember how business was done before today's generation of prima donna athletes, it is interesting to note that Johnny played all four of these games without a contract. Just prior to the next game, against the Rams, Johnny signed a three-year pact. In today's game a player wouldn't even report to training camp without a contract, much less play four games into the season without anything on paper. This spoke to two points. First, it showed the amount of respect Johnny had for the Colts and Carroll Rosenbloom. He knew that a handshake was enough. Even if he was hurt in those first few games, it was understood that he would be taken care of. It also spoke to the type of man Johnny was. He knew that he had made his money in this League so that he would have a secure future. Without a financial burden hanging over his head, he was playing purely for the love of the game. It was truly an innocent and unique time in sports history that is long gone.

With an undefeated start under our belt, the next two games were very bizarre, because they each ended in a tie. First the Rams came to visit and battled us to a deadlock. Unitas found himself in a duel with the up-and-coming Roman Gabriel. I put the team ahead with a second-quarter, three-yard run, following a 59-yard reception by Alex Hawkins. Then when we were leading 24-17, an interception of Johnny by Maxie Baughan at our 24-yard line led to the tying touchdown.

The second consecutive tie occurred in Minnesota. It was Mackey who helped Johnny tie the game on a three-yard pass in the fourth quarter. Johnny also broke another one of Y.A. Tittle's records, in this game—the career pass-completion record.

From Minnesota our unbeaten team traveled to Washington to take on the Redskins for a 17-13 victory. In the fourth quarter, the team drove 65 yards to set Lou Michaels up for the kick that would be the clinching field goal. We had been trailing 13-7 after a Gene Mingo field goal, but Matte scored on a seven-yard romp to set up the Michaels kick. For the second week in a row Johnny came up against a fantastic quarterback; this time it was Sonny Jurgenson, who was actually the second best quarterback, statistically, behind Johnny. It didn't matter, though, as Johnny was still the best, and he continued to show it.

As always, we looked forward to playing our rivals from Green Bay. In a vicious contest, our defense knocked Jim Grabowski and Elijah Pitts out of the game in the first quarter. Losing 10-0 with six minutes remaining, Alex Hawkins and Willie Richardson teamed up to score the winning touchdowns. On Hawkins's score, our very first of the game, Michaels missed the point-after because of a poor hold by Rick Volk. We were then forced to drive the field once more for the winning score. Michaels executed a perfect on-side kick, which Volk recovered. Stealing a 13-10 victory was sweet. It not only allowed us to stay in first place, but we broke the pattern of losing to the Packers as well.

The season was shaping into a showdown with the Rams in Los Angeles at the end of the season. They were having a fantastic season as well with a record that mirrored ours. We still controlled our own destiny. If we were to win out we would have an excellent chance of finally reaching the coveted championship game we had missed out on the last three years.

The way our team was playing, running the table was very easy. We started by thrashing the Falcons 49-7 in Atlanta. We followed that up with another blowout against the Lions in Memorial Stadium.

In San Francisco, Lou Michaels had four field goals against the 49ers, and Lenny Lyles scored a touchdown on an interception off of Steve Spurrier, the rookie from Florida and winner of the Heisman Trophy the previous year. Although Unitas threw a pick to start the game, which resulted in a 49ers field goal, Johnny led the team on three scoring drives to put the game out of reach at 26-9.

Then, playing Tom Landry's Cowboys at Memorial Stadium, I scored what would be my last career touchdown on the game-winning drive of the last 90 seconds. My touchdown capped off a 50-yard drive after two fourth-quarter field goals by Michaels. Although Johnny threw another three interceptions, the team rallied for a victory. The final score was 23-17.

By now the Rams had one loss and we were in the driver's seat. If we won the next game, against the Saints, we would set up a showdown with the Rams, vying for the Coastal Division crown. As we lined up against New Orleans on our home turf, it was clear that we were looking past the pathetic Saints, for we played a very mediocre game. Johnny completed only ten passes for 148 yards, and he didn't complete a single touchdown pass for the second time this season. Sure of our win, we were busy congratulating ourselves even before the 30-10 final score on being the first team since the 1934 Bears to go 13 games without a loss.

With our destiny in our own hands, we needed only to beat the Rams to clinch a berth in the new playoff system that the League had devised. We traveled to Los Angeles for the Division showdown. Once again, it wasn't meant to be. Roman Gabriel dominated the Rams' action with a three-touchdown performance. The Rams also racked up seven sacks. We did lead the game briefly in the first half, 7-3, with a 12-yard score from Johnny to Willie Richardson. But then after Lou Michaels missed a 37-yarder, Gabriel threw his 80-yard bomb, and that was it for our team.

Remarkably, we would end the season 10-1-2, with the same record as the Rams, but would lose the tiebreaker due to our dismal performance in the season finale. For the third straight year, we had competed at the highest levels in the NFL, only to go home without a shot at the big game. To go the whole season without a loss and then misstep against the Rams was unbearably disappointing.

All things being equal, the taste of coming so close once again would've driven me to prepare for another run at the title. But by the final whistle of the 1967 season, I was 34 years old, which is ancient in football years. Maybe it was time to quit, to hang up the old blue jersey, and to take this old, tired Colt out to pasture.

# THE HOPE OF A NEW DAY

Throughout the 1967 campaign, I was not unaware that my playing time was being diminished. We had won a lot of ball games under Shula's direction, so that was all that mattered. Although the team couldn't get over the championship hump in the last three years, I was having fun playing in the twilight of my career. I wasn't looked upon to carry the running game anymore, and I wasn't concerned about making my mark on the team or in the league. Furthermore, by the late 1960s, the environment that black ballplayers competed in was gradually becoming more comfortable. Not perfect by any means, it was not as bad as it had been a decade earlier. As a result, I was playing out my career and earning more money than I ever had up to that point, in relative peace. At the end of the 1967, I was definitely planning on coming back for the 1968 season.

In the off season, though, there were moments when I wondered if the team wanted me back. Shula continued to make it public that he wanted to give Matte and Orr more time on the field. He stressed how important it was for the team to get younger and quicker. I would turn 35 years old during the 1968 season, so I didn't have to be told who Shula was referring to with these comments—it definitely wasn't Berry or Unitas. I knew I had had a good run in the league. I was established in the community and wouldn't play anywhere else. I also didn't want to go through the embarrassment of being cut from the team in the interest of "getting younger." So instead of waiting to be cut during training camp or, even worse, not even being invited to camp, I decided to call it a career in April of 1968.

My decision was made easier by the fact the national TV network, CBS, had asked me to consider joining their sports broadcasting team for the 1968 football season. I was thrilled! I thought this would be a perfect "next step" in my career. It was an opportunity to stay involved in the game that I loved and to be a part of something special.

I accepted CBS's offer even though I had never worked in television before. Over the years of my pro career, however, I had done countless television and radio interviews, and I had even given a weekday sports report for a local radio station. Before that I had hosted a weekly jazz variety show at another local radio station, so I knew I could do this job for CBS; and what was more exciting was the fact that I would be a groundbreaker. Only once before had CBS employed a black man in the booth, either as talent or as anchor. Here was an opportunity to represent my race in an uncharted venue, and to represent us as successful, articulate, and full of potential. I could be a role model for black youth who wanted to play sports by reaching them through my commentary of televised games. If I did succeed at this job, it would be another small but important barrier broken for black America.

I had always respected many of the CBS broadcasters who had worked games throughout my career. Frank Gifford and Tom Brookshire, for example, were great players, interesting gentlemen, and true professionals. And who didn't like the straightforwardness of Jack Buck? The CBS commentators had always exhibited class and professionalism; it was "The Tiffany Network," after all. Being asked to join the broadcasting team was an honor and a privilege.

Joining CBS meant that 1968 was the beginning of the rest of my life. Thinking of retirement in these terms made it easier for me to acknowledge that Lenny Moore, professional football player, was no more. Football was all I had known since junior high school and, as most ex-ballplayers would attest, retirement was always a tough adjustment. When you've lived a very regimented way of life for 20 years, it becomes a habit—or, more accurately, it becomes imbedded into your psyche. Practicing at the same time every day, getting butterflies when you hear the national anthem, feeling the adrenaline when you line up for the first play from scrimmage, releasing your pent-up energy and aggressions on the field, chiding yourself for your performance every week, and getting up on Monday morning to do it all over again—this is the football life. I wouldn't have traded the experience for anything in the world, but I knew that a slower paced, "retirement" lifestyle would be extremely difficult for me. The job at CBS would mean trading in my jersey for a suit and tie, and observing football games from above, rather than down on the field; but otherwise it would mean following the same season schedule, traveling to the same towns, and keeping track of players' stats and win-loss records. If this was retirement, I thought, let the games begin!

CBS didn't train me in any way for my new position as sportscaster. I don't know if that was the standard policy or not; but to be honest, I didn't care. I had disclosed my brushes with a career in the broadcast field with those two radio gigs, so I assumed they thought I was comfortable enough in front of the microphone. Nonetheless, I had enough faith and confidence in myself to know that I could play without a game plan. Lord knows I've lived through worse things than being shoved onto the frontlines without benefit of a huddle. I did do some sound tests for the producers that spring (I found out later that Rosey Grier was in town to do the same tests in competition against me); so apparently I had impressed the producers enough to secure the offer. All I had to do was demonstrate my abilities.

Just before the beginning of the 1968 NFL season, all of the commentators, producers, and directors were asked to gather at CBS headquarters in New York to receive our final assignments. Mostly it was a chance for the guys to sit around and talk shop and to reminisce about great games in the past. To my great surprise and satisfaction, I learned at this meeting that Frank Gifford and I had been assigned a dual slot together. I was thrilled to be paired with Frank; and I would soon find out that he would be a tremendous reservoir of strength and reassurance for a rookie sportscaster.

As the meeting was about to adjourn, Bill Fitts, the head of production for CBS Sports, and the moderator for the meeting, gave us his final words of encouragement. He stated that it was a CBS tradition to end these meetings on a light note, and he asked if anyone had a funny joke or comment he would like to share. Everyone looked at each other for a short moment, and then George Connor, the great defensive lineman from the Bears, proceeded to tell what he thought was a hilarious "nigger joke."

A familiar, fiery acid began to work its slow burn throughout my body. It was a feeling that soured my stomach, in such moments—ever since that assembly in junior high school, where the students had sung "Swanee River." I had only two thoughts when George began his joke on this evening: "I must keep my composure," and "Goddammit, here we go again!"

At the conclusion of George's joke, almost everyone in the room chuckled, some nervously, some bawdily. Seeing that I was the only black man in the room, the majority of eyes tried to avoid staring at me sitting in the back. I'd like to say I don't know how I kept my composure, but unfortunately, I do. I learned the trick after years of trying to believe that I lived a life of equality in a white man's world, even though I was constantly reminded that it just wasn't the case. I had mastered the art of always keeping myself in check, no matter how intense the sting might be.

Bill Fitts adjourned the meeting with a big grin on his face, and my peers started to leave the room, glancing surreptitiously in my direction. I quietly walked out as well, trying to blend into the group, but feeling separate, like an animal on display at the zoo. I stood outside the door for a few moments, waiting for George to leave. One hundred sets of eyes were trained on me, as the people walked by, wondering what I'd do. I tried not to make eye contact with anyone; the only person I wanted to speak to was George Connor.

Finally he exited, chatting with a couple other colleagues who, as soon as they saw me, trained their eyes on the carpeting of the hall.

"George, man, can I have a word with you?" I said.

"Sure," George replied, ever the confident Monster of the Midway, who used to terrify offensive linemen and quarterbacks alike, during his heyday in Chicago during the 1940s and 1950s.

I would not be intimidated. "Man, I feel I need to say something to you about your joke in there." The pit of my stomach tightened, just thinking about that "N" word he had used—a word that sparks years of painful memories for me. I steeled myself to say what I had to say to the man: "I don't know who else you say that stuff around, but I would appreciate it if you wouldn't say that stuff in my presence again. Everything's cool; I don't have any hard feelings. As far as I'm concerned, this situation is over. I just felt I needed to say something to you."

At that point, George, who seemed a little off balance from my directness, attempted a feeble retort; but I just turned and walked away. Not bothering to wait for the elevator, I found the stairs and sprinted down them as quickly as possible.

I had told George the situation was over but, in reality, I still needed to chill out. I retreated to my hotel room and just sat there at the end of my bed, for what seemed like an eternity but was probably more like an hour. I replayed our brief conversation, over and over in my head, wondering if I had made a mistake. Since I was in New York alone, with my family still in Baltimore, and had no one to vent to but myself, I sat in my room, gathering my thoughts.

There was to be a cocktail party that evening, hosted by American Express and attended only by those in connection with the football broadcasts. I knew that again I would be the only black person in attendance. By no means did I want to attend, but I felt I had to. If I expected the CBS job to put me in a position where I could change minds and set precedents, then I needed to begin here and now. If I could open one mind about black people, our potential and our equality, now or in the booth, it would be well worth it. It was imperative that I show my colleagues that I was a man who could persevere. Man, I'd been persevering—surviving—my whole life.

As I had done throughout my career when encountered by situations like these, I thought of Jackie Robinson. He had not had anyone to vent to, either; no one to give him the strength to get through a situation like this. How did he manage? Yes, it hurts deeply, I could almost hear him say. But it is amazing how God can calm you when you ask Him for help.

In time I slowly worked the fire and acid out of my body. It was a burn that never seemed to leave my body in the same shape it was before, but my soul always seemed to escape the fire after a while. It used to be worse; it would sometimes take days to bring the fire under control, before I returned to what I considered normal. But on this night, thinking of Jackie Robinson helped me realize that George's joke wasn't the worst sort of prejudice that I'd encountered in the last few years. It had only seemed to sting more painfully, perhaps because I had my guard down, due to the excitement of my new job. You can just never get comfortable, I told myself. NEVER.

I prepared myself for the cocktail party as though I were dressing for a championship game. As I freshened up, I literally was putting my game face on, as I had done before all of my gridiron battles. I didn't know what I'd encounter at the party, but I knew I had to be ready for anything. Finally I felt I was ready to take the field. Shirt and tie: neat. Confidence level: high. Readiness to tackle the world: check.

Unfortunately, as I walked into the party, I could literally feel the atmosphere change. I shook some hands, greeted some friends, and made a beeline to the bar. As much as I wanted a shot of J&B, I knew that was what everyone expected. I had shown my composure up to this point; the hell if

I was going to blow it now. I ordered a light beer and proceeded to go through the motions of social etiquette. I wasn't standoffish, but I didn't dive into any conversations. I just wanted to make a statement, in my own subtle way—I was here to stay. No mere words were strong enough to affect me now or ever.

About an hour into the party, Paul Christman called me over to his table. I had always liked Paul, even though I didn't know him well personally. I liked him as a ballplayer, a broadcaster, and, more importantly, as a man. He was a class act. You always knew where you stood with Paul. He didn't waste time making small talk, either to be polite or to be "seen." With Paul, you got what you saw. He pulled no punches, and I respected that.

I made my way over to his table and greeted him. Paul soon took control of the conversation and said solemnly, "Lenny, I always respected you as a ballplayer. But the way you handled yourself in that meeting today showed me you're an even greater man. I really have a lot of respect for you."

Let me tell you, I was floored. For Paul to show his respect for me in public, amongst his peers and close friends, was overwhelming. To this day, his remarks give me strength. I remember that moment as vividly as any other in my life, and I am eternally grateful to Paul for reaffirming my belief that there are people in this world who care about others and who want to see our society improve. The process may be slow, and it may be painful, but we must always move forward.

I walked tall for the rest of the evening. I started to mingle some more—still reserved, still stung by George's callous joke—but much more at peace. Then the inevitable happened. George asked me over to his table. It was no surprise to me that it took a few drinks for George in order for this invitation to be offered. I took a deep breath and walked over. After some uncomfortable small talk, he started to apologize; but I could tell it was forced, as though he were just going through the motions. To be honest, I can't even remember what he said.

When he was finished talking, I reassured him that everything was cool and that the situation was over in my eyes. I excused myself from his table, left the party, and returned to my room for the night. I remember just shaking my head, as I do today, whenever I recall the incident. I wonder if George's brand of racism will ever run dry.

~ ~ ~

My first game as CBS commentator placed me in Dallas, which was the site of many racist incidents that I had experienced in the past. It was a tough town for blacks when I was at Penn State playing against Texas Christian, and it was still a tough town for blacks when I was here as a Colt, playing the Giants, in the 1959 exhibition game. There was a smell to the field in Dallas that still lingers with me even now, but I could sense it even more strongly on this day, the first time I'd been to the park since my retirement.

That afternoon in September 1968 was hot and bright. I came to the ballpark in a suit, but I removed my jacket as soon as possible. What I really wished that morning was that I could suit up and join the fray. I guess that goes back to the game's addictive qualities—it was a high that I was still attracted to. To this day, I feel a familiar rush of adrenaline every Sunday.

As I have said, I was given no training for my new position, so I did as much as I could on my own to prepare for the game. I made sure I knew the names and stats of every player and coach for both teams. I researched for days, leaving no stone unturned, for I was facing baptism by fire. Frank Gifford met me in the booth about two hours before game time. He would have had to be a blind man not to see the beads of sweat racing down my cheeks. I tried to play it off as a result of the heat, but Frank was dry as a bone. Tony Verna, the director of the day's telecast, joined us soon and walked us through the equipment, the cues, the cameras, and the general layout of the booth. I had experienced many cram sessions during my days at Penn State, but this was preparation for a test that would be witnessed by millions of people throughout the southeast United States.

After the debriefing was finished, I looked over my notes a few more times, repeating things to myself, trying to force the information to stick. There was so little time left before the start of the broadcast!

I was off in my own world of broadcasting minutiae when Frank put his hand on my shoulder and said, "Don't worry, Lenny, you'll be great. Just follow my lead. When I want you to say something—to make a comment or provide an observation—I'll tap your hand. That's all you have to remember. Past that, just pay attention to the game and point out whatever comes naturally to you."

His reassurance was helpful, but as the seconds ticked by my anxiety grew.

Finally it was game time. It was now or never. I put on my blazer, took a deep breath, scanned the crowd, heard their buzz, took the microphone, found my place next to Frank, looked at the camera, and was ready to go. Frank handled the lead in, welcoming the national television audience, making a witty comment about the sweltering heat. Then he introduced me. I looked into the camera, opened my mouth to speak—and nothing came out! I was mute in front of millions of people for what seemed like an eternity. And I couldn't do anything about it!

Frank, recognizing my paralysis, picked up the slack, made another joke, and loosened me up. Instantly, my voice came back and I was on my way.

Things improved drastically after that first game. By my fourth broadcast I felt like a four-year veteran. By midseason, it had become tradition with the broadcast crew to hang out in my room the night before the telecast to trade notes. I truly felt no one ever prepared better for the telecast than I did. Being newly retired, I had easy access to the coaches and the players and thereby gained tremendous insight. I also felt I was gaining the respect of my colleagues as a broadcaster, which was a source of great satisfaction to me.

All too soon the season was over. I wrapped up the last telecast with Frank and made my way home with the glowing feeling that results from a job done well. Tony Verna, the director who was a tremendous help getting through that first season, caught up with me shortly after our last broadcast and congratulated me on a great season. He said he'd witnessed the typical growing pains that all new commentators experience, but he added that by the end of the season, he felt there were few better. As we parted, he said he looked forward to working with me next season.

In the summer of 1969, I was a retired footballer, a "seasoned" broadcaster, and a family man. It had been a year of major transitions—not only for me but also for my family. By now, my wife Frankie and I had four children: Leslie was born in 1956; Carol was born in 1958; Toni was born in 1962; and Terri came along in 1965. In truth, though, if it weren't for those wonderful children, the apples of my eye, my marriage wouldn't have lasted as long as it did. The relationship between Frankie and me had been off and on pretty much from Day One. We had married in such a whirlwind manner—we were both too young and too naïve. Throughout our 13 years of marriage, each time that we had just about enough of each other, another child would come along. But by the time I retired from football, then took the position at CBS, I really was hopeful that there would be a turnaround for my marriage. Since I was only broadcasting and not actually playing so many games, I wasn't spending inordinate amounts of time at training camp, in practice, or on the road. I had much more time now to spend with my family and I vowed that I would work hard to strengthen our family unit and make up for lost time.

By the time I retired, all six of us were living in a starter home on Yosemite Avenue in Baltimore. Once my job with CBS was secure, in an attempt to signify new beginnings and to provide more room for the family, I asked Frankie if she would like to move into a larger house. I had my eye on a home being sold by the former mayor of Baltimore: it was a palatial house, an estate, really, that was similar to those I used to envy as I walked around Westminster during my training camp days. I really thought this would be a great place for the family to start anew. Everyone would have more space, more memories to build, more happiness in a new neighborhood that was stately, established, and a bit elite. Most of all, I hoped this house would help me repair old wounds and save my marriage.

Eager to make it work, Frankie agreed. That summer, the six of us moved into the beautiful house on Talbot Road.

In August, Frank Gifford called me and we chatted about our families, the new home, and the like. Then he asked why I wasn't at the CBS pre-production meeting for the upcoming season.

I was shocked! No one from CBS had contacted me all summer. In my preoccupation with moving into a new home and rededicating my life as a family man, I didn't really give much thought to CBS. I had expected that they would call or send a note to tell me where I should be and when to begin the new season's broadcasting. But the recollections that came to mind as I talked with Frank confirmed that there was nothing. They hadn't fired me, that much I knew—but I realized that they had never officially asked me back, either. Frank recommended that I call Bill Fitts as soon as possible to get to the bottom of this. I took the extra step and immediately booked a train to New York: I wanted to talk to Mr. Fitts face to face.

Soon I was on the train to New York, thinking of the things I would say to Bill Fitts. I knew I had done a good job the previous season, because the other broadcasters and producers I worked with had told me so. If CBS didn't want me back, fine. All I wanted was confirmation one way or the other.

I checked into the New York Hilton, right across the street from CBS headquarters. As I stepped off the elevator, walking toward Bill's office, I put a big smile on my face and greeted his secretary. Even as I spoke with her, I could see Bill talking with someone on the phone, in his office behind the secretary's desk. I politely asked to speak with Bill, and to my utter surprise the secretary said, "Mr. Fitts is not in right now."

"What do you mean he's not in right now? I can see him in his office right behind you!"

She replied coolly, "I'm sorry, Mr. Fitts is not in right now."

At that point, I knew they were playing games with me, which stoked my confusion and anger even further.

"Would you please tell Mr. Fitts that I am staying at the Hilton across the street and that I would like to see him as soon as possible?" I gave her my room number and said I'd be waiting for his call.

When I got back to my room, I turned on the television, took off my coat, loosened my tie, made myself comfortable on the bed and began to wait—and wait. As I sat there, it felt like déjà vu. Just 12 months earlier I had sat on the edge of my bed seething from Connor's off-color remark. Remarkably here I was again. That afternoon and throughout the night, I didn't leave my room for fear of missing Bill's call. But it never came.

That slow burn was starting to build up again in the pit of my stomach. I felt betrayed and wondered if CBS had been playing games with me during that entire season. When had they known that they wouldn't be hiring me for a second season—after the first game or two? At the end of the season? Why had they let me spend the summer thinking I would still have a job in the fall? Why?

I felt I knew why. Because I had stood up for myself after that meeting at the start of last season, when George Connor told his "nigger joke." CBS was probably skittish all season long, worried that I might use the broadcasting booth to comment on racial injustices or civil rights or who knew what. They must have been terrified about what might come out of my mouth next. Because my performance in the booth was solid and professional they couldn't fire me; but they wouldn't rehire me for fear that, in another season or two, I might disgrace the network in some way.

It's a hazard of blackness that paranoia emerges, every now and then, due to the lies and backstabbing and injustices that have assaulted you all your life. You get fooled or shamed by whites a few hundred times, and then you start to suspect everyone of underhanded dealings. Is it paranoia, or just becoming wise to the schemes of those in power positions?

I mulled all this over in my room that night and, still not wanting to believe I had been passed over for another season at CBS, I decided to give Bill Fitts the benefit of the doubt. The next day I made my way to Bill's office again. His secretary and I had the same exchange as the day before. I again told her where I was staying and said that I'd like to see Mr. Fitts as soon as possible.

It did not happen. I spent another entire day waiting for a call that would never come.

With a bigger home—and a bigger mortgage—waiting for me in Baltimore, I literally couldn't afford to play the waiting game with Bill any longer, so I phoned his secretary, telling her that I was going back to Baltimore, and I asked if she could have Mr. Fitts call me there.

The 1969 NFL season started without a word from Bill or anyone at CBS. I was never officially given a reason why I wasn't asked back. I had sealed my broadcast fate because I had enough self-respect to stand up for myself. It didn't matter that I had done my job well and had represented CBS with dignity and loyalty; this was what I got in return—personal snubs and unemployment.

It hurt because I had been so cautious about making a mistake. For instance, as part of the team, I had an expense account that I could have used to take television people out and entertain them as the crew traveled to a different city every week. In fact, I was encouraged to do this schmoozing as part of my job. But "entertaining," meant alcohol, and for me alcohol was strictly off limits. I didn't want to get in trouble while I was representing CBS. I didn't want to do something stupid for which I might be fired.

I spent weeks mentally rehashing other things that happened, assessing my behavior of that previous season, searching for something that might have caused a premature ending to my broadcasting career. There was nothing. I'd had a good relationship with everyone in our small broadcast/production group. It didn't make any sense to me. I felt that I should have been asked back to CBS to continue to develop my talent as a broadcaster. I had enough pride and drive to really work hard and learn about the intricacies of broadcasting. From there, who knows where my life could have gone?

But it was obvious that I would get no answers from Bill Fitts anytime soon, so I decided to take matters into my own hands. I needed a job badly, and I really enjoyed the broadcast career path that I had started. I made appointments with every major advertising and marketing firm in New York, hoping to get some work in product endorsements, or hook on with another network in a broadcasting capacity. Then I took the train back to New York, staying in the same Hilton across the street from the CBS offices.

Subconsciously I was probably hoping to run into Bill and have him say it was all just a big mistake, but that never happened.

I was not accustomed to searching for employment in the "real world" beyond college recruiters and League coaches. So I went everywhere, trying to meet as many people as possible. At least the CBS job had put me in contact with some powerful people, and I had ideas about where to go looking for work. I dropped off as many resumes as I possibly could. Considering the success I had had last football season, I thought it would be a good idea to strike while the iron was hot. I didn't want to take the chance that people would forget my popularity with football fans. I visited all of the powerful talent agencies in New York: Young and Rubicom, J. Walter Thompson, Benton and Bowles, and Ted Bates & Co.. My efforts weren't totally fruitless. I actually landed a small role in a television commercial thanks to talent agent Dominic Sayer; but I found nothing that resulted in long-term employment.

The only one of my peers to call and offer help during this period was Howard Cosell. Traveling in the same circles for a year, he found out through Frank Gifford that I was unemployed. Howard called me at my home and offered to make some calls and line something up for me. He asked when I was planning to move up to New York, and I told him I wasn't.

"That would be a major negative," said Howard. "When something comes up, you'll have to move quickly. Being in Baltimore just won't cut it."

I told him that I was desperately trying to keep my family life together, and I just couldn't move to New York. Though Howard kept trying to find me a job, nothing ever came of his efforts. But I never forgot his sentiment. He had a lightning-rod personality, but I never found any fault with him. I appreciated his concern.

I made one last trip to New York and visited Ted Bates and Company. As I dropped off my resume, the president of the company asked that I meet with him. He said that he had heard that I was going from agency to agency looking for work to no avail.

"I admire your persistence," he said, "but you are at a disadvantage." He then asked me if I'd seen the five people out in the lobby with their suitcases. I said I had.

"Those are full-time actors who have vast experience, theatrical training, and a prepared presentation. We turn a dozen of these people away each day. I appreciate your football career, but in this field it just doesn't mean much."

He watched me carefully for my reaction to what he was trying to tell me. As though he assumed he wasn't getting his message across to me, he leaned forward and said, "It just isn't the right time for blacks to be in television."

In the late '60s, agencies had been slowly introducing black personalities into nationwide television series. Diahann Carroll, Leslie Uggams, Redd Fox, Bill Cosby, and a few others were beginning to have a following; but it wouldn't be until the mid-'70s that blacks would find a permanent place on TV. It was the same for the movies; the seventies would feature what would come to be known as "blaxploitation" films, where B-level black actors had roles with adventure and heroism, rather than the standard "mammy" and servant roles that were so common until then. Sidney Poitier flourished in this era and really broke down barriers for blacks. But in 1969, according to this agency man, nothing was going to come of my efforts.

"I just don't want to see you wasting your money," he said.

At that point in time, I should've been continuing a new and exciting phase of my life. Unfortunately, it seemed my color presented a roadblock that was insurmountable. Downtrodden, I thanked this kind man for his time and took the train home to Baltimore. I blankly stared out the window on the long ride home, wondering what I was going to do. I had a huge new mortgage, a family life that was falling apart, a lot of bills, and no steady income. I was truly scared for the first time in my life and I had no answers.

All things being equal, losing out on the CBS job had thrown my life into a tailspin, and it would be a long while before I would recover.

# FOURTEEN

# A LIFE DERAILED

When Frankie and I were married, she gave up her job as a teacher to stay home and be a full-time housewife and mother. By the time our third child, Toni, came along, it was clear that Frankie needed help with the kids and the house. Since I was not at home very much in those days, I agreed to have a cleaning lady come to the house three days a week. That is how we found Lucy, a wonderful elderly woman who would eventually become part of the family. The kids loved her. It was great to have someone so loyal and dedicated helping Frankie and me raise our children.

Soon after I realized I had lost the position with CBS, Frankie told me that she wanted, in addition to Lucy, a live-in nanny to help care for the children. We had four kids now, but being suddenly unemployed, I was not sure how we could continue to pay Lucy, much less hire a second person. We could barely afford to keep the house and keep all six of us fed and clothed. How could we support a live-in nanny? Our new home was certainly bigger than our last, but it was not Buckingham Palace by any means.

I told Frankie that there was no way we could hire a nanny. She not only insisted that we could, and would, have one—she had already hired one from Jamaica. In fact, the woman was waiting at the airport to be picked up! I blew through the roof. My wife and I had many arguments over the years, with each of us sharing the blame for instigating them, but this was more than I could handle. I felt as though Frankie had lost touch with reality. She knew my job status, she knew how overextended we were. For her to not only insist on having a full-time nanny, but to promise this woman full-time employment and have her fly from another country to start working here without telling me shattered any thread of our relationship that might have remained. I told Frankie that if she went to the airport to pick up this woman, I wouldn't be there when she got back. Without saying a word, she gathered up the kids and hopped in the car, and sped off to the airport. I went to the bedroom, packed a suitcase, and left, never to return to the grand house on Talbot Street as the husband of Mrs. Frankie Moore.

I didn't have any clue about where I would go. Once I got in my car and thought about my options, I realized there was just one place to be: the club I owned and operated, Club 24, my home away from home.

In the early 1960s, Carroll Rosenbloom had come to me and posed the question, "If you were going to open a business, what type of business would it be?" I knew what he was getting at. Carroll had helped other Colts players, like Gino Marchetti and Alan Ameche, open hamburger restaurants around Baltimore. Carroll had also helped Unitas open up a string of bowling alleys, and Parker would eventually run a very successful liquor store—all thanks to Caroll Rosenbloom. In a period of time when athletes were not superstars and teams didn't use their star players for branding opportunities outside of the realm of football, Carroll was a pioneer. He recognized how fleeting success could be in such a brutal sport, and he always encouraged us to have outside interests and sources of income that we could fall back on when we retired. It also allowed the team to have another outlet for visibility. It was a win-win. Being the astute businessman that he was, he also appreciated that each of the stars on the Colts team was a magnetic figure in the community. By attaching the player's name to a restaurant, Carroll was betting that the star power would draw in and establish a consistent customer base. It was a very simple marketing plan—and it worked.

So Carroll offered to help me open a bowling alley. It was going to be at the Mondawmin Shopping Center, northwest of Baltimore. This site was perfect, located in a growing community that was ripe for a family-oriented business like a bowling alley. But after thinking further about what kind of business I wanted, I decided to do something that would parlay my interest in jazz. I thought back to those nights I spent on Pennsylvania avenue, hopping from club to club to see the legends of jazz come through town. I had built some strong relationships in those days, with the likes of Cannonball Adderley, Miles Davis, and Jimmy Smith—great jazz musicians, all. I pitched my idea for what would be called "Club 24" to Carroll, and he loved it. We soon started searching for a location and found the perfect site just off Gwynn Oak Avenue, at the upper end of Pennsylvania Avenue, which was still a happening hotbed of jazz activity. Carroll agreed to put down the seed money to purchase an existing establishment that was going out of business.

Club 24 took off quickly. Just about every night of the week there was either a local act on stage or a national name who stopped by to do a set while breezing through town. It was a magical place, and I loved being a part of it. One thing that Carroll and I did, though, was overestimate my business acumen. I just didn't have the patience to be at the bar, accounting for every pretzel, beer, and penny that changed hands. My personality is too frenetic for that. I didn't care if a waitress wanted a soda or a bartender wanted to grab a handful of nuts. It just wasn't that important to me. I soon learned that it should have been. What I found out is that if you try hard enough, chips, peanuts, popcorn, and soda can be the equivalent of three square meals. Some of the bartenders and waitresses were taking advantage of the honor system I had in place, and profits of the Club were sinking.

I also learned that while I was so involved in playing pro football, I couldn't run the day-to-day operations of a club even if I wanted to. I had to hire someone to manage the club and account for the restaurant income and expenses and make sure that it operated smoothly and at a profit. I soon learned that finding someone trustworthy who was capable of all that was easier said than done. At first I used one manager to oversee everything; but with only one person in charge of the books, money seemed to disappear. So I went with a day manager and a night manager, attempting to institute some type of checks and balances system; but that didn't work out, either. The owner of a restaurant literally needs to be present 18 hours a day to be aware of every transaction and to monitor every pour, or the owner needs someone he can trust implicitly. Unfortunately, I couldn't be there all day every day, and I never found someone who could be my right-hand man. Without my consistent attention, the business suffered. It was just too much for me at the time.

With the demise of my marriage, though, and being unemployed anyway, I decided that this was an opportunity to spend more time at the club. I would monitor things and maybe actually start making a profit. I got an apartment nearby and launched into what I thought would be the perfect profession. I tried to take a string of negatives and turn it into a positive, but it just wasn't in the cards.

My master plan didn't last long. My personality just couldn't bear being cooped up in the club 24/7. By 1970, I was intent on finding another stream of income to support my kids and to pay alimony to my wife. I looked for jobs all around town, and I sent letters to everyone I could imagine: people I had met through the Colts, fans who would beg for my autograph—yet no one could seem to find a place for me in their organization. I sent out hundreds of letters but received very little response. Most of the time I would receive a note back saying that the writer would love to take the great Lenny Moore out to lunch, but with the understanding that there was no job offer involved.

The bills started piling up and I felt myself sinking into a deep malaise. I was depressed over the dissolution of my marriage and the fact that I had to make an appointment to see my kids. It made me angry that I had to somehow find money to pay for the monthly mortgage on a huge house while also scraping up the rent for my one-bedroom apartment. I worried about the club, which was internally hemorrhaging money and constantly on edge of going out of business. I had hit rock bottom.

In 1974, with no job prospects and little hope, I sucked up my pride and went down to Baltimore's job bank. After standing in a long line, I met with an employment counselor and gave him the application I had filled out in the waiting room. He never raised his head, while scanning the application, until he noticed my name.

He looked up and said, "Are you *the* Lenny Moore?"

I said that I was.

He asked, "What are you doing here?"

I responded sheepishly, "I'm here for the same reason everyone else is here: I need a job." I was embarrassed and wished he would lower his voice.

He asked me why the great Lenny Moore needed help finding employment. I said, "Hey man, it's tough out there, and I need some money."

He asked what I wanted to do, and I said that I didn't know. I told him that, in addition to playing football, I had worked for CBS as a broadcaster and I also had previous radio experience as sports director for WSID.

Still with a look of disbelief on his face, the counselor started rifling through his files, looking for potential jobs. He finally found a position with N.W. Ayer & Sons, in Philadelphia. This was a public relations firm that was looking for field representatives to help the U.S. Army with its recruiting efforts. He said the job only paid $19,000, but asked if I was interested.

It was a large pay cut from what I had been making at CBS, but it was something. I asked what I needed to do, and he told me it was a public relations position. My next step was to report to Ayer & Sons' offices the next week for an interview.

A few days later I packed a small overnight bag and went to Philadelphia. In the firm's offices, there were dozens of other people just like me reporting for the interview. Over the course of the day, the applicants were narrowed down, and eight of us were finally hired. It was our job to travel the Eastern Seaboard and help different Army recruiting offices meet their recruiting quota.

It was hard work. Maybe during World War II there was glamour in this job, when celebrities were chauffeured around to different cities and acted as spokespeople for U.S. War Bonds. This was nothing like that. The people I was working with weren't celebrities; they were simply out-of-work salespeople. With Vietnam a very fresh memory for the country, the position certainly had its pitfalls.

My territory was Baltimore, Delaware, Southern Maryland, and the Northern tip of Washington, D.C. I was a roving representative who went with the local recruiting officer to different associations and functions to help the officer network. It took me a few months to get the hang of it; but I must say, I really enjoyed it. I loved getting out on the road to talk with different people every day. I was good at it, too. By the mid-'70s the different branches of the military were consolidating their recruiting efforts in an attempt to save money. With the amount of bureaucracy being cut, the group I was in was disbanded because the army didn't renew the contract. I can't say I was too disappointed. I had done the job for a good five years and it had run its course. It had paid the bills, but I knew that this wasn't my destiny.

This wasn't the only chapter in my life to come to a close; in 1973, Club 24 finally closed its doors. By the early 1970s, the part of town where the club was located took a turn for the worse. Drug dealers moved in. There were many times that deals went down in the parking lot and probably in the bar as well. This was something that I wanted no part of, but I found it difficult to control. What ultimately shut our doors, though, was poor bookkeeping. It was determined after a financial audit that the Club owed the IRS thousands of dollars in back taxes. With the Club barely breaking even, the neighborhood going to hell, and the IRS breathing down our necks, I decided to pull the plug. I had no remorse. The Club had had a good seven-year run, but it was time to move on. I wanted to make a fresh start in my life, and this was one cord I needed to cut.

Although I was happy to have many of these chapters close in my life, I was still back to Square One. I was unemployed with no prospects. I had gained valuable experience working with the army recruiters. It looked great on my resume having the army as a reference as well as a consistent work history, but employers weren't beating down my door. A great resume doesn't pay the bills. Not knowing where to turn next, I was hoping for a miracle. One would appear in an unlikely place.

I was astounded when, after seven years, the Baltimore Colts again became part of my life. One day out of the blue, I got a call from Joe Thomas, who was the general manager at that time. A few years prior to this, Carroll Rosenbloom had decided that he wanted to head West, and he had traded his interest in the Colts for the Los Angeles Rams with a Chicago-based businessman named Robert Irsay. With Irsay's entrance came many changes to the organization. Joe Thomas, an executive with the Dolphins, was hired as the GM for the Colts. With a few down years, he was trying his hardest to put his own stamp on the team, and he called me to ask if I would be interested in meeting him one afternoon. I didn't see why not, so I agreed.

At the meeting we made some small talk, and then he came right out and asked if I would like to work with the Colts again in some capacity. I was floored but only momentarily. I said I would love to come back to the Colts in any capacity that he saw fit. I told him that I had been out of football, for the most part, since my retirement but I was eager to return. I asked what he had in mind.

"I've been observing you for a while from a distance," said Joe. "I am aware of your work with the army. I know that you have a good reputation around town. I like the way you've handled yourself, Lenny, and I think you belong with the Colts. But there are a few conditions."

Uh-oh, I thought. Here it comes. What type of reputation did I still have within the organization?

After a frozen moment, I was relieved when Joe only wanted to give me some background on the internal workings of the Colts these days. First, he warned me that Irsay was making it a habit to come to Baltimore more often, from his home in Chicago. It was widely known that Irsay was something of a loud mouth, and every time he visited, he did nothing but muddy the waters. He emphasized that I should always be prepared for the unexpected.

The second condition Joe stipulated was that I would only report to him. There was a fair amount of politics within the office, and he didn't want me to get caught up in that garbage. He said that his hiring me was part of a project that was solely his. With the team in transition (popular players like Mackey, Parker, Unitas, and Berry were either already gone or on their way out), he wanted to have a link to the past, someone to meet with the community and act as a goodwill ambassador for the team.

Joe paused for a moment, and then he asked if this job proposal was something I'd be interested in. Without hesitation I said, "Yes!" Then I asked how much the job paid, and he said, $25,000.

I sat and thought about it for a while. That was $6,000 more than I had been making with the Army recruiters. That was great. I hesitated for a moment and thought how this salary would really help me get back on my feet.

To my benefit, Joe misunderstood my silence for a negotiating tactic. He blurted out, "Okay, $26,000!"

I was shocked, speechless. I didn't understand what had happened, but Joe didn't give me much of a chance to respond.

"Final offer: $30,000! Take it or leave it!"

With that master negotiating technique, I received a $5,000 raise before I even started my new position as Community Relations Director for the Baltimore Colts. I was home again.

~ ~ ~

The position started immediately. My job as Community Relations Director was to go out and create goodwill for the Colts. I was their man, because I couldn't say enough about the fun I had had while playing on the team. My working relationship with Joe was terrific as well. I loved going to work every day.

Unfortunately, my working relationship with Joe didn't last long. Joe was eventually fired over the backlash from the Colts trading Johnny to San Diego. Poor Joe was a straight shooter who was caught in a Catch-22. He had wanted Johnny to retire with the Colts, and Johnny had wanted to retire with the Colts; but the financial wizards in management refused to continue paying top dollar to Johnny. There was an impasse, and Joe had to trade Johnny, an act that drew fiery outrage from the whole state. Joe Thomas was the scapegoat; firing him took the attention away from the others in management.

The new GM to replace Joe was Dick Szymanski. Dick and I had played together many years with the Colts, though we were never particularly close. The distance in our relationship continued when he moved into the front office, which was fine with me. He had his job to do and I had mine. Shortly thereafter, Ernie Accorsi was promoted within the organization to be co-GM with Dick.

Even with all the changes going on in the organization, I felt my position was relatively safe. I didn't have any staff; I wasn't breaking the team's budget; I was doing what I could to keep the Colts' name before the public. Another reason I felt secure was the fact that Irsay promised me a position as an executive vice president of his new cable company.

In 1981, cable TV was coming to Baltimore, and all of the major cable companies were lined up to bid for the rights of distribution. Irsay wanted a piece of the action, too. Even with all of his business interests in Chicago, Irsay was always looking to parlay the ownership of the Colts into new business ventures in Baltimore. As the bidding was about to begin, it was announced by the city that 25 percent of the ownership of the new cable system had to be in an organization that was primarily minority owned.

Irsay must have thought that it would be to his advantage to have a minority, a former football star, be the "face" of his organization. I repeatedly told him that I didn't have any experience with this type of business, but he said that didn't matter. Sam Kravitz, another Irsay associate working on this deal, gave me a book on cable systems and told me to read up on the industry. Simultaneously I was asked to meet with the Baptist Alliance, a group of black churches in Baltimore, who were also bidding on the project. Irsay wanted to see if the Alliance wanted to play ball with his newly formed group and thought that it would be appropriate that I should be the one to initiate the contact.

To be honest, I was intrigued by the whole opportunity, although I didn't trust Irsay, a pudgy man given to fits of drunken belligerence. Repeatedly I asked him for assurance that this cable project had nothing to do with my position with the Colts. His response was that I "would always have a home with the organization." Due to mismanagement, the cable deal never went anywhere and the issue just died. Irsay diverted his attention to a fight with the city over building a new stadium.

By the late 1970s and early 1980s, the relationship between Irsay and the city powers grew acrid. Meanwhile, the Colts were mired in mediocrity. With the 1982 players' strike upon us, the team was hemorrhaging money. One day Dick Szymanski came and asked for the keys to my company car. I had a feeling I would be a target if the team was looking to cut overhead, being that I wasn't a coach or a scout, I hadn't sold any game tickets, and I had been involved in the failed cable deal. Plus Joe Thomas—who didn't leave on a particularly good note, hired me under a former regime.

Yet I was the only administrator who had any reason to leave the office on company business: Why was my car being taken away? Dick or Ernie didn't have an answer; Dick just asked for my keys on the spot. I didn't even have a way to get home. I had to call my wife to give me a ride!

It was soon after this that Ernie came to me and said I was being laid off.

"Some of the other office workers will be laid off, too," he said, as though to lessen the blow. "Once this players' strike is over, you can have your job back."

I asked what other positions were being eliminated, and he listed a handful of secretaries and office staff. I knew that these ladies literally needed their jobs for survival. Most of them had worked there for many, many years. I thought Ernie must have been joking. But the layoffs took place, and none of us were asked to return, even after the games eventually resumed. I called Ernie several times, and he would say that he had to talk to Irsay. Fed up, I finally called Irsay, who then told me to talk with Ernie. I never received a straight answer from anyone. I never received any official notice of termination.

Any small glimmer of hope I had in returning to the Colts was dashed forever when the team disappeared in the middle of the night, moving silently over a blanket of snow, as an armada of Mayflower moving vans stealthily took the team to Indianapolis.

All things being equal, the Colts should still be playing in Baltimore. Although it has been more than two decades since they left, the franchise still has a presence in the city. The Irsay family ripped the heart out of Baltimore, and even with a new franchise in town, it has never really healed.

# FIFTEEN

# LOSING LES

It was after I had left Frankie and her new nanny that I started dating the new love of my life, Erma. She was a divorced woman who lived across the street from us when we lived in our first house. Erma was one of the first who introduced herself to us. Later, as my marriage to Frankie was being dissolved, my friendship with Erma began to blossom. She was a very steadying influence for me during this time of my life. She helped me cope with the many dark days surrounding the CBS fiasco, the loss of my army recruiting job, and finalizing my divorce from Frankie. In 1974, I married Erma after we had lived together for a few years.

Later that same year, Erma was diagnosed with colon cancer. It had metastasized, so she immediately started radiation and chemotherapy to combat the tumor. Eventually she had the tumor removed. It was a long, hard battle for both of us. Sadly, it was only a matter of time before this vicious disease would eventually win.

My spirits were lifted, temporarily, when my peers elected me to the NFL Hall of Fame in 1975. Other nominees were Dante Lavelli, Roosevelt Brown, and my old "friend" from CBS, George Connor. Although Erma's health was deteriorating very quickly, she vowed that she would be there to see me inducted. True to her word, Erma made it to the festivities, although we had to be accompanied by a few nurses and medical equipment.

To present me to the Hall, I picked the only logical person: Coach Stopper from my high school days in Reading, Pennsylvania. I couldn't think of anything more fitting than for me to receive this award from the man who had given me the confidence to seek a college education and a football career. At one point in his speech, Andy said, "If I told you how good Lenny Moore is, you wouldn't believe me. I mean, good at football, at citizenship, and at caring for others." It meant a lot to me to hear those words from Andy, someone whom I always strived to make proud. Even more meaningful was the Bible verse that Andy shared with me prior to the festivities. He knew what Erma was going through, and he chose a passage from the Book of Isaiah (Chapter 40: Verse 31):

*"But they that have hope in the Lord shall renew their strength,*
*they shall take wings as eagles, they shall run and not be weary,*
*they shall walk and not faint."*

Those were powerful words for me to hear given Erma's failing strength.

My recollections of that evening are very mixed. On the one hand, I was very proud to be a Hall of Famer, but I couldn't take my mind off of Erma's suffering. And while I was honored to have Andy present for the festivities—I was concerned that my children were here to induct me without Frankie. Finally, I was thrilled that my father was alive to see me be inducted—but I was tortured by the fact that my mother was gone and I never had fulfilled my vow to ease her tragic life. With all these competing thoughts playing tug of war with my emotions, the Hall of Fame achievement was a bittersweet moment that I'll never forget.

Erma died two months later.

~ ~ ~

My children were not fond of my relationship with Erma, mostly because they felt that giving her a chance as a stepmother would have been somehow disloyal to their mother. After Erma died, I was alone. Guilt-ridden for missing out on much of my children's childhood, I wanted to make up for lost time. With that, I asked my son Leslie if he'd like to come and live with me.

Leslie had always been a brilliant young man. But where I was fortunate to choose sports as a track on which to run my life, Les turned to other fields of interest that were not so healthy. He started getting involved with drugs as a teenager, a habit that he would try to shake for years to come. As has happened to so many of America's youth, the scourge of drugs infested my son and sucked all ambition out of him. I tried everything I could. I mistakenly thought I could insulate him from the drug pushers at one point. I had him come live with me instead of at Frankie's house, believing that my experience at Penn State would be the encouragement he needed to go to college himself, but after a short stint at the University of Maryland, Les never pursued that avenue further. He just meandered, uninterested with life, succumbing to addiction. It was horrible to witness. Finally, when nothing I suggested seemed to have any effect, I had another talk with Les, saying that I would always be there for him, whenever he needed me. I didn't like his lifestyle, but he was his own man. He moved back in with Frankie.

He knew I didn't approve of his choices, but he also knew that if he wanted to change, he had to do it himself. Then one day he called me and asked if we could talk. He told me that he had decided he needed to change his life. He realized that if he was going to be a supportive son to his mother (he was back living with Frankie, who was starting to suffer from various health issues) and a responsible uncle to his nieces and nephews, then he had to turn his life around and cut those drugs loose. Les positively adored his little niece, Nikki, and he often talked about the day when he might have a family of his own. This was one of the driving forces behind him as he tried to kick his habit.

I had almost given up hope of receiving such a call for help from my son. Our whole family rallied around him—Frankie and I forgetting past grievances to help our son, and his sisters pitching in wherever they could. Through our collective faith and efforts, Les worked diligently to shake the grip of drugs, which he eventually conquered!

Then in 1991, Les became very ill. Outwardly he appeared to be a healthy young man, but his body was sabotaging him from the inside. His weight dropped dramatically, from about 190 pounds down to 155 pounds. He was unable to eat or drink and always extremely fatigued. He also complained of severe pain in his joints and muscles.

After countless visits to his doctor, the initial diagnosis was Lyme Disease or lupus. Les was put on some antibiotics and a battery of other prescription drugs, but nothing seemed to help.

Finally Les was referred to a rheumatologist, a doctor who specializes in blood diseases. By chance, another physician, Dr. White, happened to be in the office that day, and she was requested to assist in Les's preliminary examination. Dr. White specialized in the field of scleroderma and after reviewing Les's lab work, she informed us that Les had something called "systemic scleroderma."

Scleroderma is a disease that ravages the tissues in one's body and eventually hardens them beyond repair.

With the proper care that was now in place, it was only days before Les started feeling better. He finally had an appetite and was able to keep food down. He had energy and was feeling like a brand new person. When he returned the next week for a follow-up, the rheumatologist reported that Les's body was responding extremely well to the medications.

But Les's battle with the disease was far from over. Every so often he would have to have his medications tweaked in response to findings from the multiple blood tests. He would do great for six months to a year and then have an episode of the old symptoms recurring. As time went on, the disease progressed, and it took longer for Les to recover in between.

During some of the episodes, Les would experience severe cramping in his hands, legs and feet. He would also have fevers, which caused night sweats, nausea, and vomiting. He described an episode as "feeling sick in the head." This was probably because this particular form of scleroderma can cause swelling in the brain. The steroids he had to take were also causing severe bloating, and as a result, Les often took other medications to counteract the steroids.

Finally, at one horrible point in time, the doctor told us that Les had only two years to live. Our whole family was devastated, scared, and angry that this was happening to Les after he had battled for years to overcome a different enemy of his body—the drug habit.

Les's reaction to the diagnosis was more sublime: he vowed to get the most out of every day that he had left to live.

~ ~ ~

One of the things over which Les and I really bonded, of course, was football. By the mid-1990s, the Ravens had relocated from Cleveland to Baltimore, and Les and I were following the team closely. Respecting his desire to live each of his remaining days to the fullest, I would take him to the Ravens' home games as often as I could. Although it wasn't the Colts,

Ravens games offered the opportunity for Les and me to strengthen our relationship. The Ravens afforded me an excuse to spend the last days of Les's life with him without appearing to be constantly checking in on him. Throughout his illness, Les was very conscious of pity; he didn't want that from any of his family or friends. He wanted to be treated like anyone else, and we tried to respect that. As time went on, he needed the constant presence of an oxygen tank, which made getting out a little more difficult. I knew toting around his extra set of lungs embarrassed him, but I kept taking him to Ravens games and even to the 1998 Super Bowl in Miami.

By 2001, when the Ravens advanced through the playoffs that year, I was by Les's side for every game, watching the television and discussing the plays. Even in silent moments, we enjoyed just being together and trying to make every second count, knowing that our time together was limited. The day the Ravens won the AFC Championship Game, Les was more excited than ever, because it meant a rematch between Baltimore and New York for all the marbles. Sadly, he wouldn't get to see the game, as he succumbed to scleroderma on January 15, 2001.

In those last days, Les was in anguish, feeling as though his body was on fire. He was not able to hold down any food or liquids; he had a high fever, and he was struggling to breathe. He had also developed a bumpy rash on his calves, which would bleed if disturbed. Les became dehydrated as a result of constant vomiting, which left us no choice but to hospitalize him. The doctors ran a battery of tests and eventually put him in intensive care. By the next day he was much better, responding to the antibiotics and even holding down liquids and a little food. But this was the last day we spent with Les. That night his lungs became completely filled with fluid, and the doctors had to intubate him to help him breathe. They sedated him to make him a little more comfortable, but while he was sedated, Les fell into full cardiac arrest. Doctors tried for over an hour to revive him, but they were unsuccessful. Les passed away that day, January 15, 2001, at the age of 43.

The family had witnessed his incredible suffering in the last days, but it was my daughter Terri who was bravely at his side for most of it. I don't know where she summoned the strength; I knew I couldn't do it. It was hard enough for me to call him up and hear his weak voice; I could feel his frailty over the phone.

My son's passing did not surprise me, but when it finally happened it was a shock to my system. I missed him more than I ever thought possible. It is only in writing this book, more than four years since his passing, that I can finally make it through his story without weeping. Losing him was like an incision in my soul. He had become my confidante, my pal, and my conscience. Whenever I faced a dilemma at work or in my personal life, I'd call him to get his advice; he would always offer a unique point of view or suggested a different approach that would provide clarity in my thinking. He was my man.

He was a fighter to the end. I have to remind myself, to this day that Les miraculously lived nine years with the disease—seven more years than the doctors had expected. But Les is in a better place now. We never want to see our loved ones suffer, and Les was suffering endlessly. He was tired of being sick. The only hope that gets me through some days is knowing that I will see Les in another life, where that hideous disease will not gnarl his body.

~ ~ ~

With the death of my son Les still smoldering, one afternoon in the summer of 2001, my life changed when I bumped into a gentleman named Pat Panella. Pat is the executive director of the Maryland State Boxing Commission. I knew of Pat, but up to that point we had never met formally. We were in the same parking garage downtown going to separate appointments when Pat introduced himself and started making small talk. In a polite manner, he then passed along his respects for the loss of my son, which he had found out about through some mutual friends. He asked how I was doing. Although he was a relative stranger, that question at that moment produced uncontrollable honesty from me. It must have been divine intervention that I let my feelings of loneliness and frustration spill out of me to Pat. It was as if that question from Pat pulled the plug on the many holes in my soul and everything came pouring out. I told him how empty and sad I was. I told him of the lonely nights filled with despair, knowing that I'd never have another opportunity to talk with my son. I concluded by saying that I really wanted to do something for Les to keep his memory alive, but I didn't know what. Pat said that he had just the idea. He said that I should create a foundation in Les's name. I thought that sounded like a great idea, but I told Pat that I wouldn't have the first clue how to put something like that together. At that point, without hesitation, he said that he knew exactly how to assemble such an organization and he had associates who could help. Furthermore, he said that he could get all of them to volunteer their time. Before I even offered, he refused to discuss any form of payment for himself or the board that he has since assembled.

Very shortly after our serendipitous meeting, we set a lunch date to discuss the idea further. After giving it more thought, Pat said that the foundation should provide scholarships for local youths who are in need. More importantly, he said, "We'll do this for Leslie." Man, that blew me away. Here was this gentleman who I had only formally met a few weeks ago, helping me put something like this in place. I don't have the words to describe what Pat and the army of people who volunteer for the foundation mean to me and the memory of Les. It is through their hard work that this foundation exists.

On the first Monday in May 2002, we hosted our first Leslie Moore Foundation scholarship fundraiser. It was a magical evening that surpassed all of our wildest dreams. Hundreds of people from all parts of the state came to celebrate the memory of Les. To make the night extra special, the Hall of Fame fraternity came out in full support of Les as well. In honor of Les, the likes of Chuck Bednarik, Raymond Berry, Johnny Unitas, Art Donovan, Gino Marchetti, Don Shula, Ted Hendricks, Lem Barney, Roosevelt Brown, and countless others have given their time to make the event unique.

Out of this tragedy, a miracle happened. Over the past three years, the foundation has been able to raise over $200,000, has endowed five scholarships, and is currently looking to endow five more. Out of Les's demise, the lives of children throughout Baltimore will be changed for the better. I don't miss him any less these days, but the good that has come from his passing is priceless. I know he is looking down on us and smiling at what we have done in his name.

~ ~ ~

Almost two weeks after Les had died, his mother suddenly passed away. This shook me to the core. Although it had been decades since Frankie had been my wife, she was still the mother of my children and someone with whom I shared a significant period of my life.

To this day I have a hard time recalling the days and months after Les and Frankie passed. I was in a daze, a zombie going through the motions, lost in despair. The consecutive loss of life crushed my daughters.

As a result, I grew increasingly aware of my own mortality.

In mid-2001, I went in for my annual physical and subsequent tests. A few days after the results came back, the doctor called and asked that I immediately schedule a follow-up consultation, because some of the test results were of concern to him. The doctor asked that I bring along my wife, Edith, as well.

Not knowing what to expect, Edith and I sat in his office, holding hands, exchanging looks of worry. The doctor informed us that my tests, "PSAs," had come back abnormally high, which meant that my prostate was growing abnormally large. This could indicate that I had cancer. The doctor was positive that it was still early enough in the disease to treat it with radiation and chemotherapy. He said that I had the option to have the prostate removed as well, but he said it would be unnecessary at this juncture.

After everything the family had gone through, I felt punch-drunk after hearing this news. Edith and I talked and prayed about what we should do. We didn't want to choose the surgical route if we didn't have to. The doctor had said removing the prostate would result in physical changes to my body, due to the estrogen treatment that would ensue.

Of course, the option of chemotherapy and radiation didn't sound too appealing, either. Going through a routine of these treatments would have set off other complications and changes in my body. It seemed to us that having the prostate removed would give us a greater chance of beating the cancer by not allowing it to spread. Following a conversation with my doctor, Dr. Turgot Jendy, we agreed—get it out! We told the doctor that this was the route we wanted to go, and we set a date for the procedure.

It was nothing less than divine intervention that helped us choose the path of surgery, for afterwards, the surgeon came to the waiting room to tell Edith that the sack of the prostate had actually broken open, and some of the cancerous cells had latched onto the tissue surrounding the prostate. He mentioned that if we hadn't opted for invasive surgery, there was a very distinct chance that the cancer would have aggressively spread throughout my body.

This was another example of how Les's death had a direct effect on all of our lives. It forced us to treat life as a gift; as a miracle. Part of what helped the family get through the pain of losing Les was the awareness of how lucky we were to have each other. We each realized that life was not to be taken for granted. I believe that we became better people for having recognized this.

## SIXTEEN

# STARTING A JOURNEY INTO MY PAST

I t is one thing to be pleased with how your life has turned out. It is quite another thing to know very little about where you began. I knew next to nothing as a teenager about my ancestors, and this void made me feel disconnected, both from my past and from my race. My father, who was uneasy about discussing his past, should have been a resource to me. Unfortunately, he never felt comfortable enough to answer some of my questions. He took much of the history of our family to his grave as he died in the late '70s. Although I have very fond memories of him, much of what I have subsequently learned about my father from my sisters and brothers came long after he had passed away.

My father was The Man. He was the disciplinarian, the enforcer of the law. He was strict with us kids, but that may have been a defense mechanism in some ways. He was ashamed, I feel, of his lack of education and of his sharecropper heritage. He was a man of few words; he didn't like to talk, especially about his past. He wanted to forget his life as a child. I feel remorse for not having had a chance to ask questions about his childhood. It might have been therapeutic for both of us. This lost opportunity saddens me, because I wanted to know him much better than I did.

The more I found out about him and about black men in general, the more I learned about myself. In a quest for identity in my later years, I embarked upon research into African American history. The deeper I got into these studies, the narrower my focus became: what I was most interest-

ed in was black ballplayers who predated my time in the league, specifically.

Unfortunately, many of the old black ballplayers from the '30s and '40s
were dead by the time I grew curious about them. I remembered having
talked to Fritz Pollard in 1973 and again in 1979, and his insights had
helped me put some of the puzzle pieces together. Sadly, the last time I
spoke to Fritz, his mind was suffering the ravages of dementia, but it was
important to get his opinions because, as I was beginning to learn, many
black ballplayers, even in the 1980s, were unwilling to talk about the prejudice they had faced in their lives. There were one or two elderly black players who strived to let their voices be heard, which made it a little easier for
all of us subsequent players to talk openly about what we were going
through in the NFL. But most of those I interviewed still wouldn't talk "on
the record." Whether or not they were currently affiliated with a team, most
refused to speak candidly—as though it was still the 1940s and 1950s, when
any attempt at speaking the truth about racism might have led to a lynch-
ing, at worst, or being traded to a team across the country, at best.

One example of this trepidation came from my relationship with Bill
Willis. Once his playing days in the NFL were done, he secured a job with
a local municipality by running a park district. He had long since been
retired and was honored as a pioneer of the sport at his position. He was recognized as a solid community man with a spotless reputation. From what I
could tell, he seemed as safe in his job as anyone could reasonably be. As I
toured different parts of the country with my tape recorder interviewing
these ballplayers, I called Bill and told him that I would be paying a visit.

After some initial small talk, I started into the reason why I was there: I
was attempting to document the true story of what it was like to be a black
player in the 1950s. I asked if he would share his tales. Bill listened to what
I had to say, but offered little in response. When I brought out my tape
recorder, he stopped dead in his tracks and refused to go any further.
Wondering why he had such a change in demeanor, I asked him what he
was thinking. He fumbled through an apology for being so curt and then
revealed that he was deathly afraid to speak about the treatment he endured
decades earlier for fear of losing his job. I was shocked. Here was this legend who would have to try to get fired before he would lose his job, and he
was afraid of talking about the past for fear of retribution. In an effort to
make him more comfortable, I stayed a little longer, but Bill wouldn't
budge. A little frustrated, I told him I had some other people to meet in the

area and excused myself. In the car on the drive home, I ran through the day's events in my mind and began seeing a connection between Bill's behavior and my own father's. These mountainous men who couldn't be intimidated physically were brought to their knees by the psychological intimidation that had been ingrained in them as children. As youngsters, neither was encouraged to communicate their feelings and recount the events of the past—and that fear stayed with them literally to their graves. Although I didn't get the interview I came for, I left with more knowledge than I could have ever expected.

Undaunted by experiences like the one with Bill Willis, I continued my pursuit for the truth. Trying different lines of questioning with each new subject, I was able to gather some valuable threads of information. One theme that was proving to be common, that didn't really come as a shock to me, was the tendency for so many to become alcoholics. Learning this made me feel more comfortable about, but not proud of, my own drinking and "wild" behavior in the past. As a young man in Baltimore, I would drink consistently to mask the emotional pain of social disenfranchisement. I'm not an alcoholic—not now and not then—but like so many others before me, I found solace at the bottom of an empty tumbler. Liquor made some of the hurt go away or at least allowed me to forget about it for a while.

In an effort to balance my research, I also tried to interview some of the white ballplayers from the day to discuss their views on the racial quotas and other devices of segregation that the teams were practicing. It would never fail, as soon as I would snap on the tape recorder, the story would be the same: they "never really noticed" any difference in the way blacks were treated. If the black ballplayers on their team (take your pick) were having problems or issues with management, they never knew about them. It was as if everyone I interviewed had read the same script. After a while, I stopped trying to collect comments from these sources because I was getting nowhere fast.

There were some white players who did break the silence, though. Jim David, an underrated defensive back who played for the Lions apologized years ago for some of the awful things he used to call me in the heat of battle. He said that he did it intentionally to try to throw me off my game and get under my skin. Needless to say, I fell for it.

As teammates, Alan Ameche and Raymond Berry were very fair to me during our time on the team and would do their best to discuss the shabby treatment many of the black players received at the time. They admitted that much of it was institutional and very hard to change, but they regretted the treatment nonetheless. Their honesty about the situation was very rare indeed, but very appreciated.

Someone who was instrumental in helping me find out more about my race, not just from a footballer's perspective, but from a world history point of view, was my dear friend Charlie Blockson. Whenever I would come across something that I hadn't realized before, I would always call him and get his opinion. One example is the time I was surprised to learn, when I was well into my forties, that Alexandre Dumas, the famed author of such works as *The Three Musketeers* and *The Count of Monte Cristo*, was a black man. I immediately called Charlie, with amazement in my voice that is typically reserved for children on Christmas Day.

"Did you know that Dumas was black?" I asked, incredulously. Charlie just chuckled, and then gave me more examples of black authors and poets. It was the same scenario when I came upon the information that much of the basic physical science that has led to so many technical advancements we see today was first practiced in North Africa. Or when I read about the inventor of a popular product, or the composer of a well-known song—each time I called Charlie to see if he was aware these people were black, he would say, "Of course," then he'd give me more details or tell me about a book or magazine article that I could read for more enlightenment.

By connecting with my heritage in this way, and by learning about blacks that had improved our world, I finally started to feel good about myself. Two decades after finishing my four years at Penn State, I finally was invested in the curriculum that I never was able to start, because black history was not taught back then.

I was becoming more comfortable in my own skin and understanding that what I had felt as a player in the 1950s was caused by internalized feelings of inferiority. It was like rising from the depths of the ocean and being able for the first time to see land and sky and sunlight.

I began to talk to my peers who had gone through the same inferiorization process, trying to make them aware of the history that had been hidden from us for centuries. One person I talked to on many, many occasions was the now-deceased Larry Doby. We would bump into each other at sports memorabilia shows or at a charity golf outing and as a result became very friendly with each other. I noticed that he never smiled or let himself loosen up around anyone. His self-isolation made me feel very sad, and I always made an effort to talk to him. If I saw him at a tee box, standing off by himself, apart from the other three players in his foursome, I would walk up to him and ask how he was doing. I'd ask him how he was golfing, or I'd ask about his family—anything to draw him out; but nothing ever seemed to work. I wish I could have found a way to help him talk out his feelings and accept himself and those around him, as I was coming to accept myself. Larry was a great man who had withdrawn into himself, perhaps because he was afraid he could trust no one else. It is truly a shame how many Larry Dobys there are in the world.

~ ~ ~

It is not difficult to understand why so many of us are as guarded as we are, considering the fact that we must always be alert and suspicious of the many people who approach us through life. This was my frame of mind when, in January 1983, a writer named Ed Douchette from the *Tribune-Review*, a central Pennsylvania newspaper, called to ask me for an interview.

Being an NFL Hall of Famer with a reputation for being outspoken, I regularly received requests for phone interviews on various topics. Since I was between jobs at the moment, with the departure of the Colts to Indianapolis, I had a lot of time to fill. I agreed to participate. Ed wanted to know how I felt regarding the evolution of race relations on the Penn State campus, particularly since the introduction of Proposition 48 which the NCAA had put forward. As a former Nittany Lion myself, I had kept my finger on the pulse of race relations at Penn State. I was well aware that not much had changed on campus for the average black student since I was enrolled there. Coach Paterno had followed the example set by Coach Engle, in that he was very open to recruiting black athletes and helping them become assimilated to campus and was adamant that they receive a top-notch education. Thus, it wasn't necessarily the athletic department that was dragging its feet in attracting bright and motivated black students to campus, but the University administration as a whole that had much explaining to do. Some 30 years had passed since I played for Penn State, but the attitude toward black students was not improved according to some of the contemporary players with whom I had kept in contact.

Appallingly, in the early 1980s, the percentage of black students on this campus was about the same as it was in 1955. In the period from 1972 to 1983, according to the *Pittsburgh Post-Gazette*, the university averaged

9,486 students overall, with only 90 of those students being black. It was a travesty that a state-sponsored institution of higher learning, in a state with an overall black population of 8.8 percent, would have a black student body that is approximately two percent of the overall enrollment. Many felt, as did I, that the main reason for the lack of black students at the time was a lack of black faculty. There was little to attract the best and brightest black students to Penn State, and with so few black students, there wasn't much of a peer-support system in place. Without many black professors, there weren't many classes that discussed black issues. Why would a black student go to this rural university situated on top of a mountain, when he or she could go to Temple, Penn, Villanova, or Pitt?

What annoyed me more than anything wasn't the numbers, although they were depressing, but the lack of effort on the university's part to make Happy Valley an attractive place for black students. The inertia on the part of administration made me embarrassed for the university.

To make matters worse, the NCAA had introduced Proposition 48, which I viewed as another way to limit the amount of black athletes in Division 1 sports. More specifically, Prop 48 was another excuse that could be used by Penn State to limit black enrollment. It didn't take long for Joe Paterno—who was in support of the movement—and me to end up on different sides of the table in the public discussion of this Proposition.

The initiative, put in place by the NCAA, required high school student athletes to maintain a grade point average of at least 2.0 (out of 4), while taking a core curriculum of English, math, social studies, and science classes. In addition, the students would have to pass the SAT with a score of 700 (out of 1600), or the ACT with a 15 (out of 36), to gain admission. At the time, according to then-current Operation PUSH research, only 50 percent of blacks had scored over a 700 on their SAT, and only 28 percent had scored over 15 on their ACT. Meanwhile, a full 75 percent of whites had exceeded those benchmarks. Where I found fault with Proposition 48 was in the standards to which the black students were to be held.

It is widely accepted that the quality of education in urban public schools, populated mainly by minorities, is severely lacking in comparison to the better funded suburban public schools attended mainly by white students. With the new standards set in place by Prop 48, the tests may have been standardized, but the educational background of each student wasn't. Just because a black student at a poor inner-city school didn't score well in mathematics may not necessarily mean that he isn't bright, it may very well mean that he received poor preparation throughout his scholastic career. In the end, this proposition was well intentioned (and may even work in a perfect world), but as this book has hopefully shown, we don't live in an equal world. Thus, in my eyes, this initiative made it very easy to discriminate against the black athlete.

The basis of the whole movement had sprung out of an attempt to guarantee that the student-athletes entering college on athletic scholarships were dedicated students in every sense of the word. Several universities had effectively admitted their exploitation of black athletes—for the revenue to be gained through major college sporting events. The proposed initiative would make it almost impossible now for black students to be accepted in the 277 predominantly white universities or even in the 16 predominately black colleges in Division 1.

Nevertheless, a board that was overwhelmingly comprised of white universities voted this proposition in. Without a so-called "black college" represented in the rate, the whole issue seemed even more unfair.

In the midst of this maelstrom of Prop 48, with my position on racial equality already well documented on campus, I agreed to the *Tribune-Review* interview with the understanding that I would not be misquoted. I stated to Ed quite emphatically that due to the explosive nature of the subject he must "quote me correctly and in the order in which the questions were asked." Ed agreed to my terms and the interview was held.

Throughout the interview I thought the questions were very fair and I did my best to make my responses clear and concise. In the end, I felt very pleased with the discussion and looked forward to the final article.

What resulted from that interview would receive top honors if there were such a thing as a "misquote hall of fame." Although I didn't read the article immediately after it was published, many friends and family who received the *Tribune-Review* quickly brought it to my attention. It was filled with a twisting of my words that left me speechless. The article implied that I was regularly sneaking onto campus "incognito," as if I spent my time spying on the administration, the coaches, and the students. I may have driven to campus occasionally to meet someone there for lunch, but I didn't think I had to check in with someone before I visited my alma mater.

The article also quoted me as saying that Joe Paterno wasn't doing enough hiring of black coaches or recruiting more black players. As I mentioned before, in all actuality, I felt Joe had done an excellent job of continually increasing the proportion of black athletes on the team, just as Rip

Engle had done. Had it not been for these progressive coaches' thinking on the matter of equality, the overall university ratio would have diminished to an even more embarrassing level of black students on campus.

Finally, the article alleged that Joe and I had a strained relationship. I had—and have—the utmost respect for Joe. Whenever I am on campus to this day, I make it a point to stop by his home. We have never been best friends, but I don't think either one us expects that out of our relationship. It was just that, in this matter, we had a significant divide. In previous articles on the subject, it did annoy me when Joe put himself on a pedestal, through his choice of words, as though he were a representative of what is best for the black athlete. But we talked about those articles, and I was satisfied that his heart was in the right place. In addition, after Ed's article came out, I called Joe to clear the air. It was a very polite conversation that satisfied both of us. We both made sure that there were no hard feelings and that we would agree to disagree. We both wanted what is best for the university; we just had two distinctly different ways of looking at things.

Although I quickly wrote a clarification letter to the *Tribune-Review* and all other papers that pulled quotes from the story, the proverbial cat was out of the bag. I was soon reading in the paper, and receiving in the mail, many responses to my alleged position. As an example, Harry Hamilton, a black defensive back at the time, was quoted as saying that he felt "disappointment that he [Lenny] would wait until he got out into life to then turn around and throw stones." I realize that Harry was probably put on the spot with the way the question was asked; but to my way of thinking, Harry and the rest of the black athletes at Penn State should reacquaint themselves with the Lenny Moores, the Rosey Griers, the Jesse Arnelles, and the other black athletes who went before and who took the abuses so that life could be easier for today's college teams.

Shortly after the piece in the *Tribune-Review* came out, I saw Joe at a luncheon where he was being honored as the "Dapper Dan Man of the Year." In public, we stood side by side and presented a unified front for Penn State, demonstrating that there were no hard feelings. Unfortunately, that unified front wouldn't convince the fickle and partisan crowd that attended the funeral for Coach Rip Engle later that year.

The reception for Rip's funeral was to be held at the same country club in Happy Valley where in the 1950s I would have been asked to enter at the kitchen door instead of being welcomed as an invited guest at a banquet. Had I not had such respect for Coach Engle, I probably wouldn't have gone to the reception. To make matters worse, the reaction to the *Tribune-Review* interview I had done was still brewing, and I anticipated some confrontations. On the other hand, I knew I would see Rosey, Charlie, Jesse, and some other black friends at the reception; it would not only be a nice reunion with them, but it would be the height of irony to see those dear black faces in the country club, a site that symbolized some of the hard feelings we had had toward this town as students.

But as we gathered at the reception to honor Rip Engle, after our beloved coach had died, we reminisced about our playing days under his tutelage. Not only Rip, but Coaches Paterno and Torretti as well, had each gone out of their way to be fair to us young black athletes. Each coach had a distinctly different personality, but each was a straight shooter. They would not have let anything like discrimination be tolerated, either on their field or on their campus.

Coach Engle was a quiet man. He rarely raised his voice. Even in the most racially troubled time this country had seen, he provided a safe haven for the small contingent of black players who trusted him enough to leave their homes and play football on top of a mountain in central Pennsylvania.

Only once, during my senior year, did I dispute something Coach Engle had done. We were about to go on the road for a game against another college. Coach Engle was not going to let Charlie travel; in fact, he was going to replace Charlie's spot on the roster with a far less talented, and white, player. Something didn't sit right with me, and I told Rip that if Charlie didn't go, I wasn't going. Like the stand-up guy he was, Rip took me aside and talked with me about the situation, man to man. He heard me out, then he shared with me exactly what he was thinking. In a tense moment like this, all he had to do was impose his will as the coach, but he had enough respect for me to discuss the situation calmly, treating me as though I were an equal peer.

Coaches Paterno and Torretti were totally different, but equally respectful of us as black players. Coach Paterno was more of a screamer, but you always knew he cared about you. He only wanted the best for every player on the team. He is a decent and honorable man.

Coach Torretti, or "Papa T," was a monster of a man, full of bluster, who always had a funny story, and who would never turn a young man away. If he sensed that something was bothering you, he wouldn't hesitate to pull you aside, hear your story, and tell you one of his own. Invariably, you'd leave with a smile on your face.

Whenever things would get me down, on campus or later in life, I would think of these coaches, and Coach Stopper as well, and I'd realize that my actions are a reflection on them. This has always been a sobering thought, for I'd never want to disappoint any of them. They always gave me the strength to carry on.

I attended the reception out of respect for Rip. It was uncomfortable, to say the least, when I was met by some blank stares and dirty looks from the Penn State faithful—those boosters and administrators who had taken the reporter's words for gospel, and would not believe my protestations that I had been misquoted. Thankfully, Rosey and Jesse were there to ease the difficult times. We laughed things off over a drink as we had done many times before.

The greatest tragedy, in hindsight, is not that I endured the sour looks or the words of contempt, but the fact that it had been 30 years since I first set foot on that campus and yet we were still aware of academic and social boundaries that were as starkly differentiated as black and white. What a travesty.

~ ~ ~

I cannot end this tale of racism, black athletes, and Penn State—the three entities that unwittingly consumed my interest in 1983—without leaping ahead 16 years. On November 2, 1999, as reported in the *Daily Collegian* (Penn State's student newspaper), several racist emails began to circulate among the student body of Penn State University. It started with 66 students receiving the mysterious email, signed by "The Patriot," but soon the message spread like wildfire, as the disbelieving and/or curious students forwarded the message to others. Although nothing serious came of "The Patriot's" message, knowledge of the racist act put everyone on campus in a phase of high alert.

Things were quiet, until October 6, 2000, when four prominent figures at the university received letters filled with racial slurs and threats of physical violence. The addressees (a university trustee and three students, including one football player and a student leader) were African American. The letters were typed in a font that made it appear as if the letters were bleeding, and each letter was postmarked Altoona, Pennsylvania.

In time, the racist emails and letters finally got the attention of university administrators, the Postal Inspector, and the FBI. The university posted a reward of $5,000, but no one was apprehended. Then, in late November of 2000, the president of the undergraduate student government, a student of Jewish decent, received a letter postmarked from West Virginia. *The Daily Collegian*, the student newspaper of Penn State, had reported that similar letters had previously maligned the black population, but now, here was a letter oozing with anti-Semitism, including a revisionist history regarding the Holocaust.

The heat was turned up on Friday, April 20, 2001. A writer for *The Daily Collegian* had received two letters: one addressed to him, and the other earmarked for a black student leader. The letters threatened violence against members of the black community at Penn State, claiming that a young black man had been killed as an example: his body would be found in a wooded area in Centre County. The letter specifically stated: "This is a white academy [Penn State] in a white town—in a white country—and, by God, it's going to stay that way." The letter ended with the handwritten note, "Grad Day = bombs-PSU."

This letter created hysteria on campus, leading to marches, rallies, protests, student sit-ins, visits by local congressman and social leaders, countless investigations, and very ambivalent feelings throughout Pennsylvania. Then, on Saturday, April 21, to protest the seemingly slow-moving actions of the university administration, 26 students ran onto the 50-yard line after the National Anthem that began a football game. The protesters were using the Nittany Lions to bring statewide and national publicity to the smoldering racial tensions on campus.

After months of tension, nothing resulted. Graduation day came off without a hitch, and seemingly life went back to normal. What did result from all of this was a summit between black campus leaders and the university administration, to determine what they could do to promote cultural diversity on campus. After days of deliberation, a package was agreed upon that would both increase the funding for and enlarge the focus of the African American Studies Department.

Did this help the interracial stress on campus? The administration published the following enrollment figures for fall of 2001: there were 69,691 caucasians, and 8,576 minorities. It doesn't take a rocket scientist to see how this lopsided student population could make many minorities at the school feel insignificant and threatened.

This anecdote may seem eerily familiar. However, the times were not of the turbulent '60s, but the beginning of the third millennium. Have we learned nothing about civilized cohabitation on this planet in thousands of years?

My former Penn State teammates and I were very alarmed by these incidents taking place at our alma mater. We sent a letter—signed by Jesse, Rosey, Charlie, Franco Harris, and me—to university president Graham Spanier, expressing our concern and offering our help. We were ready to travel to Happy Valley at a moment's notice, if our presence as black graduates of PSU would make a difference. Ultimately, the situation was quelled before we had the chance to lend our support.

To see such racial strife at Penn State gave me great pain. All things being equal, email threats and hate mail would never have happened if, over the last four decades, the university had been more in tune with Rip and Joe's vision. What was going on now at this campus only besmirches the legacies of some great people, both black and white, whose life journeys have passed through this venerable old campus.

It's ironic, I suppose, that I can speak of Penn State now as though I were remembering a wise, dear friend, when I have written several pages describing the torment that enveloped me in my years as a Nittany Lion footballer: The classes and the exams, the fear that I would be dropped from the team, the prejudice that confronted us at opponents' stadiums. Yet from the vantage point of nearly a half-century, I can appreciate how this college experience is part of what makes me who I am today.

## SEVENTEEN

# FATE SMILES ON ME ONCE AGAIN

I t was shortly after my second wife, Erma, had died in 1975 that I received an interesting call at my office with the Colts. The woman on the other end said that she had heard that my wife had cancer.

"I happen to have the same blood type as your wife," she said, "If it would help, I would like to offer her mine."

This woman's selfless offer made me temporarily speechless. I told her I greatly appreciated her offer, but Erma had passed away. I asked her what her name was, and when she replied, "Edith," I suddenly remembered meeting an Edith about ten years earlier. That woman was working as a school crossing guard at the time, and I was working as a representative for National Beer. A co-worker of mine, Dave Johnson, had introduced us when we crossed paths with Edith on a street corner.

"Would you happen to be that same Edith?" I asked. She said she was. We talked for a little while longer, both of us amazed by the workings of fate. I didn't know anything about her, other than my memory of her being a very attractive school crossing guard. As I was talking with her, my mind's eye was filling in the pieces: her angelic face, her smooth, fair skin, and her nice figure.

As our phone conversation seemed about to end, I told her again how much I appreciated her gracious offer to help my late wife. Then I found myself asking Edith if we could meet sometime. I happened to be leaving for Pittsburgh, soon, in advance of the Colts team, to set up some PR events. I asked her if she would mind meeting me at the airport: we could have a quick conversation before my plane left.

After some cajoling, she agreed, and a few hours later, at BWI, Edith sat chatting with me at my gate. She was as beautiful as I remembered. But even better, Edith was a remarkable woman in so many ways. Ten years earlier, when we had first met, she was divorced from an unfaithful husband and raising four children on her own by working three jobs: Besides her position as a school crossing guard, she worked at a department store as a clerk and was a receptionist at Johns Hopkins Hospital. It was the latter job, at the hospital, where she learned about Erma's struggle with cancer.

Edith and I sat and talked for almost an hour until my plane was boarding. Although I was still recovering mentally from the passing of Erma and still had scars as a result of my divorce from Frankie, Edith was like a magnet to me. I felt as if I had met my other half. I sensed something special.

"Come with me to Pittsburgh," I said, knowing she wouldn't go that far.

"Oh no, Mr. Moore! I'm not that type of woman!"

I had to laugh at her old-fashioned propriety. I made her promise she would see me when I got back to town. She promised, and she followed through. Once I returned from my trip to Pittsburgh, I started courting Edith immediately. She was extremely busy, as you might imagine, raising four children and holding down three jobs; but I found ways to see her as much as I could. Being the community relations director for the Colts, I would often stop by Johns Hopkins for the purposes of building goodwill for the team. It was also a matter of building goodwill for myself, for Edith was not quite as interested in me as I was intrigued by her. Her previous marriage had left her gun-shy of relationships, and I needed to take this slowly. Also, her life was her children. She refused to let anyone or anything get in the way of her family. Like a lioness with her cubs, she was a majestic creature who was also fiercely protective of her brood.

Ultimately, we enjoyed a wonderful courtship. Edith was a great woman who truly helped to complete me. When we met for the second time, I had a job that was comfortable and fulfilling, I had reconciled with myself after the divorce from my first wife and the death of my second, and I was trying to be a better father to my children. The one piece that was missing in my life was a woman whom I could cherish, and who would cherish me in return. From the first time I had seen her, ten years earlier, I believe, I have always known that Edith was that woman.

We were together for eight months before she agreed to marry me. She had turned me down many times, but I wouldn't give up. Finally, one day we were visiting a family friend in Hershey, Pennsylvania, when we visited the Foundation building. I remarked to the concierge how beautiful this structure was and how it would be a fantastic place for a wedding. Without Edith knowing, I asked him what it would take to put together a wedding there and how much it would cost. He told me that he would be happy to put a wedding together at a moment's notice for me. He said he would do anything for an ex-Colt. The stars must have been aligned to have picked a concierge who bled Blue and White. Apparently, I had signed an autograph for his son more than ten years before. He said that he was very impressed with how polite and willing I was to make time for his youngster. Neither he nor his son had ever forgotten that moment, he said, and he would be honored to arrange the wedding.

It amazes me how many times this type of story is shared with me. I've signed thousands of autographs in my life, and one thing I tried to do, even at an early stage of my career, was to take time out and be as sincere as I possibly could be to everyone who wanted my autograph. My attention to the fans, in the few moments it took to sign my name, has come back and rewarded me a thousand times over.

A few months after our trip to Hershey, I asked Edith one more time if she wanted to get married. To my joy, she finally agreed. I whisked her off to Hershey for a small wedding at the Foundation building. A friend of mine who lives in the area was kind enough to perform the ceremony. And the concierge's preparations, from flowers to music, made the wedding a magical event. We wanted a very small and intimate wedding, so small that it was only us. Nonetheless, word got out in the hotel that we were to be wed, and as a result, we made many new friends that day as strangers came to watch the ceremony and join the festivities. It was a wonderfully spontaneous moment and an experience that I'll never forget.

Marrying Edith was a watershed moment in my life, because it literally forced me to confront all of my shortcomings. In order to be worthy of receiving her hand in marriage, I felt I had to confess everything to her. It was the hardest thing I ever had to do, for I was afraid that if I disclosed to her certain parts of my past, I would lose her forever. On the other hand, if I kept these things secret and she learned of them later, she would never trust me. So I confessed everything: I told her I had been unfaithful to my first wife; I told her that sometimes I drank too much alcohol. I was very nervous and afraid. What if I told her all about my former sins? Would she still accept me?

Today we have been married for 28 years. Shortly after our wedding, as a commitment to our new life together, we bought a lovely ranch-style home in Randallstown. Symbolically, this house has allowed me to close the door on a tumultuous past. Edith helped me become a rededicated Christian; and with her and the Lord in my life, I didn't need alcohol in my life anymore. I've been clean and sober since we met.

One of the things that so attracted me to Edith was her wonderful relationship with her children. She was a stern disciplinarian who wanted and received the best out of her children. She had put all four of them through college herself. With all the effort and long hours she put in for her children, she's never once held it over their heads. She dedicated her life to them because she knew it was the right thing to do. She is a wonderful person. Her kids have always been her priority, and she made that known to me early on.

I'll never forget the first time I met her children. I had gone to Edith's home to pick her up for a night on the town. When I arrived, I met each of her children: the oldest, her daughter, and her boys. Her daughter helped Edith get ready for our date while I sat and chatted with the boys, who were politely interrogating me. At long last, Edith was ready. Her daughter walked her out to the living room and presented Edith to me. Her daughter proceeded to pepper me with questions: who was I, what did I do for a living, where were we going, and what were my intentions?

Then, just as we were about to leave, she said, "Mr. Moore, you have my mother home at a decent hour!"

I laugh at that story every time I recall it. It demonstrates so well what a tight-knit unit Edith had created for her family. I'm just happy I passed her children's exam and she let me join the family!

~ ~ ~

The year before we were married, I suddenly became unemployed. When the Baltimore Colts left town in the dark of night, I saw my job as the team's Community Relations Director leave with it. For the second time since my retirement as a Colts football player, in 1969, I was pounding the streets again, looking for a job. The one major difference between 1983 and

1969 was my financial position. I had, by this time, worked with the Colts for years at a generous rate, and I had been able to pay off some debts. And now that Club 24 was no longer a burden, I was operating with a positive cash flow. This time, I could take a more leisurely approach to finding another job. I was in a position to take some time and collect my thoughts and find out which direction I now wanted to go with my life. I knew that I definitely wanted to be around football; I had loved being a part of the Colts again, even if it meant watching from the press box and not from the bench. The chances seemed pretty remote that an opportunity like that would come along again, however. I wouldn't even entertain the thought of leaving town to join a franchise elsewhere. Finally satisfied with my personal life and the relationships around me, my destiny was tied to Baltimore—and I was fine with that.

Regardless of my personal life, I had grown very attached to the community. The city was like a warm blanket to me. Edith and I had friends and associates here, and I knew the city inside and out. My kids and her kids were grown up and living in the area, as well; it was exciting to see them go through their life changes, marry, and have children themselves. Even though confining my job search to Baltimore might limit my choices, moving out of town was out of the question.

But as the end of 1983 grew closer, it became clear that no one was beating down my door to give me a job. I don't like sitting idle for too long, and it got to a point where I started getting uncomfortable. I was hoping to marry Edith—but how could I begin to support her without a job?

In retrospect, the main reason why I wasn't actively pursuing employment up to that point was my fear of rejection. After what I went through in 1969 when I realized that CBS did not want to renew my position as commentator, I was scared that I'd repeat those months of looking for work and facing rejection at each turn. I had had that one lucky visit to the job bank, when I was hired as an Army recruiter; but I had too much pride to go back there again. The only thing to do was to take matters into my own hands: I called the governor of Maryland, to ask for a job.

You may wonder how I had the gall to call the governor. It was not a matter of arrogance, but rather a case of total despair and loss of hope. It really was a last-ditch effort. I had no Plan B. I only knew that I was tired of begging, only to be told, "We'll call you," and, "By the way, would you mind signing an autograph?"

So one day I called the governor and requested a brief meeting. I told his secretary that I'd only take ten to 15 minutes of his time. With a skeptical tone, she put me on hold (my bad luck: she wasn't a football fan, and didn't know me from Adam). In a few moments, she came back on the line and enthusiastically scheduled a time for me to meet with the governor who, she said, was looking forward to our meeting.

The following week I made my way down to Annapolis. To my surprise, the governor had freed his schedule and was interested in getting to know me. After some initial small talk, I told him that I'd stop beating around the bush—I needed a job. He asked me what I wanted to do, what type of position I was looking for. I told him that, in my public relations job with the Colts, I had really enjoyed being out in the community, specifically meeting the young people of the city and trying to make a difference in their lives.

After relaying a short description of some of the specific projects I had coordinated for the Colts, the governor called in the director of employment for the State of Maryland, and asked him to do a search to find where I could be placed on the payroll with the skills that I had. Then the governor thanked me for making the trip and said that someone would be in touch with me soon.

Before a week had passed, I was receiving a variety of correspondence from many different state agencies, such as the state lottery and the department of education, alerting me that I was in their system and that as soon as a relevant position was available, I'd be contacted. I was impressed with how quickly the governor had made things happen, but I tried not to get my hopes up. One day, though, I got a call from Rex Smith, the director for the department of juvenile justice. Rex invited me to a lunch meeting at the Belvedere Hotel. I could understand the department of education and even the state lottery, but I didn't know where this opportunity might lead me. With nothing to lose, I went in with an open mind and a positive outlook. I was just excited to finally be meeting someone face to face.

From the first minute I met him, I knew Rex was a straightforward and open-minded man who wasn't just doing the governor a favor, but was someone who actually thought I could add something to his department. Rex explained to me exactly what his agency did. He explained how the department was attempting to reach kids at a younger age in order to nip any aberrant behavior in the bud. He said that kids would listen to me as an ex-athlete and local celebrity. He said that there really wasn't such a position on the books yet, but said that if I was interested in working there he could make it happen.

"I am interested in doing my best for anyone who will give me a chance," I said. I could feel that he was as enthusiastic as I was about working together, even though neither of us knew at the time what shape my position would take.

"No matter what the position evolves into," he said, "You will report directly to me. In the meantime, I want to ask you to do two things: keep this to yourself and go out and visit as many of the juvenile correctional facilities as possible to get a feeling for what the department does."

It felt very satisfying to meet with someone who saw my potential to help. After weeks of talking with folks whom I knew had contacts, but were more interested in playing games, I felt inadequate and embarrassed. I didn't sense any of that with Rex.

Over the next six months, I visited several facilities, from minimum to maximum security, all over Maryland. I went from the hills in the north of the state all the way to the southern border. I visited kids who had a history of assault and therefore had to sit in lock-down 23 hours a day. I met kids who are allowed to stay in an open facility where the doors aren't locked, with the understanding that if they left them, the department would find them. I took my time and really got a feel for how the department ran these facilities, and at the end of six months I went back to talk to Rex.

He asked me, "What have you learned?"

"I believe I understand what brings a child to the point of institutional supervision. I know how the system matches a child with a parole officer. I have an idea how the system determines where each child goes and why."

"Mm-hmm. And what do you think might be a solution to having so many kids end up in these correctional facilities?"

"I think we need to get to the kids as early as possible," I said, "maybe when they are as young as seven or eight years old. We need to find the kids who aren't yet really lost. Listen, Rex, I could have been one of those kids. My son, in a way, is one of those kids."

I knew I was going out on a limb being so forward about a small glimpse into my personal life, but I felt comfortable with Rex and had a hunch that he would appreciate my honesty. He wanted me to shoot straight with him, so I took his advice.

Rex was leaning forward, interested in my experience. I think he appreciated the fact that I took the initiative that I did. Clearly, this was a test, and it appeared as if I passed with flying colors. In any case, he gave me a job that might be called "roving mentor," and I'm still with juvenile services today. My clients include thousands of children, young kids who can be trusted enough to go to the Ravens training camp with me, or to an Orioles game, without the department worrying about them running off. I try to get in front of these "delinquents" as early as possible, to show them that there is hope for a better life. I try to let them know there is someone out there who cares about them, which is something so important, as I learned from my mentor, Coach Andy Stopper. Many of these children grow up in the projects, places where they are corralled by chain-link fencing. Essentially they are born behind bars, so it doesn't phase them a bit to be jailed later on. It takes someone to show them the gate to freedom before they lose all hope. I try to provide that gate and open up their world.

I've realized, the older I get, that I'm not on this earth just to worry about me. There are eight-year-old kids out there who are tempted daily to join a gang. There are ten-year-olds who think shoplifting will win them respect from their peers. There is a 13-year-old girl who is about to become a teenage mother and thinks her life is over. I'll admit on some days this is very depressing work. There are some facilities I hate to visit, because it is scary how far gone some of the kids are. Where are the adults who will care for these kids? If not me, who? I'm certainly no savior; and maybe I'm optimistic to think that a word from me will change a kid's life. All I know is that even if 20 kids ignore me, it's that 21st kid who might relate to a story I tell or an autograph I sign. This makes it all worth it; this is what motivates me to get up every morning and start the day over again.

Now that I'm 70 years old, many people come up and ask me when I'm going to retire. Retire to what? I can't sit at home all day and do nothing. I like being busy. It is just in my nature to help, and I will do it for as long as the Lord gives me the strength. I'll go to the facilities, the schools, and the homes. Whatever it takes to get the job done.

As I've explained, my high school coach, Andy Stopper, was a role model in ways that I try to emulate when I work with the kids at juvenile corrections facilities. Andy was always trying to make things better for me, and he watched over me during the good times and the bad. Never once did he judge me, whether I was on top of the world, winning championship rings, or whether I was standing in the unemployment line. He watched my back, too, and he guided me in situations where I was naïve: for example, whenever I was invited to come back to Reading to speak before a club or a group, Andy would let me know how much pay other speakers had received in the past; and he made sure I received the same compensation. I'm sure his love for me manifested in many more ways than I'll ever know. It has taken time, perspective, and maturity for me to realize exactly what a great human being Andy was, and how fortunate I was to call him "friend."

On February 15, 1989, Andy Stopper passed away from a brain tumor. He had stayed with me every step of my life; and I always thought he would be there forever. When he passed, it was almost as unbearable as having one of my parents die. I was at a loss, not knowing how to go on without him.

When Andy retired from coaching, I recited this poem at a banquet in his honor. It was a tribute to him at that moment, but I think it even more accurately describes the life this man lived:

> *"We cannot all be famous or be listed in 'Who's Who,'*
> *But every person, great or small, has important work to do*
> *For seldom do we realize the importance of small deeds,*
> *Or to what degree of greatness, unnoticed kindness leads.*
>
> *For it is not the big celebrity in a world of fame and praise,*
> *But it's doing unpretentiously in indistinguishable ways*
> *The work that God assigned to us, unimportant as it seems,*
> *That makes our task outstanding and brings reality to dreams.*
>
> *So do not sit and idly wish for wider, new dimensions,*
> *Where you can put in practice your many good intentions.*
> *But at the spot God placed you, begin at once to do*
> *Little things to brighten up the lives surrounding you.*
>
> *For if everybody brightened up the spot on which they're standing*
> *By being more considerate and a little less demanding*
> *This dark old world would very soon eclipse the "Evening Star"*
> *If everyone brightened up the corner where they are!"*

This poem says so much about what Andy stood for. He never let me forget where I came from or what heights I could reach, and I'm sure it was the same for others who knew him. He was the North Star, for so many young kids, black and white, who passed through his little corner of the world we called Reading High School; and he remained a beacon for many of us long after we graduated. Having coached for countless seasons at Reading High, he touched countless young men and women.

If I can take the experiences I've had in life and bring a little hope to the young kids caught up in the juvenile system and that even begins to match what Andy did for me, I'll believe my work has been successful.

In the end, the measure of a man is not awards, bank account balances, or physical assets. The measure comes from the number of lives he's touched. I've had my ups and downs, but I'm a better man for it and it would be a travesty not to share those lessons with others and really try to make a difference. If I leave this earth changing only a few lives it will be all worth it. I will gladly die sapped of my strength knowing that I've given it all away. I just don't know any other way.

# SOURCES

*The Daily Collegian*

*The New York Times*

*The Baltimore Sun*

*The Pittsburgh Post-Gazette*

*The Herald-Tribune*

*Sport Magazine*

*The Unofficial Colts website*

*ExplorePA History.com*

*The Penn State Football Encyclopedia*

*A Hard Road To Glory*

*The Game of Their Lives*

*When The Colts Belonged to Baltimore*

*Lion Country: Inside Penn State Football*

*From Colts to Ravens*

*Damn Rare!*

*Sundays at 2:00 with the Baltimore Colts*

*The Greatest Football Game Ever Played*